COWBOYS, FISHERMEN, *and* MONKS

Bitten by 3rd World Wanderlust

TOM MATTSON

Copyright © 2020 Tom Mattson

Artwork by: Yoshimitsu Nippashi

All rights reserved. No part of this book may be reproduced, stored, or transmitted by any means—whether auditory, graphic, mechanical, or electronic—without written permission of the author, except in the case of brief excerpts used in critical articles and reviews. Unauthorized reproduction of any part of this work is illegal and is punishable by law.

ISBN: 978-0-9983221-1-7 (sc)
ISBN: 978-0-9983221-3-1 (e)

Library of Congress Control Number: 2018913961

This book is about a trip around the world.

Contents

Chapter 1	Death in New Zealand	7
Chapter 2	Beauty Pageant in Vietnam	28
Chapter 3	Vipassana: Ten Silent Days in India	37
Chapter 4	The TranSiberian Express: Across Mongolia & Russia	60
Chapter 5	Alaska	82
Chapter 6	India: Music Box of Wonders	159
Chapter 7	Nepalese Days: Leopards of the Moon	186
Chapter 8	The Escape	233
Chapter 9	Outback Cowboy	243
Chapter 10	The Best Years of Our Lives	289
Chapter 11	The School of Enlightenment	314
	Spiritual Practice 1: Give Away	329
	Spiritual Practice 2: Face Your Fear	352
	Spiritual Practice 3: Moment of Truth	375
	The Journey Begins	390

"I can't breathe."

I woke with a start at dawn. The sun had risen orange and humongous and was spilling down swimming pool–hot. I sat up sharply, short of breath. I clutched at the hollow in my chest, fighting to inhale oxygen. There was almost none in the air. Struggling to inhale, I wracked my chest with a monstrous effort, but nothing entered my lungs. I began to panic. Suddenly a shadow split the sun and sent its rays scattering in all directions. I looked up. Ringed by a nimbus of light, a young monk stood in front of me in the new dawn brightness. His facial features were round and perfectly symmetrical. He stared down at me. His face, darkened in the backlight, leaned toward me, and the sun's light spilled out from all around him and flooded into the room.

"I can't breathe," I said to him, my eyes watering. "I don't know what to do."

It was late in the day, too late to continue trekking, but there was no teahouse in Lawichasa, Nepal. No place to sleep. I had no choice but to keep going. Truth be told, I didn't really want to arrest my ascent up the mountain anyway—I wanted to reach the next village before nightfall. The sun was already dropping down toward the horizon, and I knew I was getting a late start. I glanced up at the top of the ridge. It was a very steep climb straight up that would take me at least an hour. I started off almost trying to run it.

Big mistake.

About halfway up I hit the wall—that mysterious line, different for every person, between altitude and one's body's physiological ability to cope with it. Suddenly I was clobbered by a massive, debilitating case of altitude sickness, and I had no choice but to instantly stop flat. I waited a few minutes and tried to collect myself. Finally I started up again at a snail's pace.

It was dusk. The sun's disk sagged low in the sky and soon slid behind the curvature of the earth. It was too late now to turn around and go back to the last place with a bed. I had to press on. By the time I reached the top of the ridge it was dark and I was breathing in short, labored gasps. I was about to push on but, struggling with the altitude, I paused to catch my breath and rested my hands on my thighs. On my left a Buddhist monastery was perched on the cliff overlooking the valley below. The monastery was a popular stop on the Everest Base Camp trek, one often visited by trekkers during the day. I didn't want to miss it, so I ducked inside. The monks here don't speak, my guidebook said. They live in devout silence in residency for one to two years as part of their religious training.

The tourists had long gone for the day, having responsibly moved on to the next village at an early hour to arrive before nightfall. As with nearly everything in life, it's best to start trekking early in the morning.

The monastery was old and cold and vividly colored, as Nepal's monasteries are, in the same bright orange, blue, and yellow hues of the prayer flags that festoon the higher elevations.

The monastery was large, with several rooms and antechambers. There were no doors or even outer walls in the monastery: the whole building was open air with internal walls only. Several monks lay prostrate on their knees, their foreheads dipped to the floor deep in prayer. An enormous statue of Gautama Buddha that was three times the size of a grown man loomed large over the monastery, his gaze surveying all. A giant gold disk or medallion hung in front of Siddhartha as though to protect him.

The monks wore red or saffron robes with their bare arms exposed. It was freezing at night this high in the Himalayas, and I was awestruck that they didn't seem cold. I guessed they had gotten used to it—hot blood surges faster in freezing weather. And when you're a monk who's been enjoined from speaking for two years and spends fifteen hours a day in uninterrupted prayer, it probably doesn't look good if you throw on a windbreaker every time you get cold.

Unnerved by the gloaming slipping into pitch-blackness outside, I moved for the exit. A youngish monk, around twenty-five years old, emerged from the shadows and bisected my path. He wasn't allowed to speak, but he wrapped his arm around me and guided me back inside the honeycomb. Puzzled, I followed him into the largest chamber, the main prayer room. He lay down a pillow and an olive wool army blanket on the floor. I couldn't believe it—he was indicating I spend the night in the monastery! I knew this was not customary and that tourists were forbidden from staying here. But with night having fallen, it might have been difficult to see the trail and find a bed in the Cimmerian darkness, and this monk seemed to have intervened on my behalf.

I took off my pack and untied my shoes. There was no wall separating the main room from the nature outdoors, so I shuffled out into the dirt in my bare feet to brush my teeth. I didn't change out of my clothes into pajamas anymore—it was too cold to at this elevation, and the higher one climbs in the Himalayas, the less one bothers with things like that. Anything superfluous naturally drops away, leaving only the essentials—air, food, water, and walking. I guess that's the appeal of it. And the otherworldly beautiful scenery up here.

I shuffled back inside and sat down on a stone step. Flickering candlelight from a hundred candles or more freckled the room.

The monks read by the dim light. There was no electricity in the monastery. I was in a mysterious, very sacred place. I scooped up a candle, Victorian-nightgown style, and flew from doorless room to room exploring. Monks were scattered here and there, kneeling silently in prayer or preparing for bed.

I returned to the main room. I lay down and pulled the scratchy wool blanket up around my neck. My breathing was shallow, and I lay awake struggling with it for hours. Eventually I fell into a disturbed, strained half sleep. At altitude one's breathing and sleep are always shallow, in some gray hinterland between asleep and awake.

At dawn the huge, orange sun poured down soupy and hot. The monk smiled beatifically at me in his red robes, standing above me with his hands outstretched. I squinted into the streaming light. He was holding out a stone mug of steaming hot butter tea. Its fragrant aroma wafted into my nose. Almost completely unable to breathe now, tears squeezed out the sides of my eyes and my hands were shaking as I accepted the cup. The hot liquid sloshed over the sides and scalded my thumbs. I didn't register the pain from the burn on my hands. When you can't breathe, a skin burn is the last of your worries.

I took a sip of the tea.

I sat still for a while, feeling the warm grooves of the ribbed stone mug press into my palms.

I still couldn't breathe, but my panic eased just slightly, and after a while I noticed that my hands had stopped shaking.

A hand was resting on my shoulder. The monk didn't speak, wouldn't speak, but I could feel his inner calm through the warm touch of his hand.

"Right," I said, pulling myself together. I finally had the strength to look up and smile back at him. "I know what I have to do now."

I stood up, shouldered my pack, and walked out of the monastery.

In danger of falling prey to altitude sickness, I did something I had never done before and am personally loath to do—I descended back down the mountain to recover at lower elevation. After resting for two days and nights until I felt good again, I gingerly began to climb back up the same route I had taken, this time taking care to move slowly and stay attuned to the effects of altitude on my body. This time I didn't hit any wall and was able to progress past the monastery and further until I reached Everest Base Camp and eventually the Gokyo Sacred Lakes. I came down a different pass to Namche Bazaar and never saw the monk again.

1

Death in New Zealand

On a bright cold day in March, under a liquid blue sky, I entered Franz Josef, New Zealand. Franz Josef is a giant glacier in Westland Tai Poutini National Park on the South Island that lies in the shadow of its more famous neighbor, Milford Sound, and is primarily known for ice climbing and glacier trekking. I had touched down in Auckland, on New Zealand's North Island, and moved steadily south toward Christchurch near the bottom of the South Island from where I was scheduled to fly out to Australia in less than a week.

A green, blue, and rocky country with nothing but empty sea between it and the South Pole, New Zealand prides itself on its magnificent nature, egalitarian ethos, and a rich vein of rugged outdoor adventure activities. Since I'd arrived I had already skydived in Taupo, surfed in Raglan, white water rafted in Queenstown, and rock climbed in Wanaka. In Franz Josef I signed up to ice climb one of the upper glaciers. It was my first time to try the sport. A van picked me up in front of my hostel at eight in the morning and drove me to the company's headquarters, where a small clutch of customers and I were outfitted with boots, cleats, ice picks, ropes, and down jackets for the cold we would find on the glacier. Then we were hustled back into the van and driven to the park entrance.

We hiked an hour to the base of the glacier where the soil layer ended and the ice began. Here we paused to attach crampons to our boots. A crampon is a metal contraption that, when lying open on the ground, looks like a shark's tooth-ridged maw, a bear trap, or an open-faced waffle iron with metal spikes sticking up. We wrapped the crampons around our boots like iron maidens and clasped them shut so that the metal tines faced down to the ground. We were now ready to tread on the ice.

Where glaciers be, there are also fissures and deep crevasses in the ice—wormholes, air pockets with just a thin patina of snow covering them like a thin layer of dust on a dresser or a ring around a bathtub. This light dusting of snow masks a fathomless abyss that spans out just below your feet and stretches straight down to the center of the earth like a mineshaft. Laid across each open crevasse was a narrow wooden plank with two ropes slung up on either side for climbers to hold on to as they traversed across. These planks were no more than hole-riddled glorified driftwood, but so long as you held on to the ropes you could generally place one foot in front of the other and cross just fine.

Our motley crew that day included Morgan, a six-foot-two giant of a woman from England with a butch black crew cut who kept telling anyone who would listen that she had been a world-famous model in her teens but that now, at age twenty, her ass had grown too big for her to get any work. There was no flab on her, but she was large and fleshy, her skin marbled pink and white like a wedge of ham sucked inside airtight packaging to be sold at the supermarket. Age twenty being the only thing still holding it all together, Morgan was taut, firm, but highly unstable, like a nuclear isotope or chilled jello that was still hard but warming up fast. It could all fall apart at any minute. With her crew cut and monstrous size, I was forcibly reminded of Red Sonja or Pink or perhaps a juiced-up Sinéad O'Connor. She looked like she could plow entire fields on her own.

Then there was Andy, a tall, lanky, geeky red-haired kid of twenty-three also from England. Paul, a fifty-two-year-old German, was serious. Not one for socializing, he never smiled. Kevin, a young kid from Scotland with dark curly hair, was the only person Paul spoke to; Paul and Kevin were the only customers on an expensive three-week tour of New Zealand led by a private operator, Liz—a stern, fit, tough-talking Austrian woman of about fifty. And there were our two guides, the tall, good-looking, high-energy, on-the-make cocky guys you usually find working in places like this, in fact the same type leading adventure tours all over the world.

While we were attaching our crampons, I noticed Andy, the lanky redhead, initiate a flirtation with Morgan. Nerdy Andy betrayed every thought in his facial expressions, and I saw he thought he had scored because Morgan was speaking to him. He didn't realize that Morgan was just looking for anyone willing to listen to her tales of modeling regret.

"I was in the shows, yeah. I walked every runway in Europe—London, Paris, Milan—but now they say my ass is too big, see."

Andy adopted a grave expression and said, "Well, it looks all right to me," and managed an almost dashing smile. *Well played, Andy!* He struggled to keep his voice even, his excitement out of it, as he wrapped a consoling arm around Morgan's coat hanger shoulders.

We climbed a narrow stairway of ice steps and crossed over three separate planks that spanned three gaping crevasses until we finally arrived at the glacier we were to climb. One of the guides jerry-rigged a pulley into the top of the glacier, and we all roped in to it down below. The climb went without incident. As in traditional rock climbing, the women tended to climb better than the men. The men were more gung-ho and threw themselves at the ice wall, hacking their picks and cleats into the hard packed ice with a huge outpouring of energy and clawing their way up the face like it was sports day at school and their classmates were watching. But ice climbing is deceptively exhausting if you climb using your arms, as men typically do. It's astonishing how quickly arm strength ebbs from a bodybuilder with enormous biceps when he's hanging from a vertical wall. If you don't push up through your legs, arm strength drains away in mere seconds. Then you fall. Female beginners climb better than their male counterparts because women naturally push up through their legs. No wonder women can grind lower than men in a club.

Paul, the fifty-two-year-old German, stumbled in his crampons a couple of times. He was awkward in them—he shuffled his feet and did not lift them high enough when he walked. He lost his balance once and fell over just while standing in place. We had lunch midday. Paul sat off to one side, eating his sandwich alone. Kevin, the Scottish kid on private tour with him, went over and sat with him.

We began the second climb of the day after lunch. Andy and Morgan had paired up as partners, one climbing while the other supported by holding the rope at the bottom. There was some hand-on-the-lower-back body contact. Andy's grin seemed to say he was thinking he might get lucky that night.

In midafternoon the guides said we were done, and we packed up to leave. Threading back the way we had come, I was walking directly behind Paul, who once again stumbled badly in his crampons just as we left camp. He lurched forward but caught himself with a hard step, one hand and knee going down to the ice like a disco dancer. Kevin heard the commotion and came back to help him. Tenderly he took Paul's arm and lifted him to his feet. He asked if he was all right. Gruffly, Paul said yes. We passed the first plank without incident.

Then at the second plank an amazing thing happened. As if by fate, at the worst possible moment, Paul tripped again on a miniscule incline of ice leading up to the plank. He stumbled forward and his momentum carried him straight out onto the plank, where he landed smack-dab in the center on all fours, on his hands and knees, perfectly stable, like an ottoman.

Here is where another person might have said, *"Oh shit!"* and simply reached up and grabbed one of the two ropes that were right there above his head on either side. Paul, whether out of embarrassment or a knee-jerk reaction, instead tried to hastily scramble to his feet without holding on to anything. He lost his balance as soon as he was up on one knee, twisted helter-skelter, and plunged headfirst over the side into the ravine. I was directly behind him and was the only one who saw the hideous thing happen. In the moment I saw Paul trip and flail out onto the plank, I ran after him and lunged to try to grab the back of his shirt. I couldn't quite reach him; I missed him by about a foot. I fell against the rope on the plank and looked over the side and watched Paul's openmouthed, twisted face staring up into the bright blue sky as he fell headlong below the sightline.

There was no sound. There was no whistle in the air. It was so silent, it was almost as if it hadn't happened. I was the only one who saw it happen, but it had happened so fast, in only a second or two, that he was over and gone before I had time to yell out, "Jesus Christ! Holy shit!"

As I watched Paul's horrorstricken face drop into darkness, the plank beneath my feet swayed gently like one in a children's treehouse. I peered down into the darkness and tried to catch a glimpse of Paul, but there was nothing there except a big black gaping maw. No one else had noticed what had happened yet. It seemed like a long time passed, but it had probably only been a couple of seconds. Because the crevasse had swallowed Paul soundlessly, everything was perfectly still, quiet.

Then I yelled, "That is fucking crazy! Holy shit! Fuuuuuuuuuuuck!" in one long extended note, and what had happened slowly dawned on the face of a group member walking up behind me, and then on the guides walking out in front. A ripple of comprehension slurred their faces and then, following a moment of pure shock, snapped into place like a piece in a jigsaw puzzle. Suddenly the guides swarmed into action and surged toward the crevasse like attacking bugs, deadly serious for perhaps the first time in their swashbuckling ice-climbing careers.

The senior guide, Mike, shouted angrily at me, "Get the fuck off that bridge!"

I did register his swearing at me, which even in that moment surprised me because I didn't think it was appropriate to talk to a paying customer that way, but given the gravity of the situation, I was willing to overlook it. Adrenaline was flowing through me, through everyone in the group I imagine, as what had happened frothed into consciousness like the slow, deadly beginnings of a tidal wave. Someone screamed, there were incoherent cries, and all at once the whole scene exploded in chaos. A disaster was unfolding before our eyes, and the entire group suddenly lurched toward the crevasse in a full-blown panic to peer over the side and look for Paul.

Behind me, Liz, Paul's guide, ran toward the plank from the rear. She halted at the bridge and also yelled angrily at me to get off the plank. I went back the way I had come. A small part of me was confused why Liz was yelling at me; she was Paul and Kevin's group leader, not mine. But Paul was her responsibility; she could be fired if he bit it.

Horrified cries pocked the air like spurts of gunfire. Pandemonium reigned. A few people broke down crying and dropped to their knees. Others stood inert and stunned into silence.

Mike yelled for everyone to back away from the chasm. Frantic yet laser-focused, he began setting up a makeshift pulley on the ice near the fissure. He seemed to almost be crying—his voice was cracking as he shouted desperate but precise instructions to the junior guide who had just run up from the rear of the group.

Then we heard an amazing thing. Paul's voice rose up shakily from the depths and called out in English, "Help! Help me!"

Mike's eyes widened. "Paul! Hold on! We're coming!" he shouted.

Mike was setting up the pulley as fast as he could, hammering the fulcrum into the ice, disgorging ropes from his pack, tying complex knots, but it was taking time.

"I'm cold. It's cold. Help me! My head hurts..." Paul's disembodied voice wailed from the depths. The group jockeyed to the edge of the pit to look down, and Liz and the guides tussled with them to hold them back. The junior guide was on his walkie-talkie radioing for help. Mike was roped in now, and the junior guide belayed him into the ravine. Mike deftly hopscotched off the ice walls of the crevasse as he negotiated his way down past the sightline. Our hearts swelled with hope. Paul was still alive and talking. Mike would reach him at any moment. Paul was going to make it!

Mike called up from the darkness, "I've got him, but he's turned upside down. His head is jammed into the ice. I can't move him."

Horror rippled through the group at this nightmarish proposition. Paul's head was wedged into the V where the crevasse came back together in the deep part of the earth. The glacier was squeezing his head like a grapefruit in a vise, and considering how tight that vice was, it sounded like the grapefruit was about to explode.

"Get me out of here!" Paul screamed.

Mike was straining to pry Paul loose but was still unable to. Paul kept talking, but his voice was feebler and more disoriented now. He kept saying, "I'm cold. It's too cold …"

I could imagine the freezing temperature at that depth where the sun never shone. They were about fifty feet down, I would learn later. Suddenly Mike unleashed a primal scream in what could only have been a Herculean effort to dislodge Paul's head from the clamp where the glacier held it like a crocodile gripping the head of a water buffalo in its maw before deep diving to the bottom of the Nile River with it. "I … can't … move him!" Mike shouted up breathlessly, "I'm going to try to shimmy him sideways."

Paul was rambling now. His talking had become incessant, nonsensical. He began to speak in German, and shortly thereafter, he began to sing.

"He's bleeding internally. He's bleeding into his brain!" Mike cried up in an anguished voice.

Then I saw a beautiful thing. High up on the 360-degree panoramic glacier, tiny specks began to appear. They were other groups on the glacier that day—hiking groups instead of ice-climbing ones. From all directions, tiny ant-like figures—other guides—told their groups to stay put and then came bounding down the glacier toward us.

The ice bowl sparkled and gleamed in the radiant sunlight like an auditorium on Mount Olympus. The guides converged on our location with astonishing speed, and all at once they were among us, giving and receiving instructions. It was moving to see all the young guides so utterly focused on a situation that was not a drill.

Time passed.

Paul had stopped speaking. Liz allowed Kevin, the Scottish kid, to lie down on his stomach and lean his face out over the crevasse and call down to his friend, encouraging him to stay conscious. "Paul! Paul! Stay with us, mate! Paul!"

The kid's voice was cracking. He was extremely distressed and my heart went out to him. He seemed to genuinely care for Paul, his gloomy, taciturn traveling companion of the last two weeks. Kevin was the really good kind of person on earth.

By now a second guide had rappelled into the ravine to help Mike shift Paul. Working together they finally managed to extricate him. They tied him to a makeshift basket of rope and hauled him up out of the crevasse like treasure disinterred by grave robbers. Mike shouted that Paul was still alive, that he had a faint pulse, but when I saw Paul's body emerge from the chilly darkness, I knew he was as dead as fried chicken. His face was completely blue, his body limp and lifeless. His arms splayed backward at the elbows, dangling in unnatural directions, all the bones apparently broken. It was strange to see arms bent backward at the elbows.

Then came the second sight of the day that moved me. A blip appeared on the horizon. It hung momentarily in the air like a stationary dot, then swelled until all at once it blossomed into a helicopter. The chopper took a hard left turn at the bank of peaks and swept up the valley toward us at terrific speed. It began to circle us at astonishingly close range, searching for a place to land on the narrow glacier. The chopper's blades generated a category 5 hurricane's worth of wind that buffeted us backward, and we watched it with a mix of awe and apprehension. At the same time the guides didn't pay the helicopter the slightest heed but continued focusing on the task at hand. They unwrapped Paul from the makeshift basket. A young man of about twenty-five began urgently performing mouth-to-mouth CPR on him, pressing his palms into Paul's chest while another man searched his neck for a pulse. Tears sprang to my eyes at the moving sight of the guides working so feverishly to save this man's life. The stirring image of the helicopter struggling to land on the glacier while the wind from its whirling blades beat us backward created an arresting picture.

With no place to land, the helicopter finally perched just the front half of its two prongs on the edge of the glacier while its rear half remained suspended in midair, its blades churning madly to keep the machine aloft so that its heavy ass didn't tip backward and drag the whole helicopter over the ledge into oblivion. Unable to keep its purchase on the ice, the chopper lifted clean into the air again and hovered about six feet above the ice. Mike scooped up Paul's body in his arms and cradled it like a baby. Then he nimbly danced along the edge of the glacier until he came underneath the helicopter. A team of paramedics reached down and lifted Paul's body inside. Mike then jumped up, grabbed a handlebar, and pulled himself inside with impressive strength. With awesome agility, the chopper then elevated, wheeled, and sped back down the valley at five hundred miles per hour and was completely gone from sight within ten seconds.

One of the guides who had come down from the upper glacier walked around passing out cigarettes. When he lit mine, he looked at me with large soulful eyes and said, "Heavy, man." I asked if anything like this had ever happened here before, and he said no.

I was temporarily distracted, despite the gravity of the situation, by the sight of Morgan hunkered down on her ankles, blubbering away, her face a tearstained mess, while Andy, holding her from behind, enveloped her entire body with his lanky arms and legs like a praying mantis. It was a bizarre sight of awkward comforting. Great sobs wracked Morgan's giant frame, and she shook and trembled as Andy clutched her desperately from behind, his small spoon-shaped face peering over her bodybuilder-sized shoulder trying to look serious yet not quite able to conceal a thin smile.

Liz, who had looked furious earlier, now just looked sad and confused. *Shit, I lost a client,* she might have been thinking, but in a more literal way than the phrase is generally used. The most raw and anguished suffering belonged to Kevin; all his grief and emotions poured through his face like a sieve.

It was a somber, silent drive back to headquarters. No one spoke. The police were already there when we arrived. They said that Paul died in the helicopter on the way down. A state-appointed shrink was on hand with whom we could "discuss our feelings." Everyone ignored her: she hadn't been on the glacier with us, she didn't get to share in our experience. She ended up just sitting uselessly in an armchair, looking at her watch.

The ice-climbing company laid out food for us like at a funeral. The police jotted down everyone's contact information—byzantine foreign addresses and phone numbers they would never call but painstakingly took down anyway.

The owner of the ice-climbing company asked if we wanted anything. One person asked to have his money refunded due to the death. The owner's face tightened like a Nerf ball being squeezed. Choking on the words, he tersely agreed. I was pleased that everyone else had the dignity not to ask for their money back. I thought we had gotten a lot more than our money's worth that day.

Mike and the younger guide arrived shortly after from the hospital where Paul had been pronounced dead. The younger guide was stoic and mostly fine, but Mike, so full of easy joy before the accident, was shattered. Tears streamed openly down his face. He made no effort at all to hide or wipe them away. I had never seen a grown man cry like that before. He said that in the park's 150-year history there had never been a death on a group-led expedition at Franz Josef before. He was plainly overcome by guilt and sorrow, and I felt bad for him but also impressed that he had the confidence to show his emotions so nakedly.

People deal with death in different ways. Some, like Morgan, cry buckets, while others, like me, don't feel much beyond a certain reverence for life and a faint quickening at change and the wheel of life turning. One girl asked where the nearest church was. Someone said there was an Anglican church in town. She said she would attend the next service. Most were just quiet, not sure where to rest their eyes. Kevin suddenly came to center, smiling, and regaled us with warm tales about Paul from their two weeks of traveling together. Besides Kevin, the rest of us had only just met Paul that morning, and I don't think anyone had actually spoken to him. I believe everyone was primarily in a state of shock.

I woke early the next morning at dawn with the peculiar desire implanted in me to hike back to the place where the glacier had swallowed Paul to, in some way, pay my respects to him by gazing into the chasm of his death. I set out early in the morning alone. A soft breeze trickled down the dry land and kissed my cheek as I walked through the brisk, chilly morning air. Gravel stones crunched under my boots in the morning silence. I stuck my thumb out to hitchhike and was picked up by the very first car that drove by. I had never hitchhiked before, but as I had been told, it is surprisingly easy and safe to do in New Zealand. I was nearly always picked up by the very first car I flapped my arm at, and in New Zealand you won't be abducted and murdered like you might be in the United States or Australia.

At around nine o'clock, the ashen gray morning broke, and a soft pink glow diffused over the land as the sun vaulted high above the distant wall of glaciers. The morning light bounced off the high walls, creating a spectacular amphitheater of pink and gold light. It was cavernous and eerie—as empty, dramatic, and alien as the Ice Age.

As I began the one-hour walk to the beginning of the ice, the park remained spookily silent. Then I remembered. The police officers had said the park would be closed indefinitely for the first time in its history due to the death. A police team would come in and case the scene to determine if the crevasse crossings were safe before reopening the park to visitors. I figured I was in my rights to come here, though, because this would have been my request to the climbing company if I had thought of it the day before.

As I neared the ice field, three men approached me from the opposite direction. One was Mike! With him were the head of police from the day before and a third man I didn't know, perhaps a detective. When we met, our exchange was brief and unexpectedly uncomfortable. Mike was totally changed from the day before. Gone was the tearstained warrior. In his place stood an angry, defiant punk. He looked peeved. Perhaps he was under investigation or in danger of losing his job because he had been the lead guide on the expedition. All that sorrow for another person was gone as soon as his livelihood was at stake.

As they passed, Mike glanced at me without any friendliness and asked me why I was here when the park had been closed. I had every expectation they would order me to turn around and go back with them, and in truth I wouldn't have minded if they had because the spectral, empty park had a vaguely threatening quality about it that I couldn't quite place. I told them my reason and, oddly again, none of them challenged me or forced me to turn back. We parted ways after no more than ten seconds.

I reached the beginning of the ice shelf and immediately began to slip and slide in my sheer, worn-out sneakers. Only then did I realize that I had forgotten to bring the most basic and important item for this mission: crampons. *Damn!* But I figured, *Oh well, I'm here now.*

Fuck it. The crevasse Paul had fallen into was not too far up, and I figured I could make it, but first I would have to climb the Stair—a narrow staircase of ice steps with a sheer drop on the left side but a rope installed on the glacier side that I could hold on to for safety. I started up the slippery steps. The rope held, so even when I slipped in my banana peel tennis shoes, I didn't go plummeting over the side to my death. It was a little trippy going forward with no one around, but I did not feel like turning back just yet. My instincts (Paul's ghost?) urged me on.

I reached the top of the glacier and approached the first plank, the one before the one Paul had fallen off. To my dismay, Mike and the two police officers had removed the ropes that allow one to traverse the plank safely. I considered crossing the narrow slice of driftwood without the ropes and might have done so if I had been wearing crampons. But the plank was clearly slippery, not to mention extremely narrow, and I thought it would be merely stupid if I came up here to pay my respects to Paul and ended up following him into the abyss. I always hate giving up on any decided endeavor, but after staring at it for a good long time, I just barely pulled myself back from trying it.

I took one last look around at my beautiful solitary surroundings, utterly silent in the huge icy panoramic bowl. There was no sound from any human or animal anywhere. There was no one, nothing on the glacier but me. It was like the world before life was breathed into it. I inhaled the sharp, crystal air and reluctantly turned my back on the death pit, which was still calling to me in a seductive voice. It was like a magnet that wanted to drag me inside, in the same way the edge of a cliff seems to lure you over its side if you walk by too close to it, or subway tracks invite you to jump in just as the train is barreling down.

A perverse figment of the imagination.

But I was not going to let that motherfucker take two of us.

Paul's ghost released me, but just barely.

I wended back the way I had come until I reached the top of the Stair. The sun, high in the sky, leaned down and warmed my face. It must have been nearly noon. I paused to look out over the dry land I had walked across that morning. From where I stood high on the glacier, the trail going down to the bottom was a narrow staircase of ice steps with the glacier on the left side and a steep drop to oblivion on the right. Scalloped ice steps were cut into the face of the ice massif like teeth, with nothing but open air fanning out on the right side in a yawning chasm of death.

The glacier was an ice mountain, a living mountain of frozen water that creaked, crackled, and popped like bubble wrap when tiny capsules containing a molecule of water became so pressurized in the depths of the glacier that they burst and made audible popping sounds like popcorn. The glacier moved like a haunted house, opening up fissures below your feet and then closing them again, making it needful to be ever vigilant lest the glacier open and swallow you as it had done to Paul. There is one key difference between a real mountain and an ice mountain, though. And that is an ice mountain can melt.

I began the steep descent down the ice steps when I was suddenly met by a most horrific sight. The ice had melted in the hot morning sun and the large iron bolts that held the rope fast now dangled completely loose in their sockets. They were sloshing around in slushy pools of ice water like snow cones sold on the street in Dubai.

Shit!

The ice was no longer frozen, but I froze on the spot. I gave the rope a test pull, yanking it as though I were falling over the side and, quite horribly, the iron bolt pulled nearly clean out of its lodgings, catching only on its final two or three threads. I yanked it again and this time the bolt broke clear of its casing. The rope would not hold me if I slipped and fell over the side. I held the long, cool bolt in my hand.

With nothing left to hold on to, I would slide right off the mountain and plummet to my death.

I looked down at my tennis shoes and their toothless bottoms. Any traction or grip they once had was long gone. My feet weren't stable just standing in place in them. I had to clench my calf and lower leg muscles to stand still without slipping, as though trying to turn my legs into tree trunks with roots. I had only walked up the ice stairs that morning because I'd been able to hold on to the rope. How would I get down without the rope? There was nothing to prevent me from sliding off the slick ice steps like a slip-and-slide into oblivion.

A feeling of dread bloomed in my chest. There wasn't a soul in sight. I was screwed. I could feel it. I had no phone. I would not be able to survive a night out here in the freezing cold in what I was wearing. Even standing still just now the cold was settling into me quickly. No, my only option was to go for it before the situation worsened. I looked down at the guardrail-less ice steps. Two narrow landings punctuated three stages of steps that curled around the massif down to the bottom. Gingerly, slowly, not thinking about what came next, I shoved the metal bolt back into its melted lodgings and crammed a few handfuls of ice shards around it to try and shore it up a bit. All this did, however, was aggravate the fragile ice encasement further and triggered a splintering crack that spiderwebbed terrifyingly through the whole structure. As the splinter spread like a virus without stopping, for a moment it appeared as though it might cause the entire glacier to calve open. *Yikes!*

I gulped and pulled my shaking hand away. Giving the ice a few words of encouragement to hold itself together, I started off walking extremely slowly. Fortunately this first leg of the Stair did not open immediately onto a fall to my right that would kill me—just a long drop into a cavernous ravine that would probably break both my legs—so this gave me some confidence. I reached the first small landing safely.

Then the Stair curved around the glacier to the left out of sight, and the next series of ice steps did fan open onto an abyss that would definitely kill me if I fell. The bottom was very, very far down.

Praying to God, I tentatively reached for the bolt that anchored the next rope and found it was less melted, slightly more secure than the bolt above had been. *Hallelujah!* I exhaled long and slow in the manner of a burglar before entering a house he's not sure is empty and decided just to go for it without thinking. I took the first step. It was okay. I descended the long series of ice steps with perfectly erect posture, my eyes fixed straight on the horizon, not so much as glancing to my right into the cavernous fall. About five minutes later I reached the second small landing.

There was only the third and final leg of ice steps to go. It also featured a fifty-meter drop on my right that would be certain death if I went over the side. Expectantly I reached for the bolt. My heart sank. It was completely melted in its socket, dangling loose like a baby molar ready to be ripped out of a teenager's skull. I should have seen it—the rope was lying limp on the ice steps all the way down. It would provide no support.

As I stood on the narrow landing alone in Franz Josef National Park, for the first time I felt like I had no option, no worst-case scenario to fall back on. I had jumped out of a plane without a parachute.

Several minutes passed. I kept looking at the winding staircase, but it looked so slippery, so dangerous that I could not get myself to go forward. I was clenching my calf muscles with all my might to keep my shoes from sliding, and the effort from it exhausted me. There was nowhere to sit down. Time dripped down slowly through the hourglass. Eventually my fear ebbed away, melting along with the ice, and I became calm. I don't know why, other than the old adage that one is free only when one has completely run out of choices. I hadn't accepted this situation at all, but I wouldn't have gone forward for all the gold in the world. I decided I didn't understand the adage.

So I just floated, waited. I thought about how in the end, Paul in his delirium had started singing. Since it was in his native German, I wondered what the songs were about. Perhaps they were drinking songs from his university days, with his friends swinging beer steins at Oktoberfest in Munich. My college songs contained a healthy amount of Latin: *"amici usque ad aras ... deep graven on each heart ..." Amici* meant friendship. But what in hell did *aras* mean? It was a good thing I didn't find out until later that it means grave or tomb.

At some point in the afternoon I was snapped out of my frozen-world reverie and the universe offered me an olive branch back to the world of the living. Far out on the ice—perhaps a mile out—a tiny black dot like a computer pixel superimposed against the white appeared. My instinct told me it might be something, though it just as easily could be nothing—a bird, a scrap of shale, a rock. After a while the thing shimmered like a mirage and I imagined it moved infinitesimally. But had it? After watching it for an hour, I lost hope and looked away. My thoughts ran off again, punctured only by cold and hunger.

Eventually I looked out across the plain again. The black dot had moved! It had migrated closer and was now about a half mile away. It was a human! Perhaps a lone worker on the glacier. I waved my arms frantically and howled. It took about ten minutes, but eventually the dot stopped whatever it was doing and stood still for a moment. It was still so far away that it appeared not to move again for a long time. But eventually I saw that it was indeed coming slowly toward me. It was a man. As he approached I saw that he had a harness strapped around his waist with all the right equipment: crampons, ropes, bolts, tools. He reached the bottom of the Stair. I braced myself for a "What the hell are you doing?" upbraiding, but he was not interested in having a go at me.

"Got yourself in trouble?" he said.

"Yes," I said.

I wanted to say it wasn't the first time.

He didn't ask me to explain what I was doing here. Instead he began hammering the bolts back into the deeper, still-frozen ice. He then climbed the stairs in his crampons to the landing where I stood and hammered in my nemesis, the bolt I'd been too afraid to pass. He looked up at the cotton candy blue sky and said, "The sun always melts the ice in midday. We have to hammer the bolts back in everyday." He looked down at my sneakers and shook his head. "You can't come up here in those. It's illegal to be on the ice without crampons."

"For good reason," I said.

It occurred to me that I was very fortunate he was working on the day the park was officially closed. If he'd been furloughed, I would've been dead meat. I have no idea what would've happened to me if he hadn't shown up. I guess I would've tried to last the whole night out here. That might've gotten interesting.

He took one of my arms, and I made my way down the rest of the ice steps clutching him pathetically. When we reached the bottom I released him from my bear hug and thanked him heartily.

He turned around and continued up the ice steps, hammering in the bolts as he went. I headed back down the trail. There were no more dangerous sections and I was only about twenty minutes from soil.

That night I watched "Call on Me," the sexy Swedish music video, play over and over again on a repeat loop on a TV in the hostel bar. The last frame, of a woman's sweaty booty jiggling in your face, segued directly back to the first frame which is—a woman's sweaty booty jiggling in your face. It was so sexual that I got nauseous from watching it. It played restlessly and relentlessly all day and night in the bar. I sipped my beer but tasted nothing. The TV was so positioned that you couldn't look away from it no matter where you sat in the bar. I can't watch television—it hypnotizes me, benumbs me, robs me of my natural alertness. So I stopped watching TV from that point forward.

The various English, Swedish, and German backpackers in the bar were all chatting excitedly over the news that the park had been closed because of a death—*"Hey, did you hear someone died up there? Fell into a crevasse. It just swallowed him whole. My tour's been canceled. Shit, hope I get my money back."*

I heard this refrain constantly over the next two days. I didn't tell any of them that I had been on that tour and that I was the person directly behind the guy who died, the only one who actually saw his face as he plunged headfirst into the abyss like a kettlebell.

Morgan was holding court at the hostel, a heavily taxed tear duct system continuing to supply a never-ending stream of water running down her face as she recounted, again and again, the story for any and all listeners.

"He just fell in!" she wailed to a tour group. "It just took him!"

I stepped outside into the quiet night air. It was dark and beyond cold. The cold was satiny and it seized me in an iron grip. A minute more and it would be strangling me. I could still hear Paul's faint ghost calling to me, summoning me, urging me back onto the glacier, to the crevasse. I had looked into the chasm of Paul's death and seen only that: death. In the end death is banal. It reaches out to the living, beckons to us, and it's our job to say no. I left Franz Josef early the next morning resolved never to visit there again.

The fear of death follows from the fear of life. A man who lives fully is prepared to die at any time.

—Mark Twain

2

Beauty Pageant in Vietnam

It was the sort of bizarre, fringe experience I live for. The sort of thing you only dream will happen to you. And I reveled in it.

Why do we travel?

For the novelty of it. For the shock, the surprises, and the delicious feeling of being abandoned and lost in an unknown land, especially one more remote, where no one knows you and you know no one. When one is completely untethered and adrift, one feels everything keenly, the moment-by-moment of life unfolding is experienced acutely with your full awareness. The feeling of freedom is maximized and euphoria is made possible. Every town you walk into, every moment, is a new beginning, and you are really feeling everything.

And so it was when one night I was picked up by a Vietnamese waitress while I was, not uncharacteristically, dining alone in Hanoi, Vietnam, and through a series of unlikely events, and a dalliance, found myself a judge in Vietnam's national beauty pageant.

It was Christmas Eve, and a festive, rollicking atmosphere threaded through the pageant. There's nothing quite like Christmas Eve in a foreign country, especially in a third world country where there are very few expats. It can be wild and a really good time. No party is ever better than in an end-of-the-world type of place.

As I sat in the audience waiting for the pageant to begin, a hand grabbed me under my armpit and lifted me out of my chair like a small child. The hand then shoved me in the back toward the judges' table. I had originally attended the pageant as Trang's date but was unexpectedly thrust into the role of judge when some drunk fool didn't show up and it became apparent there were no other foreigners in the audience.

The judges were all middle-aged white men who were expats and businessmen living in Hanoi. The color of my skin was obviously my main qualification for the job, the reason I had been plucked from obscurity. As I was seated in front of the stage, I glanced down the table at my fellow judges. I was the youngest member of the panel by far but was clearly being outhipped by the others. They wore Hawaiian shirts, skullcaps, do-rags, and other hip-hop paraphernalia. One man was dressed head to toe in a Santa suit replete with a white beard that obscured his face and fell, Rip Van Winkle–like, all the way down to the floor. Although none of the other judges was under the age of forty, I of all people turned out to be the conservative one of the bunch. So I unclasped my shirt buttons and let my bronzed chest, fresh from surfing the giant waves of G-Land, free of my shirt. Somebody handed me a pair of giant, I'd say women's, sunglasses. I donned them and snapped my fingers to the servile Vietnamese manservant who was now at my beck and call and asked him to bring me a martini. I gave the dog-pound fist to the two judges seated on either side of me and was ready for whatever. As everyone looked down the table at the upstart new judge, I instinctively melted into character as Brad Pitt in the movie *Fight Club*. I snapped my fingers, did a little dance with myself in my chair, tipped my face back toward the ceiling, put my arms in the air like I just didn't care, held it all for five seconds, then put it all down. This demonstration of individuality and independence seemed sufficient to satisfy the lusty mob, because they turned around and went back to their business.

I fit right in.

It seemed destined to be a good night.

On my right Santa leaned over and gave a small smile, signaling his approval. The man in the skullcap to my left blushed, but that might have been from the box of rosé wine he had just drained. As judges we were lavished with swag, not unlike what celebrities are plied with to attend awards parties—chocolates, box of white zin, and other freebies. Another judge had polished his box of zinfandel and was slumped over the table, dead drunk.

Best of all, we were about to be treated to a swimsuit, evening-wear, and talent competition by some of the loveliest girls in Vietnam. Vietnam, as a developing country, is unassailably pre–political correctness. You have to go to a poor country to get a little honesty, a little authenticity. All of Vietnam's airline stewardesses are hot. There aren't going to be any sixty-year-old grandmas serving you coffee. All of their beauty pageant contestants are going to be *very* hot. There aren't any plus-size models in competition. The Vietnamese would just scratch their heads at that. What's beautiful about stage 2 diabetes and being a plate of pasta away from heart failure? There's no nonsense in developing countries. Because they just don't have time for it. It's a luxury they can't afford.

Trang, the twenty-year-old waitress who had picked me up, was a confident stunner and successful beauty pageant applicant due not only to her surpassing beauty but also her aggressive, businesslike personality. She looked startled only for a moment when she emerged on stage for the introductions and saw me seated at the judges' table directly in front of her with my bare chest exposed, wearing giant sunglasses, and sipping a martini. She was beautiful in a classy black strapless gown with a multitude of rhinestones glittering over its surface like a galaxy of stars tossed up against the heavens. A lone silver clasp gleamed at its back. Her understated, sophisticated dress choice was impressive, revealing her to be an elegant person, which was new information to me. We were both now far removed from the pizza and buffalo wings joint where she worked and we had met. I could tell that Trang, ambitious person that she was, believed that bringing me as her date had turned out to be a momentous coup. She lifted her chin higher, arched an eyebrow, and her face flushed crimson in triumph. Trang clearly expected me to tip her to victory. I was like a Russian Olympic judge expected to bring my horse in first, no matter how obviously I was cheating. However, I was sensitive to my role as a judge in a national beauty competition and was determined to remain impartial. This was made easier by the fact I was not in love with Trang, despite her eagerness, youth, and exotic beauty.

The judges and I gave each girl a mark evaluating her entrance. This included a lingering pause when she turned for us to take in her ass, coupled with her rapturous over-the-shoulder smile. It seems that women, even young ones, know exactly what to do with that ass when fame and fortune are on the line. The factors we were supposed to grade on were natural beauty—which scored higher than made-up or put-together beauty—dress, style, and of course the effortless flair that can only come from an attractive personality, that thing many superficially beautiful but shallow women, such as models, lack. Each girl also had to step up to the mic and introduce herself, giving her name and age. This was always given to wild whooping, yelping, catcalls, fist-pumping, someone banging a cowbell with a hammer, and jet-decibel level applause from the boisterous audience of men who had now all climbed to their feet and were cheering like rabid dogs with the stench of fresh carrion in their nostrils. The girls lowered their eyes and blushed. They only grinned wider.

They were all aged nineteen to twenty-one.

Though a large number of contestants was eliminated after the first round, Trang passed this initial test quite easily. Loyally I gave her a 10. The next stage was the talent competition. Trang lamely sang the song "A Whole New World" from Disney's *Aladdin*. She had many physical gifts, but great pipes were not among them. I knew this one would be close for Trang. Not without guilt, I purposely gave the three other weakest contestants unfairly low scores and jacked up Trang's by embarrassingly awarding her a 10. This unethical tactic barely accomplished its goal, and Trang squeaked into the next round by a mere decimal point. So much for my remaining impartial. But since Trang had brought me this far, I figured I owed her this much. I breathed easier once she was through the talent competition, since her looks and the superior dresses she had somehow accumulated (on her waitress' salary? Her just-scraping-by parents? I didn't know …) should be enough to carry her to the finals.

Next up was the swimsuit competition. The pageant hall was like a wet cave, a moist den better suited to an underground cage match than a national beauty pageant. That's the best part about the third world—it's visceral, immediate, and oh so alive. The swimsuit competition was reminiscent of *Apocalypse Now* with Asian women dancing on a raised stage in bikinis and stilettos, an image that defined Southeast

Asia—along with a vibrant drug trade and short men jumping out of holes in the ground spraying bullets from machine guns—to an entire generation of Westerners. If that image set the bar, then this swimsuit competition did not disappoint. EDM music throbbed out of speakers just behind our table that was literally rocking as excited judges bumped and jostled it, banging their bodies against it like chimpanzees. Santa bit down hard on his own hand and winced at me as if to say this was too good to be true. The room was a hotsheet boudoir, a roiling grindhouse, a far cry from America's glossy, highly produced beauty pageants. The place was a live wire—if you were here, you were really here. Just put a bunch of ridiculously hot women on a raised wooden platform that's half falling apart from being poorly constructed, play loud dance music, and done. I think every girl scored a 10 in the swimsuit competition, essentially canceling out each other's scores. It seemed too wasteful, or simply irrational, to eliminate any of the girls in swimsuits, so we didn't. The talent was deemed too evenly and judiciously distributed—by God, apparently—so we kept them all.

This is a banana republic. The rules are pliant, okay?

Next up was the evening-dress competition, and Trang did not disappoint. She was luminous in a virginal white dress that transported the audience and gave her a tenuous, ethereal quality that had no place in that raunchy room. It was a mature, shrewd choice compared with the other girls' more conventional black and fire-engine-red dresses. One girl, already the most deserving to win in my mind, wore a bewitching emerald-green dress that was diaphanous without actually revealing anything, evoking a fairylike quality, and she passed through with the highest marks. She was effervescent, the most beautiful girl, with Trang probably second or third among those remaining. Trang's creative dress choice and hardworking playing to the audience, including flapping her arms to "raise the roof," were good for second place, and she passed on to the next round. Trang was prepared to compensate for any deficiencies she had in talent with an iron will and a shameless carnival-like barkering to the audience. Shamelessness may not win in the long term, but it sure does in the short term!

Only five girls remained now, and we had arrived at the personality component of the competition, where the girls talk about their dreams for making the world a better place. This is usually the humorous part of the contest. The girls all spoke in Vietnamese, which led to the predictable result when the, I'm assuming, all non-Vietnamese-speaking judges, not understanding what had been said, simply passed the three prettiest girls on to the final, with Trang among these.

The pageant was produced with maximum energy and fueled by the vibrant, ascending energy that makes third world countries so addictive. They're raw and wild and alive. That feeling of expansion in poorer countries that are striving or still struggling to meet their potential is thrilling, electric. That same energy gets inside you too and makes you feel alive, excited to be here. Mature countries are relaxing but languid, stagnant. Developing countries are poor economically but rich in spirit. They have a forward momentum, a headlong onrushing energy that the mature ones once had but no longer do. That unrestrained energy is exhilarating.

There's always a flip side, though. In countries that aren't mature, not everything makes sense. Transportation can be late and is unreliable. The countries are less safe, less predictable. Things don't happen linearly and often don't go as planned. There is no rule that can't be bent or discarded to suit the situation, and nothing can be taken for granted. That's all part of the fun. That's when strange things happen. Like being asked to judge a national beauty pageant.

Trang stumbled badly in the final when she lamely sang another Disney song—"Part of Your World" by Ariel in *The Little Mermaid*. I squirmed with discomfort and tried to crawl inside my shirt. But her dress was one for the ages—an incandescent ice-blue gown illuminated with hundreds of tiny diamonds that glittered like Tutankhamen's tomb. The dress' hemline was especially exotic. Veering from her left knee at a sharp forty-five-degree angle up to the peak of her iliac crest above her right thigh, it revealed the whole of that perfectly formed leg, which should have been awarded national heritage status. It was only the diagonal cloth plunging down to her opposite knee that cloaked her private area from view. I'm not sure what she was wearing for panties, but it was strategic. It was the most glamorous dress I have ever seen. Rita Hayworth moaned in her grave. But it was the more effortless, perhaps slightly more beautiful girl in the green dress who sang the prettiest song and won. Trang placed third. Ambitious person that she was, I think she was a little mad at me for not pushing her all the way to the crown. I never told her that but for my ruthless fixing of scores, she never would have made it out of the second round.

Vietnam is a country where marriage and family are of first importance, and one of the first questions Vietnamese people ask is whether you are married and have children. If you say no, especially if you are female, they respond with the greatest pity and concern, asking sincerely, "What is the problem?" In Vietnam it is not appropriate to respond "Back off!" mostly because such responses don't work. The Vietnamese always win, just as they've won all their wars through history against richer, more advanced invaders—the Ming Chinese, Mongolia, Japan, France, and the United States. Now, as then, they hold all the cards and seem forever in the stronger position. Many women traveling alone in Vietnam, even the most defiantly independent, eventually admitted that these personal questions got them down a bit until they finally just answered that they were married and their husband was resting back at the hotel. For lesbians and militant ultrafeminist types, answering this way goes down like glass in their throats. The Vietnamese then respond with an ingratiating little laugh and the utmost relief—disaster has been averted: you are not single.

Oh, I don't know what for! I'd just like to see something different. It's always the same here.

—Penthe, Ursula Le Guin, *The Tombs of Atuan*

3

Vipassana: Ten Silent Days in India

I was a modern-day Siddhartha. I lived a high life in Los Angeles, replete with an apartment on the beach, house parties, and a glamorous job at Hollywood's first and most storied movie studio. Yet I was restless and unhappy—senselessly, wastefully, inexplicably so. I did a lot of yoga but felt that the Indian teachers were corrupt and only wanted to grab Western girls' asses in yoga class (I wanted to too, but I *didn't*). So I decided to go to the real India and meditate for real salvation. Just as Siddhartha renounced all his wealth and possessions, I renounced Manhattan Beach, surfing, and tanning on the white sand beaches to search for the ultimate solution to man's suffering. My suffering was … I don't know why I was suffering. House parties, apartment on the beach, gorgeous willing women in bikinis dancing in my apartment and clutching margaritas, good job. What's not to like? I had good girlfriends—*really good* girlfriends. I should have understood this was the good life. Why couldn't I just appreciate what I had?

Probably the very fact I couldn't appreciate or see what I had, what all these good things meant, was the source of my suffering. Basically, I just wasn't present.

I was on the beach in Goa, India, when my friend Heather from London called me about a very intense, very old school of meditation called *vipassana* that she was keen on doing. Vipassana is the most difficult and intense meditation course of all, she said, and my interest was instantly piqued. Vipassana was founded by Prince Siddhartha Gautama, a prince born into great wealth in India who was unable to reconcile why his trappings of great privilege and wealth nonetheless left him so restless and unhappy. ("I'm listening," I said to Heather, noting I felt the same way.) The prince renounced all his wealth and possessions in 530 BC and at the age of twenty-nine, set out to walk across India as a peasant in search of the ultimate solution to humankind's suffering. ("Still here," I said, noting I was the same age.) Siddhartha was ambitious and prepared to go as far as necessary, do whatever it took, to uncover the root cause of suffering and fix it. Intelligent and highly resourceful (check, check), he resolved never to stop until he found the answer and fulfilled his quest to end universal suffering.

Siddhartha grew up with great wealth. His father, King Suddhodana, had three palaces with lotus ponds built for Siddhartha: one for the hot season, one for the cool season, and one for the rainy season. The prince wore costly robes, ate the most delicious food, and enjoyed music and all the pleasures on offer of the day. At the age of sixteen he married his cousin, princess Yasodhara. It was a happy marriage.

When he was twenty-nine, Siddhartha wanted to know what life was like outside the palace walls. His father, whom he trusted most in the world, tried to prevent it, but Siddhartha stole out and took a chariot ride around the city, driven by his servant, Chandaka. On the ride he saw a weak, bent old man, seriously ill, moaning with pain. Then he saw a body being trolleyed away for cremation. He was shocked by what he saw. The vivid harshness of reality partially awakened him on impact, and suddenly his destiny seemed laid bare before him. He became convinced that there must be a way for humankind to free itself from suffering. He decided to give up his princely life and search for this path.

After taking this decision, he was told that his wife had given birth to a son. Wanting to see the child before he left, Siddhartha went to Yosodhara's room and found her asleep holding the baby in her arms. He was afraid to wake her in case he could not bring himself to pursue his plan. His newborn son was another tie keeping him here. He ordered his servant to saddle up his favorite horse. They rode to the river Anoma and crossed over. Here Siddhartha shaved off his hair and beard and gave his royal robes and jewels to Chandaka.

"My lord?" Chandaka said.

"I don't need them anymore," Siddhartha said, smiling at him.

He put on the saffron robe of an ascetic and set off into the wilderness.

Siddhartha wandered the vast steppes of India for years, experimenting with trial and error such as extreme fasting with other seekers that brought him within an inch of his life. Extreme forms of self-abnegation, such as fasting for over a month, had long been favored by India's Vedic and Jainism religions. One day he fainted from hunger and nearly didn't regain consciousness. A shepherdess emerged from the forest gloom, leaned down through the ether, and proffered him a small bowl of milk and rice. She lifted a spoonful to Siddhartha's mouth and he sipped. Seeing him eating, his five fellow ascetics turned on him in anger and abandoned him. Now Siddhartha was all alone in the wilderness.

Realizing he would die from starvation before uncovering the truth, he pulled himself back from the brink. Understanding that he was still following the same outmoded, conditioned methods of the past, Siddhartha finally broke free and forged his own path. Only then was he able to discover the connection between man's misery and his personal thoughts. No one had ever looked before at the connection between the two and noticed their equivalence: the misery of the thought is equal to the misery you feel. Therefore, Siddhartha reasoned, if you changed the thought, or simply didn't think, your feeling would change. The feeling follows the thought. If your thoughts are positive, happiness follows you like a shadow that never leaves. No one had ever considered before that the messenger bringing the plague—your thoughts, your mind—might in fact *be* the plague. The answer was the simplest and also the most insidious, hidden in plain sight all along. *The enemy is your mind, nothing outside of it.* In brilliant Agatha Christie form, it turns out *the messenger is the villain*. The one bringing you bad news *is* the bad news and not whatever or whomever the message is about. The contents of the message are never your problem. The problem is only ever the negativity in your mind, not your real-life situation.

In seeing this, Siddhartha made a radical new discovery that transcended the standard meditation of the day, called *aspana*, which practiced quieting the mind through breathing and mantra repetition of the chant *om*. Siddhartha went on to achieve enlightenment under the bodhi tree and become the Buddha when he delivered his first sermon, "The Setting in Motion of the Wheel of Dharma," to a handful of supporters outside Varanasi. He returned home to visit his wife and now seven-year-old son. Siddhartha then spent the next forty-five years traveling around the Ganges basin instructing all who wished to be taught, in royal courts and peasant villages. The Buddha ignored the traditional Indian social order. He taught people of all castes. His disciples included not only rulers and priests but also casteless people and Untouchables.

He taught what he called the Four Noble Truths. They teach that suffering comes from trying to hold on to what is unholdonable. Everything inside and outside ourselves is constantly changing, and there is nothing to which we can cling forever or with which we can permanently identify. Life is like a rushing river: you might as well try to hold on to the current. They also require individuals to never say or do anything that causes harm or pain to another person. Yes, the Buddha was actually wealthy, spoiled Prince Siddhartha before he became one of human history's most famous figures, influencing everything from Western philosophy to most of today's major religions.

One reason that spiritually minded Westerners are interested in Buddhism and the religions of the East is that the formal teachings of the Christian church either don't know or don't teach the true meaning of Jesus' words. The grim Catholic Church–invented stuff about sinning, the need to ask for forgiveness, judgment, Jesus dying gruesomely supposedly for our sins … These messages carry less resonance with young people today, which may explain the exodus toward secularism and why an army of Westerners are instead drawn to Buddhism, Zen, yoga, and meditation—Eastern mysticisms that predate Christianity. Ironically, today's Christianity is missing the very thing these people seek: spirituality—to feel closer to God. And if your organized religion doesn't help you feel closer to God, then by God you will look for Him somewhere else.

Siddhartha was the first enlightened person on record. More than five hundred years before Jesus said it more esoterically, and thousands of years before Eckhart Tolle said it, Siddhartha said, "Do not dwell in the past, do not dream of the future, concentrate the mind on the present moment." That is the bedrock of today's most advanced spiritual teachings, and most people have no idea it was first said thousands of years ago by the Buddha himself.

Some other Siddhartha chestnuts:

> The mind is everything. What you think you become.

> We are shaped by our thoughts; we become what we think. When the mind is pure, joy follows like a shadow that never leaves.

> Happiness does not depend on what you have or who you are. It solely relies on what you think.

> All human unhappiness comes from not facing reality squarely, exactly as it is.

> No one saves us but ourselves. No one can and no one may. We ourselves must walk the path.

> Peace comes from within. Do not seek it without.

I was intrigued by this ten-day vipassana meditation course because, first of all, it sounded full-on, which is what I wanted. I was not likely to encounter dilettantes there. And because the course was based on the personal discovery of the Buddha himself, I was assured I wouldn't be wasting my time in some ersatz ashram with some old "yogi" pervert hack with a beard and poor English dry-humping the hot young Western girls in the downward-dog position (the doggy-style position) in quasi-bullshit yoga classes all across America every day. This was not *Eat, Pray, Love*; I was not going to find myself uncorking stemwinders about my ex-husband with a Texan named Richard over delicious curries while mopping the floor. No, this was the real shiznit. As vipassana is the most extreme of all the meditation courses on offer in India, I figured it would also be the most worthwhile.

On my last day on the idyllic strip of beach paradise known as Goa in Southern India, I tossed the volleyball to the Israelis, so serious and competitive even about beach volleyball.

"There's no war here, guys—relax," I said.

They scowled at me. Even all the weed they smoked out of hookahs in the open-air lounges at night didn't seem to chill them out. I said goodbye to Delphine, the gorgeous, statuesque, six-foot-tall French stunner I'd met on the beach here.

I kissed her, smiled, and said, "See you later."

She nodded okay. I packed up my swim trunks and left the beach for good in favor of Hyderabad, a bland, dirty metropolis in the center of India that would rank next to dead last, ahead only of Mogadishu, Somalia, on the Travel Channel's "World's Best Places to Visit."

The sign on the entrance of the vipassana center in Hyderabad, India read:

> Strive ardently, oh man, and burn!
> Purity comes from burning away the dross.
> Gold must pass through a crucible before it can be refined.

It occurred to me that the exact same sign could be posted over hell.

I wondered what was in store. I had done no research and had heard only vague rumors of extreme hardship and suffering in vipassana. I learned upon entering that for the next ten days we would not be permitted to speak—not a single word to anyone at all—other than a brief forty-five-minute period after lunch when we could meet with a teacher in the main hall and ask questions about the meditation technique that we didn't understand. Questions were expected to be concise. Meandering dorm room–style verbal masturbation would not be tolerated. The teacher was much closer to a Sphinx than your garrulous high school English teacher. Any other talking during the entire ten days was strictly forbidden. Also, as my poor friend Heather told me in harrowing detail, you were not allowed to leave should you decide the course wasn't for you. Once you signed on the dotted line and passed through those gates, you were required to stay the full ten days come hell, high water, or jihadists from neighboring Pakistan. Heather, God bless her, on her fourth day jumped over the wall before dawn, got to the highway, ran down a car, and escaped! I wish I was making this up, but I'm not.

Heather had wanted to do vipassana badly and had been the one who convinced me to go, but when she went, she hated it. She asked to leave on the second day but was told no. She was effectively being held prisoner against her will until the end of the course. Desperate, on the third day she pleaded with them again to let her leave. Again she was denied. On the fourth morning she rose before dawn and snuck to a wild corner of the compound that was littered with broken machine parts. She climbed on top of the parts, and clambered up over the wall in the dark. The ashram was miles from Hyderabad's city center, in the middle of nowhere, but it did adjoin a road. She flagged down a car, bundled herself in the backseat, and slipped into the city at first light just as the compound was stirring. She caught her own midnight express *the fuck* out of there.

We were also ordered to avoid making eye contact with anyone during the course on pain of some horrible punishment we were assured we would not want to experience. Men and women were strictly segregated. We could only just barely glimpse the women, tiny as ants, across a great gulf in the meditation hall, their faces hidden behind Indian veils they were forced to wear.

These rules were put in place to cut down on distraction so that we could concentrate on the difficult matter of focusing the mind. You don't need the Buddha to tell you that when you are imprisoned and cut off from the world for ten days and forbidden to speak, a woman's pair of sultry green eyes staring at you through the slit in her niqab could be quite a distraction. Instead of enlightenment you might find yourself pondering the shape of her jutting protuberances and lush valleys beneath her tentlike hijab.

For the first three days we practiced *aspana*, the form of meditation in vogue before Prince Gautama came boogying along. Aspana is still the meditation technique most widely practiced today, where you focus your attention on your breath moving in and out of your nostrils and gradually become aware of the tactile sensation of air passing over the viscous inner lining of your nose, softly abrading it, in and out. And when you notice your thoughts have strayed back to the sensational French girl you took to bed last week in Goa, gently dismissing the delicious thoughts from your mind and returning your concentration back to your breathing again.

Focusing on the repetitive in/out of your breath is still the fastest way to stop a restive mind. It's the reason people say, "Breathe" to someone who's panicking; it's wiser than most people are aware. Breathing is powerful precisely because it's involuntary—it happens automatically. You can't *not* breathe, and you can't *do* it either. It just *does* on its own. You can't turn it on or off if you try. Breathing embodies the mystery of being alive more than anything else. The upshot is that you can't focus on your breath and not be present at the same time. It's impossible. To focus one's attention on one's breath is to be present. Consciously paying attention to your breathing pulls you into the present moment, which is enlightenment. Therefore you can enter a state of enlightenment anytime simply by focusing intensely on your breathing. For as long as you focus your attention on the in/out of your breath and your mind doesn't wander, being present stops the mental diarrhea of thinking.

Siddhartha, before he became the Buddha, discovered that he could quiet the mind through aspana but that it was incomplete. When faced with a difficult situation, anger or fear still welled up inside him. These feelings he named *sankara* and set about how to unwind them. He found that all misery comes from an attachment made between thought and object—either wanting something you don't have or fearing something that you don't want. These desires, these attachments, are only happening at the thought level, meaning they're not real, they're just illusions, holograms. Real things are tactile; you can touch and feel them, such as the earth, wind, trees, other people. Thoughts are not reality; they're just ephemera, vapor, meant only to pass through and not stay, in the same way the breath passes through your nostrils but doesn't stay. It moves. It enters and leaves. Thoughts are meant to leave, to keep moving. Like the chairs on the Haunted Mansion ride at Disneyland, they move by really, really fast until they disappear in that tunnel at the end. The point is they don't stick around. They're not supposed to, you know, really *haunt* you for years on end. You're not supposed to *hold on* to the chairs. Obviously you let them go, and they disappear in that tunnel.

We began vipassana, Buddha's discovery, on the fourth day, and it flung us out beyond where aspana had met its limit. That's when the ecstasy began. After all the concentration on the breath passing over my nostrils, the membranous inner lining of my nose had become so sensitized that I felt as though I'd snorted mint mouthwash; my nose's inner filament tingled as though it were being abraded by a stiff ocean wind. The teachers told us to direct our attention to our upper lips and feel the tingling sensation when our breath exhaled over them. At this point, after four days of acute awareness, my perception had sharpened to such a point that I could feel a million tiny pinpricks on my upper lip every time I exhaled.

Next we were told to apply our focus over our whole face to see where else we could feel the tingling sensation. They told us to focus on our scalps, notoriously one of the hardest places to feel the tingling. I had a kind of beginner's luck, and not only could I feel a million tiny pinpricks of light, like a million tiny pricks from a loom all over my face, but the top of my head felt like it was bathed in a white fire. The carbonated, fizzy sensation on my scalp was genuinely intense. Make no mistake, this is an ecstatic sensation. If everyone knew how to do this, there'd be a lot less opium in New Hampshire. It was pure, natural bliss.

Our minds had been sharpened to such a degree that we were now able to detect the rushing river of light that gives our bodies form. Our bodies are very much unsolid and immaterial. This rushing river of light is literally everywhere—it's the matrix of our existence, the amino building blocks of the universe. The feeling of particles of light rushing through one's body is so intense and good that you know the universe must fundamentally be good to produce something so brilliant and radiant and euphoric. It is so much more powerful than any evil out there. Even now I can still access the tingling sensation on my face whenever I want to with only a few moments of concentration. Like riding a bike, if you've done it once, you can do it again. That file is uploaded in the folder labeled "Enlightenment," and I can pull it up whenever I wish. Once you know, because you felt it in vipassana, that your physical body is an unsolid rushing river of light, then you can resurrect the joyous, sparkling feeling that's like real-life magic and experience the ecstasy all over again.

After focusing on our heads, we were instructed to direct our attention down our arms, over our chests, and down our legs to our feet to see where else we could feel sensation. I had nice success with my shoulders, elbows, and wrists. My elbows in particular were highly sensitized, their gelatinous collagen a hotbed of sensation. The fizzing, firing sensation in my elbows was so potent, so intense, that it bordered on unbearable—the unbearable lightness of being. You could fairly call it an extended orgasm. The feeling of ecstasy is that good.

The teacher said that if sankara, the seeds of misery, rise close to the surface, they can result in a block in an area where you previously felt sensation but suddenly no longer can. Powerful tingling in your scalp or back, for example, might suddenly pack up and leave town. If that happens, you should not mourn the loss of the blissful sensation—that would just be another attachment.

"Be patient," the teacher said. "Continue the practice, do not resist the loss, and wait for the feeling to return again."

What exactly is enlightenment? According to the dictionary it is "to receive intellectual or spiritual light"—*to enlighten*. My understanding, probably like most people's, was that it means happiness. In the West, happiness—that thing so available and yet so elusive—is life's ultimate goal, the solution to life's sudoku. Of course, what the West doesn't know is that happiness cannot be a goal; it can only be right now.

Happiness cannot be pursued. To pursue it implies you don't have it; you're separate from it. You can only be happy or not be happy now, in the present. Happiness is largely a choice. You're happy now or not at all.

Let me explain. The Buddha's great discovery in the end was simple, as all the great discoveries are. Namely, one's physical body is hardwired to reality. If thoughts are by their very nature false, like words from a silver-tongued serpent, the body remains true and continues in its perfect alignment with reality. Your physical body and the universe are literally *one*, both made up of the same starlight, the same particles of light called photons that zoom around the universe and are its, and our, building blocks. Your body is a living thing *seamlessly stitched into the universe at large of which it is an inseparable part*. This fabric of the universe, it and us, is actually just one—called reality. If your body is woven into reality with no seams between them, it explains why you can trust your gut over thinking and your gut is never wrong. Your gut is jumper-cabled directly into the universe, and thus it reflects the universe's timeless, infinite wisdom.

Thinking, on the other hand, is problematic. Thinking by its very nature is false. If a thought is negative, you can't trust it. A negative thought causes a corresponding feeling of stress inside the body. That feeling of stress is just nature's way of telling you that the thought is false. Stress has a function: it's a fire alarm telling you that your thoughts have strayed from reality and that it's time to bring your attention back to the tactile, physical world, the only thing that's real. Take in your surroundings. Have a look around. Take a deep breath. Breathe in the fresh air. Taste the cup of hot, pungent coffee in your hands.

Siddhartha discovered a simple and rather encouraging equation: worry = false thought; or worry = not true. Simply stated, this is true every single time without exception. Surely this is even better than $E = mc^2$! And behold, the wheel of dharma was born.

At four o'clock every morning we were ripped out of deep, dreamless sleep and woken into pitch-darkness by someone banging a huge bronze gong outside our door. *Gong! … Gong! … Gong!* No matter how many mornings I went through this I never got used to it. The shock of it was like being birthed into hell. The price of enlightenment is steep.

Every morning also brought a brutally cold shower in the predawn darkness. All the rooms in the ashram were cold shower only. This may have been because cold showers were standard issue everywhere in the subcontinent except for the expensive hotels, but it also might have been because hot water was considered too much of a sensory pleasure for the course. As a rule, no outside pleasures other than those gleaned directly from meditation were permitted. Women were not allowed to wear jewelry. Men were not allowed to beat off. We were not even allowed to read or write at night, though I was usually so exhausted by the time my head hit the mattress that I fell dead asleep immediately anyway. Second-time vipassana participants were forced to sleep on the floor; they didn't even get a pillow. Pillows were ridiculed as being too luxurious.

Meditating started at four thirty in the goddamn morning and went straight through until eight o'clock every night, with only three daily meals of dal bhat in between as break. Second-time vipassana participants didn't get dinner; they received no food at all after twelve thirty. We had one hour off at lunch, and I usually scarfed down my dal bhat in ten minutes and ran back to my room for forty-five minutes of deep sleep. Altogether we were doing fifteen hours of hardcore meditation every day, nearly every waking hour of the day. Meditation was all we did. It quickly became grueling despite the ecstatic tingling feeling. The continuous, unbreaking concentration was hard work. I left sessions damp with sweat.

The forced silence and lack of any comforts whatsoever makes vipassana repellant to dilettantes. Vipassana is yuppie-proof. The inscription over the entrance about passing through a crucible is no joke. They mean it. As I said, you won't find any *Eat, Pray, Love* types here. There's no pasta, no gelato, no Balinese frenemy shaking you down to buy her a house. Vipassana is closer to a concentration camp in Dachau than anything else. You have to be pretty tenacious to get through it.

I was one of only five Westerners in the course amid a sea of Indians, around 150 students in total. The other Westerners were a young man from Venezuela, his pretty girlfriend from the Czech Republic, and a young Israeli couple. The Indians clearly weren't enlightened because, despite the explicit instructions to avert our gaze from others, they gaped openly at me as usual. Occasionally, when I became annoyed, I stared them down until they looked away, but I usually just acted like a hot chick and pretended I didn't see them.

There's something sexy about a man in a dress. Yes, you read that correctly. When I first arrived at the course, a *dhamma* worker, or manservant, provided me with a *langyi*, a long cloth sarong that is tied around the waist, because my own clothes—tank top and shorts that exposed my arms and legs—were deemed scandalous. Wearing the langyi turned out to be a liberating experience. Indian men wear theirs without underwear. I did so only the first time until I discovered I wasn't skilled enough to keep the family jewels from spilling out across the linoleum every time I sat down. During my first meditation I glanced down and saw my whole apparatus splayed out across the white marble like a Scandinavian cheeseboard. I wore boxer shorts after that.

I'm straight, but there's something freeing and genuinely empowering about wearing a dress (from the waist down, anyway) and feeling it carry and billow around your ankles when you walk like Cobra Commander's cape or Nero's toga. One feels goddamn wonderful and powerful in a cape or a kilt or a toga. How the hell did we ever let these great things get supplanted by jeans? In a langyi one feels lithe, supple, regal, sexy … like a prince and an assassin at the same time. I felt like I could cross my legs and sip a cup of tea like the prince of Persia, then stand up and break a motherfucker in half like an assassin, and then sit back down and calmly finish my tea, possibly read a little Proust. In the langyi one has that kind of mobility—an athletic, assassin litheness. Walking around in that dress, I felt like I had powers I didn't have.

We were supposed to sit on the meditation mats in disciplined stillness without shifting our legs for up to two hours at a time. For beginners this created considerable pain in our legs and back, more than one might expect. The lifelong meditator can sit still on a mat all day and feel like he's in a Jacuzzi; but for the first-timer, muscle stiffness and cramps set in quickly. It was not forbidden to shift one's leg position during meditation, but we were highly discouraged from doing so. If you moved, you might be struck by one of the abusive priests. As a result, when a session finally ended, several participants were slow to rise. One Indian tried to stand up too quickly before lunch one day and collapsed on the spot as if he'd been shot. He hit the floor hard with a loud *thwack* like a plump Mexican child whacking a piñata with a stick. The Indian shuddered on the floor for a while like a fish on land. He lay crumpled in a heap, quivering like jello in an earthquake. The other Indians filed out past his convulsing body and ignored him completely. No one tried to help him up or even so much as looked at him. The Indians care even less about each other than we do. I lingered for a while to watch him. After everyone left the hall, he slowly tried to stand up again.

On the seventh day they threw us into a dungeon. We each had our own cell in a circular cellblock that was shaped like a concrete birthday cake. They stuffed us inside narrow two-by-four-foot cells with walls that were too close to lie down in any direction. It was like solitary confinement in *The Shawshank Redemption*, but much smaller. My cell was a coffin. Huge metal doors swung shut on our freedom and we were plunged into biblical darkness. Sound reverberated throughout the cellhouse. Someone started hacking and coughing. It sounded like he was spitting up blood. A fat man in the cell next to me started to cry. He did not, however, call out for his mother. That was me.

When I was finally released from the cell a few hours later, I fell out into the corridor like a broom falling out of a closet and was met by the sickly, frightened face of a diminutive Indian man who looked like the incarceration had really taken a toll on him. We were not supposed to interact or speak to others, but we both must have looked so horrified at what they had just put us through that, glancing at each other a little askance, his lip quivering as though it were caught on a fishhook, we both spontaneously broke into grins and then burst out in full-blown laughter.

I doubled over, howling at the ludicrousness of the exercise, and he did much the same. I fell back against the wall. We laughed without care as though it was the funniest thing in the world that we would voluntarily sign up for a course that threw us inside a dark jail cell. The little Indian man was so white with fear that he looked Caucasian. He stood no more than fifteen apples high and my heart went out to the poor bastard. We both lightened up as we laughed, and the tension drained from my body like a punctured pustule. Other miserable Indians looked at us sourly as they walked past on their way out of the cellhouse. But we didn't care. Our laughter was a tonic for the harshness of the exercise. The experience was definitely incentive never to get sent to prison. French literature be damned, there is nothing romantic about it.

The dungeon was affectionately called "the pit" by the dhamma workers who tended to the place. That afternoon some of the prisoners began farting in their meditation cells. Soon others joined in, farting in deliberate sequence. I was astonished—they had cortical control over deployment. Like musical notes on a xylophone, a symphony of protest was being staged in open rebellion against our managers and this unexpected incarceration they had foisted on us. The metaphorical walls were beginning to break down. We were reaching our limit.

On the eighth day I sensed an easing in all our moods. The Venezuelan lifted his eyes—they had brightened considerably, hope having returned to them—and he nodded to me. The Israeli guy, usually so serious and self-consciously pious, looked up at me in passing and smiled warmly. In that smile I realized he was a good guy.

Was it that we knew the end was near? Or had it worked, had this experience elevated our consciousness, allowing us to better appreciate our lives? We could see out the end of the tunnel now, could see that they weren't going to throw any more heavy shit at us, anything gnarlier than the dungeon. We knew we were going to make it; we were going to get the hell out of this place.

I lifted my face to the clear blue sky and thought of Heather climbing over the compound wall. I had great respect for her for doing that. The human spirit's will to get free, to smell freedom and reach it at any cost, even if it means washing up on some distant shore with nothing, but free. The will to break out of a heavily fortified compound and flee over a squalid stretch of empty land on the outskirts of Hyderabad, India …The drive to find the place where you belong—was all very inspiring to me. My instinct was usually to stick out less-than-ideal situations instead of climb over that wall and escape. I looked up. It was a very high wall indeed. It would have attracted compliments from the Château d'If. *Bravo.* I wondered how the hell she had gotten over it.

I found it hard to concentrate in the cell. It was supposed to draw you deeper into vipassana because you couldn't be distracted by visual stimuli, sights and sounds, couldn't be tempted to look around if you were alone in a blacked-out jail cell. But robbed of sight, I was more tempted to look around than ever. Peering into the sepulchral blackness, unable to make out anything, I scratched and scraped at the walls enclosing me like Edmond Dantès. I found I needed the others around, the teachers watching, to keep me honest. I was more restless than ever inside the cell. Judging by the farting mutiny, others were too. People didn't want to meditate inside a jail cell plunged in primordial darkness. Perhaps this was the test, but if so, the teachers never remarked on it.

Somewhere on the edge of darkness, like a distant star viewed at the farthest reaches of the Hubble telescope, a corona bloomed where no light should be. I squinted at it until it came into focus. It looked like a warm shower, a comfortable bed, and hot food that wasn't dal bhat. It looked like pancakes, eggs, bacon, and hot coffee. What is it with the Mesopotamian cradle of civilization and dal bhat anyway? Can we get something else to eat around here please?

On the afternoon of the tenth day, the teacher brandished a bullhorn from inside his robe and bellowed that we could now look at each other and speak again so that we could "reassimilate to the outside world" before departing the next morning.

The only form of live interaction we had during the ten speechless days was an hour-long lecture from Goenka, the global head of vipassana, delivered to us every evening at eight o'clock via DVD on a television set in a cramped room with perforated-board walls and bloodred carpet that must have been two hundred years old. It was the same bloodred carpet Dracula had shipped over from Transylvania to his new home in London.

Each evening Goenka spoke about what we had learned that day and put the techniques into context so that we could better understand what we were meant to accomplish. Goenka told us that there are vipassana centers all around the world, from Germany to Australia, California to Japan. These ten-day vipassana courses take place in every major country on earth, so if you want to do it, you don't have to go to the original one in Hyderabad as I did.

All vipassana centers are built and run on donations. Goenka said that for any spiritual practice to be pure, it has to be free from commerce—any religious teaching that requires you to pay is already tainted because in that moment it has become a business. I agreed.

Growing up I had always looked upon my family's church with suspicion, the way the priests dwelled pruriently over the collection plate as though it were more important than the sermon, which in retrospect it was. I'm sorry, but there's something a little weird about passing around a dinner plate and asking people to reach into their pockets and drop a couple of crumpled dollar bills on it while a hymnal choir sings in the background. We didn't even get a clown, an ape in a tuxedo, or a bear dancing on a beach ball for those dollar bills—what gives? During the week the church deacon regularly phoned our house.

"We'd like you to increase your commitment," he said.

A pimp in a strip club says the exact same thing.

When I heard the deacon calling, I walked over, took the phone out of my mother's hand, and gently laid it back in its cradle.

Thanks be to God.

When I was fifteen years old, I snuck into our pastor's office and discovered secret documents in his desk drawer that said the pastor of our modest little church was milking the congregation for $85,000 a year! It was an investment banker's salary at the time, a staggering sum for a preacher of a tiny parish to be earning, a guy who essentially works one day a week. Yes, I'm sorry you have to work on *Sunday*. Buckraking the collection plate, I thought. Outraged at his peeling money off my mother to fatten his already exorbitant income, I told my mother not to give the man another dime. We stopped going to church after that. We started going to the beach on Sundays instead, and I started surfing.

God is in the ocean, let me tell you. I discovered that the world is God's church, His real church. If you can't have a black gospel choir singing the soundtrack to *Sister Act* every Sunday morning, then the next best thing is standing up on a plank of wood and riding it down a cresting wave in the Pacific Ocean. Sitting out there in the rolling waves in the miracle of our planet, cloud and sunlight raining down on me like I was inside one of Mary Poppins and Bert's street paintings, I felt life couldn't get any better than this. Splendiferous sunsets unfurled headlong over the endless rippling water like God's masterwork and were overwhelming in their beauty. For atheists, in the ocean you're also not far from the primordial ooze, gunk, and goo in the dank mud below that you believe we came from.

Vipassana workers are all volunteers with the idea that giving back through service is more valuable to your dhamma (similar to karma) than giving back with money. Requests for donations are not coercive as they often are in places like this, and it was encouraged only to give what you could afford, whether it was one dollar or a thousand. I purposely gave just one dollar to test this theory and was not met with the slightest attitude that it was unsatisfactory. I gave a more generous amount after they'd passed my little test.

Perhaps you are wondering, was this semitraumatic, wordless ten days worth it?

In a word, yes.

For the next three days after the course I felt uncommonly light, as though I wasn't carrying around my usual body weight around. I felt half as heavy—transparent, see-through even, as insubstantial as rice paper. Thoughts, too, were very breezy, not sticky, did not snag on my mind. They drifted in and out like the empty illusions they are. I saw my thoughts as from a third-party point of view, as though I was standing on a high vantage point looking down at them far below. I saw that thoughts are wholly separate from me, that they have no density or material body in the real physical world. Thoughts are imaginary. Only the tactile world is real.

A feeling of spaciousness and corresponding aliveness expanded out inside my body, giving me an airy feeling of weightlessness, and I felt nearly light enough to lift off the ground like a balloon. After being imprisoned and silenced for the last ten days, I appreciated the startling vivacity of life that much more.

The French girl, Delphine—six feet tall, beautiful, sweet, fun, skin fragrant, body smooth—was waiting for me in Bombay. When she opened the hotel room door, she said I looked different, and I know she wouldn't have said it if it wasn't true.

She's French. They don't bullshit like we Americans. French women are no shrinking violets.

All that time spent focusing my attention on the breath passing over my inner nostrils, on the particles of light that make up the stars in the heavens, the cells in our bodies, and everything in between, had finally allowed me to absorb the great unimportance of thinking. I felt like I'd had a lobotomy. More distance from thought meant more space inside my body meant freer and lighter which meant more happiness. Most of all, I felt *awake*, intensely awake. Driving-off-a-cliff awake. When you're that awake, you are close to God. Because when you're totally awake, you're totally present. And because you're so present, you feel so alive. Heaven could almost be described as a state of full, intense alertness.

Thinking back on those three days after vipassana reminds me of it even now: no attachments, a feeling of pure excitement for where we were at, the pleasure found in each other's company, a cigarette and a soda at a street-side café—all such beautiful things. I loved the people I met on these travels. People are decent and good wherever you go.

There is no path to happiness: happiness is the path.

—Siddhartha

4

The TranSiberian Express: Across Mongolia & Russia

The Russians wouldn't accept any money other than their precious Russian rubles, not even American dollars. Boris the Blade was threatening to shut off our credit and stop serving us food if no more rubles were pressed into his fleshy palm.

Wide-eyed and incredulous, I asked him, "But how will we eat?"

Boris' face twisted up in perverse pleasure and he laughed, his pale blue eyes, usually dead as a reptile's, shining with mirth for the first time I'd seen them. Sympathy and mercy are not emotions closely associated with Russians, it would seem. As the TranSiberian train flung itself west from China into Mongolia and then Russia, there were progressively fewer ATMs at the increasingly forlorn outposts the train stopped at in remote Siberia. It had been four days since we'd last seen one. I had run clean out of rubles, and I wondered how I was going to feed Abby. Abby—lithe, blonde, feline—was thin already. But I knew she was tougher than she looked.

I had met Abby at the ends of the earth in Jasailmar, the most distant outpost in Rajasthan in northwest India on the doorstep of the vast Thar Desert bridging India and Pakistan. Jasailmar is an ancient medieval walled-fortress city, an incomparably romantic place lifted straight out of the pages of *The Arabian Nights*. Beyond the medieval fortress was nothing but empty sand for over a thousand miles and caravans of Bedouins walking all day under the sun, wind, and nothingness from one far place to another. Jasailmar and Prague are probably the two most romantic cities I've ever been to, with Paris and Istanbul behind these. If you want to see a true labyrinth-bazaar straight out of the fantasy novels we loved as children, with mules clacking up stone alleyways carrying sheaves of hay, hidden doorways, mazelike passageways and the thrill of getting lost inside, a real one exists in Fez, Morocco.

One day on a cobbled backstreet in Jasailmar I was looking up at a mysterious stone tower with a single glassless black window when a pretty girl with a too-large camera around her neck appeared beside me looking up at the same window.

"It's like an Arabian fairy tale, isn't it?" I said to her.

We chatted for a minute and discovered we had both signed up for the same camel safari leaving the next day. Or perhaps she was still considering which one to sign up for and I convinced her to go with mine.

Her name was Abby. She was traveling with two girlfriends. They were all from St. Paul, Minnesota. One of her friends was a short blonde, and the other was a studious-looking brunette who looked like Thelma in Scooby Doo and told me her favorite books were *Midnight's Children* and *East of Eden*.

On the first day, as we rode our camels west across the sweltering desert, I noticed that Abby's camel had wandered far away from the pack. It was walking in a wide elliptical orbit out where Pluto would be if the rest of us were the sun. She was nearly out of view far to the south of us. She was draped over her camel's hump like she had passed out. Her body was limp and lifeless and half dangling out of her saddle. She looked as if she was about to fall off. A camel is a very tall animal; if she fell it would be a long drop to the sand. *Yah*! I thwacked my camel with my riding crop and rode over to her.

"Are you okay?" I asked.

Her mouth hung slackly open, drool collecting in one corner while her tongue lolled out the other side. Her body was bundled over the camel's hump like luggage, her left cheek pressed hard up against the hump. She was wearing a pink T-shirt and oversized plastic sunglasses with purple lenses. She looked interesting.

"Are you dehydrated?" I asked. "Do you need water?"

She didn't respond.

"Are you ill?" I pressed. "Do you require a doctor?"

"Shut up," she said, reluctantly coming back to.

She slowly unwound her long body and sat up straight. She cocked her head sideways at me, the purple lenses of her sunglasses glinting in the sunlight.

"I'm rubbing my clit against this camel's hump. I'm masturbating and have been having a rolling orgasm for the last two hours." She looked straight at me. "You broke my concentration."

"Oh, wow," I said. "Well then, carry on, soldier. As you were."

A tattoo that said *loststar* was on the underside of her wrist. I looked at the camel's ugly face and its hump thrusting up so prominently on its back.

Wow, I thought. *I'm going to have to do better than that giant beast.*

What ensued was three days of romance in a sort of Bedouin lifestyle in the desert. We had only camels, a few rugs, a little food, and nothing else. We didn't even have tents. The desert was warm at night, and we slept out under the stars. The heavens were a cascading rush of stars, a black waterfall of diamonds.

Our Indian guide built a fire each night and prepared simple meals of hot soup and bread. He fashioned himself a roué, and one night around the campfire he invited Abby to go off in the darkness with him.

"Go for a walk?" he asked, gesturing toward the primitive darkness that from where we sat in the middle of the desert looked as deep and infinite as space.

It was obvious he tried this number on all the young female clients, and I had the thought it might have worked once long ago. Abby smiled politely and then turned to me and nodded into the darkness.

Do you remember the movie *The Mummy* with Brendan Fraser? The ubiquitous black beetles in Egypt that emerged out of the sand to devour the villain? Those same black beetles, called scarabs, are all over the Thar Desert, except they don't like the light. They hid under the sand all day while the sun scorched and, like vampires, came out at night. And when they did, there were billions of them. It was very much the same as in *The Mummy*.

After Abby and I made love one night, I climbed into my sleeping bag. The fire had burned low to just embers but still emitted a faint light. That faint aurora of flame was like a crucifix protecting me from the great Satan beneath the sands, as the beetles did not surface so long as the fire gave light. Abby lay spent on a rug next to mine. In a postcoital endorphin bath beside the flickering, dying embers, she pulled a blanket over herself but passed out before climbing inside her sleeping bag. I noticed it vaguely as I passed into a deep sleep.

I woke at first light, unable to sleep beneath the ferocious sun. Abby slept longer. The fire had long since burned out, and she had slept the whole night exposed on top of her rug in the open. When she finally roused and climbed to her feet, I'll never forget it, something like one hundred beetles flowed out from under her body where they had nestled there during the night for warmth like baby chicks.

Ewwww.

The hideous black beetles had burrowed under her belly during the night, and when Abby stood up, a block party's worth of beetles, each the size of a kitten, fell off her torso and neck and then fanned out, scattering in all directions. They hesitated for just a moment, then leaped in the air and dove headfirst into the sand, submerging themselves and gone.

I recoiled in horror. It was my worst nightmare. Abby just laughed—a rich, full-throated laugh. She didn't give a fuck. Abby was pretty wild. I loved it. That camel safari across the vast empty desert, most truly in the wilds of nowhere, was one of the most remote and romantic destinations I found myself in during these long wandering years. Without any doubt, it left its rich aromatic imprint on my imagination.

After three days we returned to Jasailmar. When we entered the gates of the medieval city, we were swarmed by over two hundred children. They saw our elephant trunk-length cameras and wanted their pictures taken. Abby and I snapped hundreds of photos and showed them the digital images. The children squealed and laughed with delight at seeing themselves in the images.

Then I went on a pilgrimage alone to the north to Dharamsala to meet the Dalai Lama at his annual lecture that's open to the public every March. While it was exciting to brush my hand along the holy one's hairy leg beneath his robe when he strode past me in the garden's dappled courtyard—touching God, essentially—his lecture, relying mostly on reading from some massive Buddhist tome that made *War and Peace* seem like a one-page story treatment, was soporific and boring. They should've given him the hook and flown in a Shakespeare performing summer troupe instead. Realizing how stupid it was to have gone to the mountainous north to see the Dalai Lama when Abby was still in the country, I raced back to her in New Delhi. After two torrid nights together in Major's Den hostel, Abby flew home.

Some months later, she surprised me by flying to Beijing to meet me. I had told her my travel plans and she decided to join me on the three-week TranSiberian Express train odyssey from Beijing, China all the way to Prague, Czech Republic, in Europe. We would cross an entire continent together and see some of the world's most far-flung and exotic cities.

We boarded the old-fashioned steam engine train in Beijing. The train looked like something out of *Murder on the Orient Express,* from some antiquated age. It wasn't modern, but it was vintage and beautiful and dare I say, perfect—a nineteenth-century train for a nineteenth-century journey.

On the second day we crossed the border from China into Mongolia. Mongolia is an absolute kick. It has but one city, the capital Ulaanbaatar, the rest being just grassy steppes, nomadic horsemen, and *gers*, the primitive straw huts the people sleep in that are like Native American tepees. Abby and I spent two days and nights exploring the vast, empty grasslands of the Mongolian countryside. It was the most beautiful country I have ever seen if we don't talk about mountains: it was stark, pale, empty, windswept, green, and piercingly peaceful. It was utterly silent. Mongolia is so primitive that there are no machines outside the capital. If I have ever found Shangri-La in this world, Mongolia outside of Ulaanbaatar is it.

We slept in a ger, and I kept us warm during the freezing nights by stoking a tiny furnace in the hut's center with log after log. The furnace was something out of a thousand years ago, certifiably medieval, and it burned wood the way your grandmother smoked cigarettes. Black smoke billowed out of the stovepipe furnace and swirled around us in the tepee, choking the air and our lungs. It was like smoking a thousand Marlboros a night. Abby eventually succumbed to the cold and the turbid, eddying smoke and began to cough consumptively. I kept waking up in the night to refill the stove with a fresh cache of wood to stave off our freezing to death.

It was June.

I couldn't imagine how cold December must be. Everything must be frozen solid. It must be an absolutely white world. I'd love to see it; it must be startlingly beautiful. Mongolia was very private, intensely bucolic, and almost painfully beautiful. It's almost entirely uninhabited—a throwback to an earlier, more mythical age. Mongolia has less distraction than anywhere I've ever been. I was almost living the Native American life I've always secretly yearned for. I was a hunter, felling the largest, most dangerous beasts, and Abby was my Pocahontas or Woman of the Hearth, scantily clad in leather and feathers—feral, gamine, fiercely independent, wickedly profane, and sexy as hell. At night we slept naked in an enormous white woolly mammoth fur on a hard cave bed. And I've never been happier.

I would have been very happy living in *The Clan of the Cave Bear*. That life would have suited me fine.

The TranSiberian Express

The simplicity of spending every day riding horses and hiking around the empty green savannahs that stretched from Ulaanbaatar to China with no infrastructure in between—no roads, telephone poles, cables, nothing—was the perfect way to relax in a truly lost world that is essentially no different than North America sixteen thousand years ago when the great ice calved just enough for the first human to limbo through somewhere around present-day Montana. Can you imagine what that person saw? The strange beasts and supersized animals that roamed uninhabited America at that time must have been head-spinning to see. Mongolia is like that pristine country. Without the strange magical beasts, though.

Preferred mode of transportation in Mongolia: still the horse.

We crossed the border from Mongolia into Russia two days ago, and as the train hurtled west across thousands of miles of Siberian wasteland—the most desolate, bald country I have ever seen—the world itself seemed to expand.

At each of the increasingly few stations, the train stopped for a mercurial length of time. The stoppage times were always different, and since we couldn't read the Cyrillic timetables, we never knew when the train was going to depart until it did. There was no whistle, horn blow, or announcement from an attendant that the train was about to leave the station. Usually we saw the Mongolians running back across the platform before we noticed that the train had imperceptibly started crawling forward. Within thirty seconds the train would be at full speed and completely gone and we would be left behind.

Abby was more nervous about missing the train at these brief stops in remote Siberia than I was. I was more insouciant and simply *believed* that I wouldn't miss the train. I loved to stay out on the platform as long as I could, perusing the many food items, clothing, and trinkets, and watching with fascination as the Mongolians leaped down from the train at every stop laden like pack mules with rugs, blue jeans, sneakers, denim jackets, dresses, belts, boots, fragrances—fashion knockoffs of everything one might find at Macy's department store. Because the train only stopped for a few minutes at each stop, there was no time to set up an actual shop, so the Mongolians themselves were the pop-up shops. Their bodies were the stores—their outstretched arms the coatracks the Russians shopped off of. Eager Russians traveled from great distances in barren Siberia to be on the platform when the train arrived to buy these heavily discounted Chinese knockoffs.

I picked up a pair of Hermès jeans for myself, the Hermès label emblazoned across the ass in gold stitching like a tattoo. The zipper and button snap broke within a week, but I kept wearing them anyway because, you know, they're Hermès. A couple of months later someone told me that Hermès doesn't actually make jeans. In Russia the prices of goods are terribly high in proportion to the low wages, fueling demand for these counterfeit items. Inflation was out of control and the value of the ruble fluctuated wildly even within days. That year Moscow was named the world's most expensive city—shocking considering the relative poverty of its citizens.

The day before the train crossed into Russia, the Mongolians knew what was coming, and they were ready for it. They spent the waning hours of daylight before we arrived at the border urgently hiding all their rugs, blankets, blue jeans, sneakers, denim jackets, dresses, and more inside every nook, cranny, and crevice of the train—nooks, crannies, and crevices an ordinary passenger would never know existed. The spectacle of their stashing all their smuggled goods inside the bowels and recesses of the train was an aspect of the journey I'll never forget. The goods were so many and available hiding space so little. The Mongolians knew every alcove, cavity, cubbyhole, wrinkle, knot, and fold of that train. They pulled up the floorboards and crammed large quantities of clothing and shoes *under the floor* of the train. Screwdrivers were spun thousands of times in service of sealing the floorboards back into place.

After they ran out of space under the floor and in their own sleeping cars, the Mongolians pushed their way *into the guests' rooms* and started hiding as many clothes as possible *in other guests' storage containers*. We watched nonplussed as our fellow ticket-buying passengers, these Mongolians who didn't speak a word of English—not even yes or no—shouldered their way into our room without knocking and, without a word, pulled our bags out of our storage bins, tossed them aside, and began cramming their clothes and contraband items inside our storage containers instead. The rooms on the train were tiny with two bunkbeds along each wall, four beds in total, and only two storage bins under the two lower bunks. The room was so small that there was hardly enough space to walk between the two bunkbeds.

The Mongolians jabbed their thick fleshy fingers, the fingers of Qing dynasty eunuchs or Franciscan monks, at our backpacks and then at us, indicating that we should store them elsewhere, either leave them in the middle of the floor, or sleep with them in our beds. They didn't offer us anything in return for seizing our storage space but were so insistent that we gave in pretty quickly and just watched the outlandish spectacle in utter fascination. I mean, where else can you see this?

We crossed the border into Russia in the middle of night. I was awoken in darkness by a loud gestapo-like banging on the door. Three tall, grim-faced officers crashed into our room like a breaking wave and shined flashlights in our faces like Rolf's Nazis in *The Sound of Music*. We cowered in our bunks. I looked up groggily, for a moment not knowing where I was. All was shadow and light playing across the ghoulish faces of the Soviet soldiers strutting across our room in the darkness. They were immense, tall as Titans. They dragged heavy metal-ribbed flashlights across our bedframes, making horrible jangling noise to frighten us. The man in front was the spitting image of Dolph Lundgren: six-foot-six with a square jaw like an Easter Island moai statue and short white-blond hair meticulously spiked upward.

For a moment I was ushered back to the Soviet era as the evil cast of *Rocky IV* strode across our small room—Communist giants, terrifying. It was only the third time our room had been invaded without our permission that day, but this was the first time it was truly scary. Their faces were grotesque, misshapen in the wobbly, spectral light. Dolph Lundgren loomed over us, the very picture of Soviet enslavement, the top of his head nearly grazing the ceiling. He opened his mouth and barked out harsh, guttural commands. Two underlings took our passports and then began turning the room upside down. They turned on the lights, looked under the beds. Nothing. Then they opened the storage containers and a nimbus of light emanated from them. There it all was: piles of contraband clothing gleaming like jewels, the cache unearthed.

For a moment Dolph Lundgren stared at the booty in silence. He inhaled sharply, making a hissing sound, and then he unloaded a long booming, vituperative rant in Russian. I thought the two lieutenants would start removing the contraband from the storage containers, but they did not. Instead they walked back out into the corridor.

Five minutes later they returned with a Mongolian man and a woman. It seemed that the Russians believed they were the ones who had hidden the smuggled goods in our room. We were lucky they didn't think it was us. It was our room, after all; they could easily have arrested us if they wanted to. Dolph Lundgren interrogated the couple outside in the corridor for several minutes. The Mongolians seemed to understand what he was saying, though they didn't say a word. At some point Lundgren took them off the train, and I never saw any of them again. I thought the Mongolians were returned to their room later, but now I'm not so sure. I looked for them on the train over the next few days, but never saw them. A sacrifice to the gods of corruption. Perhaps in this game two Mongolians are sacrificed on every TranSiberian train journey in exchange for allowing the racket to continue. That and a payoff are the price of using the TranSiberian Express to smuggle fake Chinese goods into Russia.

The lieutenants came back to our room, returned our passports, and then, surprisingly, left the contraband with us. The chests stood gaping wide open, the smuggled goods exposed like refugees in the cargo hold of a ship. Before leaving, one of the lieutenants noticed a few more contraband denim shirts the Mongolians had hung on a hook behind our door. He said something in Russian to the other lieutenant and they both chuckled and looked at us sympathetically. Then they left, never to return.

They didn't confiscate any of the goods, though they put on quite a show of searching each car with maximum chaos, dragging huge, metal-ribbed flashlights across bedframes to inflict the greatest possible terror in the guests. I laughed thinking about some rich American complaining about this shocking treatment. Dolph Lundgren and company would probably pick that American up and throw them out the window of the surging train. Russia was a sketchy place. I got the feeling you didn't want to mess with it too much. I suspect that everything we saw was staged in some way with money exchanging hands in shady customs offices at the border. A mysterious bargain had been struck, never to be explained. We were in Russia, where corruption and Potemkin village–style misdirection are second nature.

The visa to enter Russia as a tourist was by far the most difficult to obtain in all my travels. If you overstay your visa, the Russians don't simply fine you and slap you on the wrist the way most countries do. They throw you in the clink. Russia is not exactly a welcoming place for strangers. There appeared to be no immigrants at all from what I could see. I saw no people of color. This has ensured the Russians look exactly the same as they did when *Rocky IV* came out. Russia is like a time capsule—if your smartphone fell down a drainpipe, you'd never know if it was 1961, 1991, or 2021. If the DeLorean from *Back to the Future* took you back in time to Saint Petersburg in 1961, the city would look no different than it does today other than a single KFC and Pizza Hut on the main street.

One of the delights of the TranSiberian train was the dining car. Abby and I spent many long, slow hours in it playing cards, eating, and just talking. It was idyllic. Whenever we crossed a border into a new country, the dining car was traded out and replaced with an entirely new car with a motif, decor, menu, and chef from that country. The car wasn't just redecorated but completely switched out and a new one installed. This always happened late at night at the border crossings, so I never saw exactly how it was done, but both times I was awoken in darkness by a horrendous gnashing and ripping sound of metal gears being torn apart—a terrible rending of metal that lasted for forty minutes.

In each country—China, Mongolia, and Russia—the dining car was decorated in elaborate detail. In China, calligraphy scrolls, dolls with exquisitely drawn features, and paintings adorned the car. The Mongolia car was very indigenous with Native American–like tribal headdresses, wooden totems, necklaces of animal tusks, and large parchment tapestries of warriors riding horses across vast open plains. The Russian car had an enormous black bear's head the size of a Volkswagen stapled to the wall. You could never forget about the bear head while here because its sinister yellow eyes followed you around the room wherever you sat, like Big Brother's. In fact, we were in Russia, so it probably was Big Brother. Animal furs, paintings of privation and hardship, Russian soldiers running through snowy forests to halt the advance of Germans in World War II, and elegant Russian nutcrackers adorned the walls.

Each new car also brought with it a new chef. All the food was delicious. It wasn't the usual prepackaged, microwaved swill you get on a train. We had real human chefs cooking real meals in tiny kitchens. The prices were expensive, which precluded the Mongolians from eating in the dining car, but the food always surpassed my expectations and was nearly worth its exorbitant cost. The Russian chef, Boris the Blade, was a real character. He didn't speak any English, but he made the most sumptuous, bountiful Russian borscht soups: cornucopias of potato, cheese, sour cream, hunks of beef, and vegetables filled right up to the brim, none of the halfway skimping nonsense you get in the States. These were hearty, full bowls of soup fit for a tsar. One bowl of Boris's borscht was a meal.

Flat beams of pale yellow sunlight slanted through the windows of the dining car as Abby and I spent hours relaxing and getting to know each other, ordering food, doing crossword and sudoku puzzles, then after an hour or so eating again. If I hadn't just been emaciated by giardia from the poisonous tap water of India, I would have gained a lot of weight from the enormous amount of food we consumed in that dining car. Abby ate enough to feed a water buffalo for a year and didn't gain an ounce; she remained as skinny as a Rwandan.

Those carefree, unstructured hours in the dining car were perfectly happy and as free from restlessness as I have ever been. There's something about the simple, meditative nature of long-distance train journeys, especially one with very few stops over vast, alien terrain like the TranSiberian Express. With no place to go and nothing that has to be done, one can fully relax and just sink into the sublime Zen nature of trains. The lack of available options, while the train soothingly and, all-importantly, continuously rumbles on beneath your feet, renders life perfectly adequate as it is. There is no hungering for more in life while on a long-distance train journey. Dissatisfaction is suspended. You have everything you need. It was a blissful existence, and for that journey across an empty continent Abby and I were lifted clean out of the stream of time.

Our tiny room had two bunks, four beds in total, and we roomed with two strangers. The organizers had thoughtfully paired us with two other Westerners. One was a young blonde woman from Norway getting her PhD in music history—not music, but music history. I learned the different permutations of the harp through history, including the much maligned but ultimately misunderstood dulcimer. The second was a young American college student, age twenty, boldly traveling across Russia alone. He was happy he didn't need a fake ID to drink in Russia. I told him in Russia they would let you drink yourself to death at any age and no one would try to stop him. He grinned.

As Abby and I had just met in India a month ago and she had just flown in from Minnesota to join me on this trip, things were red hot. Each night the train cut the lights at exactly 11:00 p.m. to force the passengers to go to sleep. I'd wait one minute, and then climb up into Abby's bunk above mine. There was no other place to go and do it on the crowded train. There were no private or unoccupied rooms. The train was chockfull, and every room had four occupants. The train had less available space per square foot than a rabbit warren, beehive, or anthill. There were no private places where a couple could go at all, except the public bathroom, which was a cramped, foul-smelling space. We did it once in the smoking car when no one was there. We were in a poor country, so the smoking car was never empty for long. Abby just shrugged down her jeans, bent over, and slipped her fingers through the steel grate where the cigarette smoke passed out of the train. She gripped the metal grate white-knuckled, and we humped like livestock for a few minutes until a smoker walked in. It was very *Anna Karenina*. When the man entered, Abby said I should have just kept going and he would have turned around and left. That was an eye opener for me. I was getting an education.

Our room was so small—no larger than a dry freezer at Applebee's—and the space between the pair of bunk beds so narrow that the Norwegian music student was mere inches from our faces when Abby and I did it in the dark. Since I only ever waited a minute to climb into Abby's bunk after the lights went down, I doubt any of our roommates were asleep yet. The Norwegian woman faced away from us. I imagined her lying there with her eyes open, exotic seventeenth-century musical instruments floating through her mind like sugarplums. I could have reached out and placed my hand on top of her head, she was that close to us. Abby and I tried not to make a sound. The Norwegian never fidgeted; no one did.

When out on the platform at the brief stops, I occasionally pretended as though I hadn't noticed the train start moving again to give Abby a scare. Then I'd run over and jump safely on only when she was screaming at me hysterically. I laughed at her terror at my nearly being stranded in Siberia.

Just a bit of fun, I thought.

The train stopped for a different amount of time at each station, and it was difficult to gauge how long a stop would be because we couldn't read the Cyrillic timetables. There were no timetables in English. The Russian language doesn't use the Roman alphabet or even our numbers, so the Cyrillic characters are completely inscrutable. Incredibly, none of the staff on board spoke any English. The TranSiberian Express is an exotic and marvelous creation but still a fairly primitive one, frozen in time, which is part of what made it so fun. There was no translator, no English-speaking guide on the train, so the duration of each stop was entirely unknowable to the Western passengers, causing us never to wander more than a few feet from the train on the platforms lest it start up and leave us behind. Stoppage times could range from as long as thirty-three minutes to as brief as two minutes, though the average time seemed to be around five to seven minutes—fairly short. The length of stops was mercurial and followed no discernible pattern. It could be short one time, long the next, short several times in a row, or short, short, long, short. The stop times weren't based on any logic we could guess at. We never saw goods or fuel being loaded onto the train that would necessitate a longer stop, and the train didn't stop for longer in cities than it did at small outposts. It was a mystery. We were in the dark.

Boris the Blade was laughing, his dead, reptilian eyes alive and dancing for the first time I'd seen them. This American and his skinny girlfriend were going to starve, and what could be more delightful than that? Boris was overjoyed, to put it mildly, and even did a little dance in his apron to prove it.

"Boris, you're pretty spry to do a Riverdance like that," I said, but no joke would get him to feed us unless we somehow came up with some rubles.

We were halfway across Siberia now, with halfway left to go, and Boris had just cut off our food. There would be no more border crossings or kitchen car changes to save us. Abby and I had both completely run out of rubles, and Boris would no longer accept our American dollars in payment. He'd accepted our US money extremely reluctantly the first two times—the second time I had to press the money into his cold fingers to get him to take it—but by the third time he refused to accept it anymore. In no way would he accept our Chinese or Mongolian money, swatting at it derisively and saying something in Russian that might have meant "worthless." Boris the Blade spoke no English at all, not even yes or no, but he did manage, using profane gestures, to convey that Chinese and Mongolian money weren't good for anything beyond wiping his ass with, and his use for American dollars didn't run much higher. I repeated that we had no more rubles and we were hungry. Boris belly-laughed up from his diaphragm and walked away.

At the next, slightly larger stop in the barren Siberian wasteland, I was determined to find an ATM, knowing we would soon starve. I had no choice but to venture out and look for one, risky as it seemed with the unknown stoppage time. Abby followed as I stepped off the train, only to discover that the tiny station at this remote outpost was on the other platform on the opposite side of the tracks. We had to climb up and over a bridge that connected the two platforms and was high enough for trains to pass under. We did this, stepped inside the station, and *eureka!* An ATM stood there. It was the first one we'd seen in nearly a week. Abby inserted her ATM card and punched in her code for her daily maximum of $500. The machine declined the transaction.

"Fuck!" she swore. "We have to get back on the train."

"No," I said. "Try it again with a lesser amount, just two hundred."

She shot me a disapproving glare but punched in her code again. It worked! The machine belched out the equivalent of $200 in rubles. Yes! We could eat!

"Let's go."

"Just a moment," I said, as I slid my card in to withdraw the same amount. I got my rubles, and we ran back outside.

The train on the opposite platform was moving.

"Oh fuck!" Abby said. "That train is moving. Which one is our train? Is that our train?"

There were two trains side by side on the opposite side of the bridge that looked identical to each another. One of them was moving and picking up speed, while the other was standing still. The moving train was on the far side of the still one. We could see it moving through the gaps in the first train, but couldn't climb through the gaps—we had to run back over the bridge.

"Shit, I think that's our train," I said.

"Go! Run!" she screamed.

Taking the steps three at a time, I bounded up and over the bridge. Abby was an athletic girl, and she was right behind me. We ran down the other side.

"Is this our train?" she yelled. "Is this the right one?"

"I don't know!" I shouted. The train had picked up so much speed and was moving so fast now that it was almost too late, too dangerous, to try to hop it.

"Make a decision!" she screamed.

"Get on!" I yelled, and without looking back, I lunged for a silver rung outside one of the boxcars.

Grabbing it with one hand, I was on, my feet resting by just my tiptoes on a tiny one-inch foothold. My heels and the balls of my feet were suspended out in midair. The train was now barreling along at a healthy forty miles per hour or so, definitely too fast to jump on, or off, if I had chosen the wrong train. Frantically I looked over my shoulder. Abby was on! She was a little way down from me, clutching a silver rung on the next car over.

A train attendant must have glimpsed me through a window because a door to my left slid open. A thick arm reached out and gripped my wrist. I hopped to the step newly available and was inside. Two enormous Mongolian female train attendants stood there. They slammed the door shut, and started roughing me up. They punched me in my body and face and yelled at me in their language for being so stupid, so crazy for riding on the outside of the train as it moved into hyperspeed when I was supposed to be on the inside. They seemed to think I was joyriding outside the train like some American adrenaline junkie, like Patrick Swayze in *Point Break*.

"No!" I shouted.

One of the women clotheslined me against the wall while the other moved in and robotically barrel-punched me in my kidney, but I had strength born of desperation and I shoved them both away.

They did not speak English, but I pointed at the door and screamed, "There's another person out there!"

I thrashed at the door, ripped it open. And there was my Abby, looking pretty calm out there given the circumstances. She was still holding the rung outside the speeding train. The train must have been rocketing along at ninety miles per hour or more, terrifyingly fast. Like a professional rock climber or transforming insect, Abby had flattened her body against the side of the train to keep the gale wind forces from blowing her off into oblivion. She needed to jump from her little foothold and rung to the one I had been standing on beside the door. Athletically and, I will never forget this, with no hesitation, she nimbly leaped through the air from her foothold to mine. For a moment she was airborne, touching nothing with either her hands or her feet, both her arms crooked at the elbows and both her legs crooked at the knees, suspended in midair, suspended in time, as the train bolted forward like a bat out of hell. She was fearless. She landed perfectly like an angel. And then I took her in my arms and swept her inside the car. The door slammed shut, and once again the Mongolian attendants started beating us on our arms and faces.

Abby and I looked at each other, kind of exhilarated, kind of crazed. We laughed and ran off together down the train, flying through passageways searching for the dining car, for Boris the Blade, for a passenger we recognized, anything that would tell us whether or not we had jumped on the right train. We had boarded somewhere near the back and nothing looked familiar. We ran through car after car, but there was no dining car. No hot soup, no Boris the Blade. I started to panic. "Oh shit, this is the wrong train," I said. "This isn't our train. All our shit's on the other train …"

"Wait," Abby said. She was cool.

We streamed through car after car, flinging open doors and not bothering to shut them behind us. Then I saw someone I thought I recognized. "I think I've seen him before …" Then someone else. And suddenly we were back in our car, and all was well.

"What happened to you guys?" one of our friends asked. Our roommates sat there grinning at us, completely unaware of what we had just been through. But there may have been a certain sparkle in our eyes, a windswept whimsy or ecstasy in our faces that seemed to say it all. Our friends cocked their heads, leaned in, looked closer. Abby and I looked at each other and started to laugh. We had had quite a thrill—the thrill of a lifetime.

When you arise in the morning think of what a privilege it is to be alive, to think, to enjoy, to love …

Remember that very little is needed to make a happy life.

—Marcus Aurelius, *Meditations*

5

Alaska

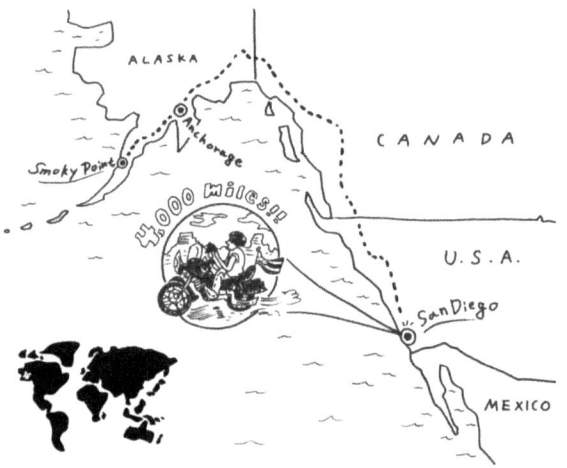

It was night. I was taking a ferry up the Inside Passage from Washington State to Alaska. I lay shivering on the deck of the ship, staring out at the black water and stars. I'd skimped on paying for an overpriced room aboard the ship, electing instead for the cheapest option available, which was sleeping outside on the concrete deck under the night sky. Black ocean waves smacked against the hull of the ship and spackled me with spray as I lay shivering. Though my sleeping bag was rated to 0 degrees Celsius—supposedly fit for Base Camp IV on Mount Everest—my teeth were chattering and I was shaking inside the bag, too cold to fall asleep. A frigid ocean wind buffeted the ship all night long, strafing my face. I tried to burrow deeper inside the sleeping bag but there was no deeper to go.

The ferry moved on imperceptibly through the close night, and I was still shivering more than an hour later. I knew from the last two nights on the deck that it would take at least two hours for my body to warm enough to the down inside the sleeping bag for me to pass into sleep. And yet those 120 shivering minutes turned out to be an unexpected blessing. Though I lay freezing, the sky was extraordinarily beautiful, illuminated by millions of stars, countless pinpricked holes in the dark curtain of night. Other than in the depths of the Himalayas, I have never seen so many stars in all my life.

I stared up into multitudes, a stronghold of stars. The rich tableau of starry night sky was so enthralling that I felt I could look at it forever, a riddle I would never comprehend yet couldn't tear my eyes away from. The planets and countless shooting stars, at least one every few seconds, fired my imagination and left me breathless with awe.

As I lay on the hard deck wearing a headlamp I glanced at my copy of *Wuthering Heights*. A classic as I understood it, it topped all lists of romantic novels, but it just wasn't for me. Halfway through, I couldn't do it anymore and flung the book overboard. By then I was immersed in Brontë's murderous moors and violently romantic way of thinking, so while I usually don't litter, I thought Brontë herself might appreciate the hot, careless act of hurling her novel in the remorseless sea.

During the day I stood out on deck in the stinging wind under a pale sun that emitted no warmth and kept my eyes peeled for sperm whales, which we had been told there was a possibility of seeing. In my deepest heart I hoped to see something chilling and massive like Ahab's whale itself, see it smash the ferry into driftwood and send bodies flying into the gelid sea. Part of me wondered what that would look like.

I never saw anything other than a few porpoises.

I had bought a used Kawasaki Vulcan 750 cc motorcycle. I had feverishly negotiated its price down from $7,000 to $4,000. The irony is that I ended up spending far more on repairs and logistical costs than if I had just bought a brand new bike to begin with. No one has had their motorcycle break down in more isolated, remote parts of the planet than I have.

Continuing my quixotic year when I quit Sony, questing for knowledge and desperate to expand my world, I found myself on the Vulcan driving north from San Diego to Alaska on the Pacific Coast Highway—US Route 101—during a sunless, surprisingly cold month of June. June, it turns out, is not a warm month on the California coast. Who knew? It was freezing.

It was overcast the entire way. The sun never poked out once until I reached Alaska. I would be cold the entire summer—for six months straight—a harbinger of things to come. I loaded the bike onto the Alaskan ferry in the port city of Bellingham, Washington, near the Canadian border, and looked forward to a chance to rest my sore ass on the ferry for a few days. An ocean journey is always one that's closest to my heart.

I had noticed another bike lashed against the hull in the cargo hold next to mine, so I knew there was another rider on board. A rider usually isn't too hard to find in a contained world such as a ship at sea, because riders usually have a certain appearance—facial hair, tattoos, an antiauthoritarian loner glint common among the biking community. When I saw the leather jacket with the bald eagle and the word FREEDOM the size of a billboard marquee emblazoned on the back, I knew I'd found the other rider.

It didn't hurt that I was wearing the exact same thing.

I approached him in the ship's bar one afternoon and introduced myself. He had seen my bike in the cargo hold too, and we quickly made a plan to meet outside the docking bay when we arrived in

Haines, Canada, and ride on to Anchorage together. His name was Rosie. He was around forty-five years old. He was a pit boss in a casino in Reno, Nevada. Being older, he had an enormous souped-up, tricked-out motorcycle that was closer to a spaceship than a bike. It had a huge wraparound windshield that blocked out all wind, a CD player and satellite radio playing a steady stream of baby boomer hits like the Eagles, a heater at the torso and legs like a Mercedes, even a seat heater, and a massive ass for luggage that rivaled a Datsun's. I looked down on his bike with disdain. At that level is it even like riding a motorcycle anymore? You might as well just slap two more wheels on it and call it a car. My rough-and-ready Vulcan was closer to a bicycle with a jet engine tacked to the back with bungee cords than a motorcycle. It was lean, stripped down to the nuts, with no extra features. Its only extra feature was myself. My windshield was closer to a geisha's fan than an actual windshield—it didn't even block out any wind because it was only as high as my nipples. Heavy, frigid winds gusting out of the North Pole beat my face relentlessly like a fraternity's hazing paddle for the next seven thousand miles. But I wouldn't have it any other way. If I'm riding, I want to feel it all. Why else do it? Otherwise just buy a car, jackass.

As we moved further and further north, during the frigid, teeth-chattering nights on the deck of the ship I gazed out at the lightless coast, black and forbidding, haunting and calling to me at the same time. Finally one cold afternoon we reached Haines. Haines is a tiny port—I wouldn't call it a town—in northern British Columbia, Canada. Despite having an official population of six hundred, you'd be hard-pressed to find two people. The town consists pretty much of the port itself, a tiny motel, and the road out.

From here it was an ass-murdering eight hundred mile haul to Anchorage. Although we're only talking about Haines, in northern

Canada, to Anchorage, Alaska, the distances in Canada are so vast that this ride is roughly equivalent to a third of the way across the United States. I had no idea until I got here that Alaska is a jaw-dropping two thousand miles north of the US-Canada border. That's two-thirds of the distance across the United States.

This far above the sixtieth parallel, it was light almost twenty-four hours a day in summer. It only got dark for a couple of hours between two thirty and four thirty in the morning, and even then the sun just barely dipped below the horizon. Its pearly orange lid sat right at the sphere horizon, its scalp sliced just finely enough by the sharp straight line of the horizon that you could see flares flying up from solar storms on the surface of the sun.

When the ferry docked, I swooped down into the ship's hold to collect my bike. The other bike was already gone. That was fast. I wondered if Rosie had taken off without me. When I rolled my bike out, he was in the parking lot waiting for me. He sat astride his motorcycle, which was already turned on and roaring in idle, his sunglasses on, arms folded high across his chest, his face granite, ready to go. He looked impatient. This was the moment he had been dreaming about, possibly for years.

I knew the feeling.

As the bikes I had in those years were all bought used and cheap, they also had a great deal of mechanical problems, not the least of which was frequent trouble starting in cold weather or when the bike had not been started for several days. Both conditions were in place this time. After turning the ignition a few times without success, my bike as lifeless as a sarcophagus, I looked up and met Rosie's hard, disapproving glare. He was not a man who made much room for other people's needs. I tried to ignore him.

"Come on …" I verbally cajoled the bike.

Castigating the motorcycle, you won't be surprised, didn't work. Finally I pulled out the choke—a kind of last-stop measure to start a bike—and the Vulcan belched and hacked its way to life.

The choke, on the left handlebar, is literally a string, like the one on the end of a tampon. Yanking it floods the engine with gasoline, like a surge of heroin to an addict's bloodstream, and can goose a cold bike to life like beating your fists against a dead man's chest and screaming, "Come back, you fucker!" will bring him back to life in the movies. The problem is if you use too much choke, you drown the engine in too much gasoline and soak the ignition wick, making it too wet to spark, just as wet firewood won't make you a campfire anytime soon.

The altimeter, another important instrument on the dashboard, hovers at just above two on a healthy bike. My altimeter was hovering a hair above zero. If the needle touches zero, the bike automatically dies. My bike was a speed bump, a pothole, or just catching a chill away from death. I grimaced. It could cut power at any time.

I glanced over at Rosie. He had been watching me hatchet-faced for the last five minutes. When I finally pulled out the choke and the bike coughed to life, he nodded brusquely. He said he thought we could do all eight hundred miles to Anchorage in one ass-killing ride. No breaks, just murder through it. This was not really feasible—about the most a rider can get away with in one day is five hundred miles, maybe six hundred if he's a masochist. But Rosie's implacable face told me he wasn't joking. I realized he rode often enough that his ass had transmogrified into wood. For anyone who doesn't ride consistently, as I didn't, your ass becomes seriously uncomfortable after only a few hours on a bike. The longer you ride, the worse it hurts until it's so painful that knives of shooting pain are radiating out from your butt over your entire body like a fistful of pinched nerves or being stung by a swarm of jellyfish. It's hell, it really is. You have to pass through an extraordinary crucible of ass pain before you come out the other side and the powers that be transform your mushy ass from cookie dough into wood.

Only then can you call yourself a rider.

My companion rode parallel with me on the empty double-lane road like Peter Fonda and Dennis Hopper in *Easy Rider*, sometimes slightly ahead, sometimes slightly behind. We drove seventy-five miles per hour, but our bikes were close enough that I could easily have reached out and touched him. We rode in sync, as though both controlled by one brain. Like a harmonious musical chord made up of two adept motorcyclists instead of notes on a scale, we weaved in and out, in front and behind each other, riding in figure eight patterns like ice-skating partners but on a road instead of an ice rink, our collective one brain calibrating our rhythms without our having to do anything to make it so. Exposed on the highway with the ability to reach out and bump fists while hurtling along at seventy-five miles per hour creates a bond, a symmetry between bikers that doesn't exist between car drivers.

Most car drivers seem to hate each other. The exoskeleton frames of cars dual-function as conductive antennae that give people license to channel their frustration and hatred at the people in the other metal exoskeletons around them. With no concern, thanks to no chance of meeting each other face-to-face, their rage can flow freely, safely, and most importantly, unabated. Screaming at or berating strangers is somehow accepted in our advanced civilization as long as you are in a car. Following this to its logical conclusion, people would probably like to attack strangers on the street if only it were socially permitted. We haven't evolved past the bloodlust of gladiators in the Colosseum. We just built cars.

But bikers all love each other. It's a lovefest, man.

Once while I was riding in the far north, a black man rode into the same gas station where I was refilling my tank. Snow lay on the ground.

I stood shivering next to a gas pump. The tall black man dismounted his bike. He was wearing snakeskin boots. I glanced at his Indian motorcycle. An entire crocodile's skin was spread across the seat of his bike. He was wearing a thick silver fur coat. "I like your Carhartts, man!" he called to me. We clasped hands, and he reached out and hugged me. A stranger whom I had just met five seconds earlier.

It can happen with another biker.

Bikers are like prenatal twins separated at birth, newly reunited. There's an automatic respect that exists between bikers without being spoken, one linked to our small number and the ever-incumbent danger of death, the omnipresent chance of becoming a pancake on the asphalt two seconds from now *anytime we're riding*. We all know that every time we straddle the saddle and bolt down the interstate at ninety miles per hour with no armor, just jeans, wifebeater, and black leather jacket, we're putting our lives in God's hands. It doesn't have to be said. Gripping those handlebars, the only goddamn things keeping you alive, knowing full well that if your hands were to slip off the grips for any reason at all, you'd be just a bloodstain, a grease spot on the highway, there's some subtle understanding that, in some way, we're all trying to touch God, no different than Michelangelo was when he painted the Sistine Chapel. God resides in the thin line between life and death.

When bikers see other bikers approaching on the opposite side of the highway, without exception they ritualistically drop their left hand down into a low V victory sign in greeting—a universal greeting between bikers in all countries around the world that reinforces the bond between you and every other biker you pass on the other side of the road. You automatically and irrevocably belong to the same club.

Interestingly, if you talk to other bikers at gas stations, both of you scuffing your boots against the concrete bank of gas pumps while your tanks refill, in motel lobbies at check-in or check-out or at the stand-up coffee and doughnut breakfast, in diners over bottomless cups of hot coffee and hash browns drowned in bacon grease, or at casino blackjack tables, you find that you somehow share a similar life philosophy and have certain basic things in common. You may come from different socioeconomic backgrounds, yet in some foundational way you are the same person. Bikers are freethinkers—iconoclasts. All serious bikers share an abiding love of freedom, a real devotion to it, and a very deep patriotic love of America, or their own country. Patriotism and love of freedom run hot-quick through our blood like molten quark-gluon plasma, the hottest goddamn thing in the universe. We bleed American. Fuck yeah. When I ride, the American flag is plastered to nearly every inch of my shoes, bike, gear, saddlebags, helmet, and clothing. It's hard to see anything other than stars and stripes. I look like Apollo Creed straddling an oblong rocket between my legs.

And then there's the mystical experience, what we really ride for, when you leave the interstate behind and find a secondary road through dense, dark nature. Yellow-and-gold trees spin past dappled in spindly gold sunlight, swaying tranquilly in the breeze, with no other sound than the hypnotic purr of the cruising motorcycle and the wind kissing your face. Something about the movement of the bike, your face screaming down the wind, and that rich, close nature as God intended it—the Bavarian forest, the wheat-streaked golden field—sweeps you into a world that's much more beautiful and mythic than our own.

On the road we were traveling there were no intersections, no stores, no gas stations, and no infrastructure other than the road itself for 140 miles. My bike's tank was only good for 100 miles. Using the reserve tank I could squeeze out maybe 120 miles on one tank of gas at the absolute most. Because I'd bought my bike used, it was old and no longer worked optimally and ran out of gas much sooner than I expected. Rosie's bike was large and brand-spanking new—he could do 200 miles on a single tank of gas easy, he said.

Back in Haines, having been warned that the next 140 miles had no gas stations, I bought a red plastic gas can, the kind sold at Walmart, filled it with gas, and lashed it to the back of my bike with bungee cords. When we reached 100 miles in, I waved Rosie off the road. He waited as I refilled my tank from the spare can.

I had felt nervous for the last ten miles. There is no more worrisome feeling to a biker than the prospect of imminently running out of gas. One moment the bike is running fine. Then suddenly it jerks violently, as if it's been kicked in the nuts, and rockets forward for just a moment with its last gasp of life before instantly cutting power and dying, all its gauges collapsing to zero, a microcosm of the future death of the universe. I had run out of gas on the road before; it's not a pleasant experience. After it happens it takes at least ten minutes for enough gas to trickle down from the reserve chamber into the main tank for the bike to start up again, and while you wait, there's nothing to do but stand idly by and twiddle your thumbs. Once the bike sputters back to life, then the clock is really ticking. You have only fifteen or twenty miles to find a gas station before the reserve tank runs out, and then you're properly fucked. As I poured gas into the tank and gave it time to trickle down into the engine, Rosie's chin drooped to his chest in a catnap.

After ten minutes I fired up the bike again. I nudged Rosie awake, and we rode on together for perhaps another twenty miles. That's when it happened. As we rounded a big leafy bend in a tight curve, I looked up and saw a true American bald eagle flying low overhead, twenty feet up. It was my totem. It was mystical and beautiful. I felt strongly that it was here for me. It was amazing. It was spiritual, positively ethereal. I pulled the right handlebar tight into my chest and had the bike so low to the ground that I caught the g-forces that allow one to accelerate inside a tight curve. I was just straightening out when I heard, or rather felt, a faint *click* somewhere deep inside the bike, not in its bowels but somewhere deep in its soul, inside the engine. Suddenly the bike's acceleration died, the engine disengaged from the gas pedal, and the bike rolled to a benign stop, the engine still purring away as though nothing had happened. Odd. I rolled my right wrist down on the throttle, and the engine surged as usual, but the bike didn't move an inch. Then I opened up the gas full throttle. The engine roared like a racecar, but the bike didn't budge. The throttle and gas had been disabled from whatever makes the bike go forward.

In one moment everything had been fine. In the next, apropos of nothing, my bike had suddenly died. It was still on—the engine was running—but it no longer had any power. Rosie circled back. I told him what was wrong.

"I never heard of that. That sounds bad," he said blandly, and I had a feeling he was right.

If he, a serious rider, hadn't heard of it, then it probably was bad. It dawned on me that this wasn't something I was going to be able to fix with the rudimentary set of socket wrenches in my tool bag.

I shrugged, sanguine.

I looked around and breathed in the sharp Yukon air. It was crisp and fresh. Rosie had no more patience for me. He said he was going to continue apace to Anchorage, hauling ass for the next seven hundred miles without stopping until he got there. Damn, that is one long ride. Sayonara, dude.

Rosie had a phone with a SIM card for Canada. He let me borrow it so I could call AAA emergency service. Fortunately I had remembered to upgrade my US coverage to global, their highest level of coverage, just before I left the United States, or I would've been completely screwed, because you can't change your service and use it on the same day. AAA bragged that at this, their highest tier of service, they would come anywhere on earth to pick up your broken bike. *Let's see*, I thought. It was hard to get any more remote on the planet than where I was except possibly the Gobi Desert or Midway Atoll. We had gone the last one hundred miles without seeing any other vehicles or any sign of civilization other than the road itself.

Luckily his phone rasped out a signal. Someone picked up and I gave them my location as best I knew it—"One hundred and twenty miles inland from Haines on the road to Alaska, somewhere near Kluane Lake, wilderness, middle of nowhere."

They put me on hold for a long time. Rosie fidgeted. He hated burning daylight standing upright like this. Finally AAA came back and said that the closest place with a mechanic was Destruction Bay.

"Destruction Bay," I repeated. Rosie whistled. *It's not me who's fucked,* I could see him thinking. He took his phone back, nodded a brisk farewell, and took off like the survivor in our postapocalyptic future with better equipment and more water. As he rode away I yelled after him to give me loose slot machines if I ever came to Reno. He dashed a finger off his forehead like a pilot, and I never saw him again.

Now I was truly alone on a desolate highway in the middle of nowhere, abandoned. I looked around at the wide expanse of nothingness. I was marooned in the Yukon.

Everybody wants something. Late in the day, around eleven o'clock and still light outside, Jude Blanchette, the lone mechanic in Destruction Bay who had been contacted by AAA, pulled up in his truck and tied my bike to his tailgate. He proceeded to drag my poor bike thirty onward miles to Destruction Bay.

In the cab of his truck, Jude, whom I didn't know from Adam, and beginning from zero pleasantries, began telling me the lurid story of his life—he was a disgraced Vietnam vet who'd been convicted of murder and spent the last eighteen years in a federal prison for shooting and killing two of his own men one night "in the shit" in Nam, as he called it. He admitted without remorse that he'd killed the two guys in his unit on purpose for fun, for sport. He confessed all this to me within the first five minutes of our meeting. Jude had spent the last half of his life in a military prison.

"Was it Guantanamo Bay?" I asked him.

He craned his neck around and stared at me with dead, reptilian eyes. He didn't say anything for a long time. It was getting a little awkward so finally I shrugged and raised my eyebrows in a "Well?" expression.

"No," he finally said.

When Jude was released from prison, he retreated to the most isolated, immutable part of the world he could find, a place bleak and destitute enough to match his black heart, which just happened to be where my bike broke down.

Jude, speaking softly, gradually moved the conversation from murder to money, apparently his two favorite subjects. "How much money do you have?" he asked.

"I don't know," I said vaguely. "A few bucks." I chuckled uncomfortably and glanced over at him to see if he was chuckling alongside me. No such luck. I wasn't sure whether he wanted to know if I could afford to fix my bike or if he was just after my money. I hoped it was the former, but my heart already knew it was the latter.

There was nothing between us but five inches of empty space. I thought about him murdering his two best friends eighteen years ago just for fun, for sport.

I wanted to ask him, "How did it feel when you killed your friends?" But I already knew his answer. *Good. It felt good, Tom.*

Suddenly I was glad I was wearing an A-frame wifebeater, shit-kicking cowboy boots, and a scarred but indestructible leather jacket with a huge American flag emblazoned across the back. Grime, soot, and oil from the road were baked into my face. I was unshaven and swarthy beneath a moisturizing layer of dirt. I smelled like gasoline. If you lit a match to me I would have exploded. I probably didn't look completely easy to take down. I'm six feet and 180 pounds. Yet Jude stood six foot four and 240 pounds, built like a Samoan linebacker. I was puny next to him.

"I could fix you up, get you back on the road," he said with persiflage, as though he'd said it before.

"That's great!" I gushed, relief flooding over me.

"For a thousand dollars," he said.

I stared at him, but this time he was looking straight ahead.

"What …?" I said. "The deductible is only two hundred dollars; AAA pays you the rest."

Jude waved away my words with a soft motion of his hand before I'd finished speaking. He was practiced in all responses from experience. Nothing I said was going to throw him.

"Do you know how long AAA takes to reimburse me?" he said. "Nine months. It's not even worth it. I'm not going to spend the money on the parts myself and wait around that long to be paid."

I knew he was evil, but his argument almost made sense even to me. I said, "I'm not going to give you a thousand dollars. The whole bike isn't even worth that much. I don't have it anyway. I only have three hundred dollars on me."

That part was true—I only had $300 left in cash on me, and I knew there was no ATM in Destruction Bay. I hadn't been expecting to see one until I reached Anchorage, which now seemed as far away as Alpha Centauri.

"Then," Jude said lightly, "we have a problem."

I sighed. I looked at him sitting across from me. This time he was looking straight at me, his neck coiled around with that dead, snakelike coldness in his eyes. I knew things were going to get a lot worse before they got better.

When Jude pulled into his house, I turned down his extortionist bid again, and his expression hardened. He unhooked my bike from the hitch of his truck, rolled it inside his garage, and pulled down his garage door and locked it right in front of me as I stood there watching.

"Want your bike back? Think about it," he said, looking at me with what can only be described as a vast reservoir of hate.

He walked inside his house and shut his door.

Standing there in my cowboy boots with my duffel bag and $300 in my pocket, I turned and walked up the hill to the main highway, turned north, and walked about twenty minutes until I reached Destruction Bay. Its lone gas station appeared ahead of me on the left.

I walked into the tiny office. Bells jangled from the top of the door, as they do in small towns. A slender, late-middle-aged man sat behind an old brown desk circa the 1970s. Beside myself, I told him what had just happened.

"Jude knows the value of a dollar," came his memorable reply, followed by a slur so pungent it made my eyes water.

The slender man looked me straight in the eyes from his seated position, one of his eyebrows arched high like Mr. Spock's. He said nothing more, but in that moment he had told me he knew exactly who Jude was and that he wasn't on his side. He would prove a key ally in the days ahead. I soon learned that he was the gas station's owner. Fortunately he also rented three rooms out back that functioned as the godforsaken town's only motel. Two of the rooms were already taken. There was just one left, and I grabbed it. If that room had been taken, I'm not sure what I would've done. I may well have had to sleep in the forest that night. When you break down in the wild and are left at the mercy of insane locals in Appalachia or something like it but worse, things can turn south in a hurry.

I set my alarm for 4:00 a.m. and woke up in the middle of the goddamn night. It was freezing cold even in the tiny motel room, which had only the thinnest sheet siding for walls. Shivering, I pulled on my jeans and opened the door and walked outside, where I was plunged into icy darkness. I walked down the highway to Jude's house in the dark, a stranger in a strange land.

It was utterly silent. The scuffing of my boots against the pavement made the only audible sound. I eased down Jude's gravel driveway. Tiny stones crunched beneath my boots. The garage door was locked. I tiptoed around the side, walking ever so slowly so as to avoid making noise. There was a side door. Holding my breath, I twisted the knob. Eureka! It opened. I exhaled and slipped inside. Vague memories of summers in my youth in Michigan at my grandmother's house drifted up out of the limbic system—a birdbath in the front yard; an attic; a delicious, perfect wood smell; an enormous Oz-like hot-air balloon in a long open field in front of the house; fireflies and crickets chirping all night long in the warm languid summers outside the bedroom window. It was Dorothy country, Jem and Scout country—a beautiful childhood. People in the country don't bother to lock their doors at night. They know the neighbors.

Not this neighbor.

I ran my hand flush along the inside wall of his garage until it fumbled across a switch. I flicked it up. The room crackled and spit to life in a dim halogen half glow. And there she was, my motorcycle—or what had once been my motorcycle. It was now a filthy dead husk that looked as though it hadn't been ridden in a hundred years. It was dirty and lifeless from being dragged behind Jude's truck. The bike having been my loyal companion these last many months, I felt as though I were rescuing a kidnapped lover that had been abused and was lying there unconscious. The bike in my sight, the need to save her before dawn took on a new urgency. I looked around for keys to open the padlock on the front of his garage. Inside the garage of a stranger who had killed two men for sport and gone to prison nearly twenty years for it, a fresh sense of terror swept into me as I rifled through the toolboxes on his workshelf. I couldn't find any keys. *Damn.*

I picked up the bike, and wheeled it around. It was extremely heavy with a full tank of gas in it. It strained against my body's ability to maneuver the bike's handlebars inside the tight space of his garage without using the kickstand. If the bike banged into anything or fell over and clanged onto the floor, it would be game over and I'd be dead meat. Luckily the width of my bike was infinitesimally lean enough to squeeze through the side door, as though the maker of the doorway had built it precisely with my motorcycle in mind.

Jude's house lay in a gully, and I would have to push the bike uphill to get it onto the highway. It was a very steep driveway.

I was standing directly in front of Jude's front door now, just five yards from it. His house loomed over me, frighteningly close. Sunlight bled out across the horizon. Suddenly an enormous fear rippled through me. In the country older men tend to wake at dawn, and I had a feeling Jude was one of those early risers, creepy bastard that he was. If he caught me, who knew what he would do? He had certainly shot and killed men for less. He would have an excuse this time too: he could simply say I was trespassing on his property. In America they let you shoot people for that. It's called "home defense." He could probably kill me and get clean away with it, especially in a place like this with no policemen for six hundred miles.

I gave the bike a good push up the hill. It didn't budge. Not a centimeter. An icy rivulet of mercury slipped down the back of my spine like a cup of icy rainwater poured down the back of my T-shirt. *Shit.* My heart sank. The Vulcan was too heavy to push up the hill. I simply couldn't do it. Suddenly my options looked very bleak. I looked at the sun—it was rising! And damn fast too. A primal fear welled up inside me. I looked back at the house and its darkened windows. Jude would be up at any second and look out his window and *see me standing in his front yard.* It felt edgy and dangerous. I imagined the shotgun Jude kept beside his bed.

I kept glancing at the house, waiting for the lights to switch on and Jude to come bursting out the front door and shoot me dead, knowing he could legally do it. There were no neighbors, no other houses nearby. No one lived within shouting range, and more to the point, no one cared. The place was named Destruction Bay, for Christ's sake. There was a reason for it. It had *earned* its name. The census said the population had dropped from fifty-five people in 2006 to thirty-five in 2011. You tell me what happened to those twenty people. On second thought, no need. Jude. That's what happened.

I didn't know what to do, so I just let the bike roll back down into the gully. I paused to think. I decided to try and get a running head start to get the motorcycle up onto the driveway's forty-five degree angle.

I ran, holding the bike upright as best I could. The machine was so heavy that it nearly tipped over, and I had to stop and brace it against my hip with all my strength just to keep it from falling over. If it crashed into the ground, it would make a huge noise that would wake up Jude. I cursed the bad luck of having just refilled the tank before the bike broke. On an empty tank the bike was literally half as heavy. Most of its weight comes from the gas.

The sun was splashing down now and had nearly lifted into full light.

Inhale, exhale. Breathe in, breathe out. I calmed myself, tried to slow my racing heart, and decided just to take things very slow. I crouched down nearly to my heels and coiled all my strength in my core like a panther. Then I pushed up from my legs as hard as I could. My thighs quailed beneath the weight of the bike. I thought they would crumble. I felt the front wheel move infinitesimally. The bike advanced up the hill an inch! I squeezed the brakes on the handlebars tight to maintain the inch I'd gained and prevent the bike from rolling back down into the ditch.

Yes! I'd made an inch. I rested for thirty seconds. Then I coiled my core and pushed up hard through my legs again. The bike scratched up the face another inch. I clamped down hard on the brakes. I realized that if I did this all night I might eventually reach the top of the hill, perhaps in four or five hours.

Push, clamp down on the brakes to preserve the inch I'd gained, rest, push again. Wax on, wax off. As I repeated the process, somehow I was able to do it faster. The hand-eye coordination required to keep the awkwardly shaped oblong bike balanced upright so that it didn't tip over to one side, symbiotic marriage of man and machine, improved with repetition. I cannot remember a feeling of greater relief or joy than when I realized I was going to be able to get my bike off his property. At around six o'clock I reached the top. It hadn't taken four hours; it had taken one.

I made one last huge lunge and pushed the heavy bike onto the pavement. Yes!

I turned around.

Reader, I shit you not, his lights were on.

Fuck! I had been so engrossed in the work that I had completely forgotten about his house for the past hour. I'm glad I hadn't turned around and seen his lights on while I'd been pushing the bike because I very well might have panicked and dropped it over.

Light streamed down from his second-story windows like light streaming down from a rift in the clouds on the rim of a raging storm. Suddenly a terrifying hulking shadow split the right-hand window. Someone was up: it was either Jude or his wife. I couldn't see who it was, but the stooped shadow, scent of evil, and betting money all said it was Jude. He seemed to have just risen and not yet looked outside. That was a stroke of luck—enough sunrises had inoculated him to their beauty and he no longer looked outside first thing in the morning. If he had just glanced out his window, he would have seen me standing in his front yard, completely exposed. He was probably stumbling bleary-eyed to the john. In this case, it was probably the call of nature that saved me.

I straddled the bike, and stretched my warm blue-jeaned crotch over the familiar well-worn seat, that motorcycle seat that was more of a home than any other I have known in my life. Like the well-worn diner booth where I began each morning with a cup of hot coffee, that seat was all comfort and self-knowledge. I kicked off the pavement with both legs like a swimmer kicking off the deep end of a pool and got the bike rolling. As I scooted down the pavement, I swiveled at the hips and flipped the bird back at his house. *Fuck you, Jude.*

I figured I had at least ten minutes before he came downstairs and discovered that the bike was missing. By then I'd be nearly at the gas station. After an adrenaline-fueled, nerve-wracking, frisson-sending fifteen minutes holding my breath to hear heavy boots running up the pavement behind me, Jude with shotgun in hand, ready and willing to shoot me in the back, an open grave somewhere nearby, I finally glimpsed the gas station up ahead of me in the dim morning light. I looked back around into the hazy dawn. A mist had crept in. I couldn't see a thing beyond twenty paces back. I heard no footfalls, no thudding of footsteps on the pavement behind me.

Scarcely daring to breathe, I rolled the bike behind the motel and covered it up with some branches and leaves the best I could. I peered around the side of the building.

Jude was there.

I couldn't see him in the mist, but I felt his presence as surely as you can feel the presence of a stranger inside your home. I slipped inside my room, exhausted, and lowered the blinds so that Jude wouldn't be able to look in my window.

My brain was whirring. In my mind I was still rolling the bike uphill one inch, two inches at a time in the close, threatening dark. Light bled out over the horizon. I stood a few paces from Jude's front door, waiting for it to open, waiting for it to open … Suddenly the door flew open wide, but no one came out. Scared, I looked inside and saw only a dense black maw, a thick clot of darkness. A sick feeling emanated from it and I turned away in fear. Then I was pushing the bike uphill again, teetering under its weight. It was getting harder and harder to hold the bike upright without it falling over on one side. Suddenly my arms were flailing and I couldn't hold the bike upright anymore. Thinking about it again and again in an endless loop, like I had to do it again, like I had to do it forever, I fell into a troubled sleep plagued with nightmares.

I woke in the morning and for a good three seconds had no idea where I was. I looked around and just couldn't place it. Then it all came rushing back to me. I groaned. I got up, checked to make sure my motorcycle was still behind the motel—it was—and then took breakfast in the gas station's restaurant, the only restaurant in town, also owned by the rail-thin gas station owner, a person who I instinctually felt was an ally in this hellish place. Though I could be wrong: I had been betrayed by nearly everyone I had known so far.

I didn't fear Jude in the daylight now that I had my bike back. I could feel, as you can in the Darwinian animal world, that the pendulum, the leverage, had shifted back in my favor now that I had reclaimed my property. I also felt, true or not, that I had sanctuary on the gas station lot. The gas station was my church, my Notre Dame. I felt like standing in front of the gas pumps and screaming, "Sanctuary!" and waving a flag of some sort. The gas station owner was my priest, the father who had barred the church's doors against the evil that hunted me just outside its walls. Remembering his comment from yesterday I gleaned that no one liked Jude, and this gave me some confidence. Like a vampire unable to walk in sunlight, Jude would not be able to trespass onto the gas station lot and shoot me in broad daylight, though he knew I was here.

The gas station owner let me use his phone. I called AAA again. I told them that they had screwed up and their accredited mechanic was a convicted murderer and extortionist. I probably lost my shit on the phone and started screaming at AAA to get me the hell out of here. *What the fuck is this place?*

With that they put me on hold for a long time. Finally they came back and said that the next closest AAA-accredited repair facility was in Whitehorse, Yukon Territory, some six hundred miles back the direction I had come. In case that didn't register, six hundred miles is a hell of a distance. They said they would send a truck and that it would arrive in two days. It would cost me a fortune despite the insurance, because the insurance had a coverage limit of one hundred miles and the distance the truck had to cover exceeded that by a measure of twelve, but the cost could be deferred until later.

"Whatever!" I screamed. "Just send the guy!"

I was spooked to hell by this point, a basket of frayed nerves.

Whitehorse. There's more truth to a name than you might guess, and you don't have to be a mystic to know that Whitehorse sounds a whole hell of a lot better than Destruction Bay. Yes, Whitehorse would do just fine.

Two days later a AAA flatbed truck pulled in to the gas station from somewhere far away. The guy was nice and I could immediately tell he was normal. Finally! A normal person! What the hell does it take to meet a normal person these days?

He lashed my bike to the bed of the truck like a bagged dinosaur. He said they would store it in a garage in Whitehorse and charge me $100 per month until I came to pick it up, whenever that might be, even fifty years from now. With no repair services capable of fixing the bike within six hundred miles, I abandoned my motorcycle to the Yukon. There *was* a way out of Destruction Bay and fortunately it wasn't in a body bag. An eighteen-wheeler stopped for gas on the way to Anchorage, and I asked the trucker if I could hitch a ride with him. After three days in Destruction Bay, I had only $150 cash and a duffel bag of clothes. I was footloose, freer than ever, but I had lost my only friend, the motorcycle.

The delay had created another problem that threatened to undo my entire reason for going to Alaska in the first place. With the loss of the three days in Destruction Bay, by the time I arrived in Anchorage the fishing season had already begun, and I had missed the hiring window for the floating canneries at sea. The hiring season had ended three days ago, and all the recruiters for the fishing industry had pulled out and left.

I was alone in Anchorage with no motorcycle, no job, and no other purpose for being here. I had come all this way to get hired for the fishing season and I'd literally missed the boat.

Thanks, Jude.

So I did the only thing I knew to do. I've found in life that it often comes down to one thing, which is just the next thing. I went to city hall in Anchorage to inquire about any leftover fishing jobs. The clerk at the counter told me the same sad story—all the recruiting for this year's fishing season was finished. I was too late. The workers had all been flown out to their floating bergs of migrant labor in the middle of the Pacific Ocean, and I couldn't join them because the companies that arranged those flights weren't arranging any more. There was no way to get out there even if they would employ me. Besides, they had filled their quota.

No need for you. Go home, surfer.

There is something mystical that happens in life, though, and that is you are never completely out of options. If I have learned anything from these travels, it is that. The woman at the counter lowered her eyes to the sheaf of papers in front of her in the sign that it was time for me to move on. *The circus left town last week and you missed it, bub.*

I tried once more.

"Is there anything else I can check?"

"No," she said and looked down at her papers again in the universal sign that means, *It's time for you to leave now.*

I didn't move.

Time passed. I kept standing there. After a while she looked up again. It finally seemed to get into her head that I wasn't going anywhere. Presently she set down her pen and said, "Well, there's a job board in the back you could check."

I walked to a perforated corkboard at the back of the room. Everything on it had been ripped down. Only a few tattered shreds of paper remained under pushpins. There was just one ad left on the board. I squinted at the handwriting.

Large looping letters, leaning right, suggesting an analytical, even creative person. Good sign.

The ad was signed Chuck and promised a real fishing job aboard a boat in the ocean, like the *Deadliest Catch* on the Discovery Channel. It was exactly what I had come to Alaska for and what I had been unsuccessful finding on subscription job sites before I had come, which had all turned up goose eggs. I seized a phone on the table and dialed the number.

A man with a low Texan drawl picked up. "He-llo."

"Is this Chuck?"

"Ye-p." The *p* sound popped over the phone like a chew toy being ripped out of a baby's mouth.

"Is the job for crewman still available?"

A pause on the other end of the line. I held my breath, pressed my eyelids tightly shut. *Come on. Come on.*

"Where are you?"

"City hall."

"I'll be there in ten minutes."

Click.

He'd hung up. I listened to the dial tone on the other end of the receiver. A rush of excitement flooded my body like a rush of gasoline flooding the engine from the choke. Woohoo! Here we go! Suddenly I had a reason for being in Anchorage.

I had lucked my way into a set-net fishing job in Bristol Bay in the southern Bering Sea working for intrepid lifelong fisherman Chuck Robertson. Chuck was originally from Texas and still counted family there, but he'd relocated to Alaska as a child when his father became a fisherman. When his father passed away, Chuck had kept right on fishing. His mother lived in Anchorage.

You might think these jobs on fishing boats are easy to come by, because who the hell would want to do this kind of work, right? Quite the opposite, in fact—these jobs are very much in demand, as all jobs are. I had spent a month in San Diego researching jobs on Alaskan fishing boats, trying everything to secure a crew job before I left, even paying for a few subscription lists at ninety dollars per month promising fishing jobs and boat captains' private phone numbers.

One of them I subscribed to, AlaskaJobFinder, said:

> With so many people eager to earn large paychecks in the short crabbing seasons, jobs can be scarce because of their popularity.
>
> We have information how to find jobs offshore working in the processing plant where many crabbers get their start.

> You will learn about what the Bureau of Labor Statistics calls the world's most dangerous job. For the adventurous-minded the Alaskan fishing industry is hard to ignore.

These words sent a shiver of excitement pulsing through me, a quicksilver thrill, and when I read them I knew I wanted to do it. None of these paid lists ever yielded a lead, though. They all came up donuts. Very few of the phone numbers worked in reality; they were old and out of use.

The two times I got an actual fishing boat captain on the phone, their answer was the same: "I'm all filled up for the season, sorry. I have my crew ... And how the hell'd you get this number?"

Not one captain needed an extra crewman. One captain was kind enough to explain to me that these jobs are enormously popular and that once a crewman secures one, he tends to hold on to his spot season after season. I only got the job with Chuck because, by some lucky miracle, his crewman had quit the day they were scheduled to fly out to the Bering Sea to start the season, leaving Chuck holding the bag. Chuck couldn't do the season on his own, so he'd been forced to cancel his flight and spin his wheels in Anchorage until he found a new crewman. Chuck said that his ad had sat on the board for three days without anyone calling.

"*Three days!*" he repeated, disbelieving.

How could that be? Because three days ago the recruiting season had ended and everyone in Anchorage knew it, so no one had bothered to come around city hall looking for a job since then. It was pure luck his ad was still there when I walked in late, because actually it was a very attractive job. I couldn't believe my good fortune. By being here at the wrong time, I was actually here at the right time. Even my motorcycle breaking down and being tormented by Jude suddenly had new meaning. Anyone on those floating flotilla hellholes in the middle of the Bering Sea gutting fish would have given their left nut for the job I'd just gotten by walking in late. Ha!

When Chuck hired me, I thought I would be going out on one of the drift boats seen on the Discovery Channel's *Deadliest Catch* specials, where you work like a Mexican donkey for twenty-two hours a day and the moment your eyes accidentally close during a shift because you're so exhausted, your ankle gets tangled in a stray rope on deck and suddenly you're whisked overboard and your body hits water so icy cold that it doesn't immediately feel cold. Your lungs are stabbed through by venomously cold Arctic water, you're dragged to the bottom of the ocean in mere seconds by the plunging cage, and less than five minutes after your ankle was first ensnared, you're fish food. The mackerel will be plucking out your eyeballs like olives and licking your skeleton clean. It was fully my intention to get on one of these hellion live-or-die fucker boats. I wanted to undergo the harshest testing of manhood I could find. Why? "Embedded in the DNA it is," Yoda might say.

When I first arrived at Smoky Point I had a really hard time, to put it mildly. At that point it had been all of three days since Chuck had picked me up at city hall, and he kept asking me to do mechanical repair work that I had no experience in such as fixing his tractor engines, outboard motors, and ATVs. I can no more understand an engine than I can *Finnegans Wake*. Chuck seemed to take it for granted that I knew how to repair complex machinery, but I had never touched anything more complex than an espresso machine before. I have the soft hands of a piano player that had never done a real day's work in their lives. The gap between Chuck's assignments and my results, compounded with spending every waking moment with someone who was basically a perfect stranger, caused me considerable strain early on. For the first two weeks I was beside myself with grief, wondering what the hell was wrong with me and why would I choose to put myself in such a ruthless, miserably unfun situation?

After two weeks of flailing with engines and motors and accomplishing nothing, just experiencing cascading, endless humiliation, fishing finally began and things started to improve. No longer foundering with machinery, I fell into work I was able to do and turned out to be good at. I liked fishing, and anything you like and spend time at, you're likely to be good at. It's pretty much as simple as that—enthusiasm is a wonderful gift to quality.

Chuck had hired me on for the summer salmon season of set-net fishing, where you're allowed to cast up to three nets within a thousand meters of shore anywhere you want along the coastline. I wouldn't be on a "drift" boat, where one sleeps and eats and spends all their time on a boat that must legally keep drifting through the water. We were fishing close enough to shore that I was always able to see land, so even if the boat sank I would probably be able to swim to shore, unless I succumbed to the freezing cold water first. One time I lunged after a fish a little too enthusiastically and my momentum carried me straight overboard after it.

"No!" was the last thing I heard Chuck say as I hit piercingly cold water. Hitting water that cold feels like falling through a glass coffee table. I was wearing gaiters, the fisherman's rubber overalls, but the water gushed in over the top of them and went straight through my T-shirt. An icy rush of frigid seawater impaled me like a lance through my heart. When I breached the surface I found I couldn't breathe.

The water was so cold that it had shocked my lungs into malfunctioning. I gasped for air that wouldn't come. Like a fish attempting a last-ditch effort to escape our net, I burst skyward and gripped the lip of our boat with one hand. I tried to pull myself up with my other hand but lacked the strength. As I faded back into the icy blue, a pair of orange rubber gloves reached down from above like deus ex machina. As I fell beneath the surface of the water, the gloves grabbed me by the front of my gaiters and lifted me up inside the boat.

Chuck and I spent days, months, driving the boat up and down the coast, moving our net from place to place prospecting for fertile fishing grounds, a swatch of sea that was stuffed with fish. Fishing is fickle. It's a little like an Easter egg hunt. Chuck would scout a location that he hoped lay in the path of some great diaspora of fish churning downstream from their breeding grounds at the source of the Egegik River high up in the mountains. We'd plant a net and leave it and then motor back to check the first net we'd already set that morning in front of Chuck's cabin. There was always great anticipation when we pulled a net up from the water after being away from it for some hours—would it be teeming and stuffed to the gills, so to speak, fraught with fish? Sometimes it was and sometimes it wasn't. It was prospecting, which made it fun. And sometimes frustrating.

Chuck was older than me, but he looked ageless. At first I had no idea how old he was because his beard was still black, his face wrinkle-free, and most of all, he was as strong as a water buffalo, moved swiftly like a bull, with purpose like a cyborg, and he always walked with his hands balled into two fists like a boxer ready to punch anyone who made the mistake of passing by too closely.

Chuck could lift a drum of oil with at least as much brute strength as I could. So I was stunned to learn that Chuck was fifty-nine years old. He could have been thirty-nine and I never would have questioned it. Chuck told me that his father had possessed the same Zeus-like strength and undiminished youth straight up until age eighty when he quit fishing. Then he declined all at once and was dead within a year. Showing no trace of concern, Chuck said he expected to go much the same way.

He leaned against the gunwale, tilted his face back to receive the sun, basked in it for a moment or two. Then he took hold of the outboard motor, and we sped off to the next spot.

The roughest, most intense boats one sees on the Discovery Channel are the ophelia snow crab and king crab drift boats that depart for the gray gelid seas of the Arctic every winter between November and March. The stormy, treacherous northern seas and perilous wet, iced-over decks in winter add yet another sticky dimension to these boats' already immense danger. These are the boats where every year deckhands die at a steady clip.

I saw the drift boats out on the horizon, backlit in the setting sun, dragging enormous hauls of what must have been millions of fish. That was volume out there. When a drift boat's nets are in the water, the rule is that the boat must keep drifting—like a shark it can never stop moving. If you find an El Dorado of fish being belched out of the Mariana Trench, you can't just sit your boat on top of it and hoard the treasure for yourself, engendering hostility from everyone else. The only spot you can legally bogart for yourself is the one directly in front of your land or house; this is considered your "yard." Keep your boat moving or face the consequences of the fishing version of insider trading, which can result in the loss of your fishing license, though I only ever saw aerial police patrolling the skies once, on the first day of the season. That flyby was more like a starting gun than a warning shot. I never saw the authorities down here again.

There was no justice or remorse in Smoky Point, way out on the far edge of the world. Smoky Point was without any doubt one of the earth's far-flung corners, slung way the hell out on the Aleutian Island chain, America's most distant outpost, the farthest edge of empire.

Chuck said he bagged a shark in his net once by accident, but that's like finding the Hope Diamond in your garage—one in a billion. Chuck and I found the net heavier than usual once and pulled up a whole baby seal. The seal was dead. Its cheeks were caked white: it looked as if it had choked on its own vomit. It was absolutely terrifying, like a horror movie. But 99 percent of the time we pulled up only salmon.

There are five types of salmon in Alaska:

1. Chinook, more commonly known as king salmon. These are giant and can weigh up to one hundred pounds (about forty-five kilograms) in Alaska. Chuck and I caught a king salmon every thirty fish or so. They are not as valuable because of the lower quality of their meat, but it's a thrill to see their enormous size.
2. Chum, more commonly called dog salmon because of the poor quality of their meat and their grotesquely ugly faces, which make Munch's *Scream* look like Natalie Portman by comparison. Chum have no value, and companies do not want to buy them. As you may have guessed, despite being ugly, they reproduce in higher quantities than ants and maggots combined, and naturally, the preponderance of fish we caught were chums.
3. Coho, also known as silver salmon. These are the fish found in the clear-running rivers of Alaska and the Yukon that wild bears feast on. They were the rarest fish in our catch, and as so often goes with being the rarest, they are also the most valuable. Silvers fetch the highest price at market and are the most delicious.
4. Pink, also called humpies. These salmon are more plentiful than silvers and have a rosy taste consistent with their name.

5. Sockeye, or red salmon. These fish were our bread and butter. They are the most abundant sellable fish in the catch and the one most sought after by buyers. While slightly less delicious than coho, sockeye are no slouch on the taste buds and bring more money because they are larger than coho (fish are sold by two factors—type and weight.)

Each silver we caught was worth about three dollars on average, so every fish we caught was money. When Chuck held up a writhing fish and looked at its greasy head, he saw three dollars, or two dollars if the fish was a runt. At midday when our brail bags were breaking beneath the weight of a full boat teeming with fish, Chuck steered the skiff out to sea and drove us to the tender.

Tenders are the enormous buying boats that park themselves about a mile off coast. Fishermen up and down the coast wagoned out to the tender once a day to sell their hauls of fish in exchange for receipts that they could hand in for cash at the end of the season in Anchorage.

Each day Chuck and I waited in line behind other fishing vessels for our turn to deliver to the tender. When we reached the front of the line, hooks like giant squid pincers unspooled down from a tower above and we clipped them to our brail bags. Then they hauled our catch, which weighed a thousand pounds per bag, clear up into the sky. After the last bag, Chuck clipped himself in at his belt like a rock climber about to ascend the Dawn Wall at Yosemite, and he too was whisked up into the sky on a wire like an actor in your local theater production of *Peter Pan*. Chuck nimbly alighted on the aft deck of the ship and the tender's buyer, a large man in orange gaiters, scribbled out a receipt for our fish.

The whole business was all about this receipt, the same pink carbon copy one is handed in a Las Vegas pawnshop. The receipt was handwritten and as analog as the one an eight-year-old hands you from his lemonade stand on the street corner. I stared at the old-fashioned carbon copy with our delivery's weight scribbled in pen. It would be so easy to counterfeit. Chuck wrapped his long fingers around the receipt and I glimpsed the corners of his mouth turn up slightly in satisfaction. It was clear that Chuck loved his work and loved getting paid for it. Chuck folded the cheap piece of paper with immaculate care like a fifth grader wrapping a love note he's going to pass to the girl he likes in homeroom class, and slotted it inside a hidden pocket in his gaiters. That receipt was what the mass grisly murder of fish is all about.

The price of fish was in the middle of a long decline that had been precipitated by the rise of farmed salmon, which had succeeded where most new businesses do—by undercutting the complacent mainstream by offering the product at vastly lower prices. At that year's price of $0.47 a pound, and with each fish weighing on average five pounds, each fish we caught was worth $2.35—not bad, though still the worst price fishermen had ever seen and far below the 1990s heyday when everyone was getting rich in Alaska fishing for $1.27 a pound. Chuck said he had gotten so rich in the '90s that he had bought an airplane and flown around like an oligarch.

"Where's your plane? I want to see it." I teased him.

"I didn't want to squander my youth by being responsible," Chuck said wryly.

He smiled. "The problem with owning a plane is gas. Filling a plane's tank is very expensive. No one tells you that when you buy it."

When the price of fish skidded, Chuck went broke and had to sell his plane and the other fancy toys he'd accumulated during the gold rush. Some clever entrepreneur had created farmed salmon in the putrid swamps of the American bayou, added pink dye to the slithering monsters to make them look like real fish, and offered them at slashed prices, creating a multibillion dollar enterprise that drove down the price of freshwater salmon by 70 percent to its now historic lows and left Chuck's industry on the brink of collapse.

During the summer the Bristol Bay fishery sent us a memo that said:

> The analysis indicates that the outlook for the future is grim. Low fish prices and modest salmon returns are likely to continue and the economic disaster these have wrought will continue if the fishery is left unchanged. A substantial increase in the world's supply of farmed salmon over the last decade and a decline in the productivity of Bristol Bay sockeye salmon stocks threaten the economic viability of one of the world's great salmon fisheries and the region that depends on it. These conditions have placed the fishery and many communities within the Bristol Bay region on the verge of financial insolvency.
>
> The fishery is nearly financially insolvent. Last year, permit holders on average earned $4,000 after operating costs, but before deducting for debt service on vessels and permits. There isn't enough wealth available in the fishery to support the number of participants and the average annual incomes it once did.

As dire as the situation had become for Chuck and the other fishermen, freshwater salmon had recently been making a small comeback thanks to the emerging organic and free-range healthy food trends. People had begun learning about the cesspools that farmed salmon are harvested in and giving more thought to what they put in their bodies.

After seeing the dark creatures bubble up out of the bile in videos myself, I won't touch farmed salmon. They don't spawn naturally in the ice-cold rivers of interior Alaska; they're harvested in the dirtiest, filthiest Southern swamps you can imagine. Before the pink dye is added, the fish look like turds, creatures that autogenerated from the slime, like maggot-moths. Of course, after they're dyed and that little piece of green paper is laid on top (it's supposed to look like parsley?), and especially after people compare the farmed salmon's price with the Alaskan salmon's, they no longer care where it came from and are happy to buy it. People don't mind dying five years earlier in the distant future if they can save a buck today. As always, though, if there is one unfailingly true axiom in life, it is you get what you pay for.

The fish surged downstream and slammed into our net, and then they struggled, writhed, and thrashed around trying to get free. Chuck told me that a number of years ago some animal rights activists had agitated for lawmakers to investigate the effects of being captured on fish (other than being eaten, presumably). The activists' arguments broke down when scientists were unable to prove that fish suffered in the same way that mammals and birds do when they're caught and bleeding. Of course, watching blood spurt out of those fish like a spigot hose and pool in the bottom of our boat was like watching a crime scene. The fish didn't scream like lambs, but that's only because they don't have vocal chords. I held up a fish as it convulsed and bled out down my arm and searched its eyes for meaning, some sign of ineffable pain, but found none. They thrashed around like Jacob and the archangel, though, that's for damn sure.

Picking each fish out of the net was like a little sudoku or geometry problem, and as the season wore on I got better at figuring them out. After being captured, a fish thrashes around like Rain Man on an airplane, hurtling itself like ordnance under and over the net and rocketing through holes until it ends up in a tightly wound ball of netting, its face ludicrously popping out of the mesh webbing like a bank robber wearing pantyhose to conceal his face. In the beginning, struggling to unravel this fish ball was as frustrating as negotiating a Rubik's Cube. I couldn't do it and kept handing my fish over to Chuck in defeat to remove. He'd sigh in faux, or probably real, disappointment. Then with dexterous fingers he extricated the fish like a Brontë sister darning a sweater.

When the fishing was really cooking and hundreds and thousands of fish were streaming downriver and plowing into our net, the whole thing would light up end to end in plumes of flying water like the fountain show at the Bellagio. Fish steamed into our net like flies onto halogen rods, and the whole ocean tilted up on an axis as though it were being hoisted into the sky by the moon's gravity. When fish hit the net, they bucked and burst skyward in a last-ditch effort to escape, a final surge of their last energy, but the net always held them fast and dragged them back to the surface. The fish continued to struggle, which only ensnared them further. Soon they would be in our brail bag, and in a few hours more they'd be on the tender in a massive refrigerated hold the size of Andorra with a billion other fish, and a week later they'd be on your dinner plate.

You're welcome.

I was rather surprised when at some point midway through the season, I discovered I was actually enjoying myself. It was the first time I had enjoyed myself in a good long while. Slowly improving and gaining expertise in fishing over the course of the summer was satisfying in a way I had not expected. The reason being that fishing, while simple, is also immersive and meditative. The task is elemental—to catch fish—and the work, while repetitive, is also mysteriously soothing, and even given to creative inspiration. You can submerge yourself in the dream state while doing it. While fishing all other concerns gradually fade away until they disappear completely and nothing is left except fishing and peace as you sit out on the glassy water, clenching a squirming animal in your fist.

Late at night we'd be out on the water, with the sun arcing down and the heat of the day off, water placid, still as a lake. It was after midnight and still light. At these times, quietly picking fish from the nets, not talking because we had fallen into a groove from sixteen hours of ceaseless work and counting, past the tired point so no longer tired and well into my second wind, my arms muscular and body lean, and looking forward to bowls of microwaved popcorn when we got back to the house, I was happy. Because the work was physical, just challenging enough to be interesting, and perhaps most importantly, endless, the rhythm defanged and sandpapered away thought. Nothing remains after thought is gone except a deep sense of contentment.

Chuck usually called it a night around one o'clock, and then we headed back to his cabin where we microwaved popcorn and listened to music on XM Satellite Radio, relaxed, and slept until our daily wake-up at six a.m. Chuck had been fishing at Smoky Point for over fifty years and he had eased off the throttle a little in recent years, sacrificing a few extra fish for a little more downtime in his comfortable crib at night, which was fine by me. I got at least four or five hours of sleep each night, more than the norm during fishing season when most crewmen on the drift boats got closer to two hours of sleep, whipped by tyrants in a mad Ahab-like frenzy to catch as many fish as possible during the three-month season. Since there was no limit to the number of fish you could catch, but the season had a hard starting and end date, there was no incentive, other than mutiny, for a captain to allow his crew to rest.

Our nearest neighbor, Rick, was a cowboy fishermen who just couldn't bring himself to hang it up at night. Rick was so greedy that he left his nets in the water all night long while he slept, which was against the rules—you're supposed to pull them up. Over the course of a night and that many hours going unpicked, the fish, unable to move, which is essential to the survival of a fish, eventually died in the net.

Chuck and I came out one morning to find Rick and his crewmen struggling to pull up the most massively full net of fish I've ever seen. It was full to bursting, nearly too heavy for three men to hoist, and when they finally lifted it out of the water, the bottom of the net broke. Seven hundred dead fish dropped through the bottom to the ocean floor where they rotted in a watery grave.

"Nice," Chuck said.

Rick took a step back and wiped the sweat off his brow. "I don't do good work but the good news is I don't do much of it," he said.

Then he added, "My head hurts—I think it hurts if it's either too full or too empty."

"Are you sure you want to pursue this?" Chuck asked.

Rick looked at me. "I used to be my harshest critic, but then I married my wife."

"How is Courtney?" Chuck asked.

"I love her but she's so crazy she could haunt a nine-room mansion from the front porch."

Chuck shook his head.

At least we were killing fish for food, but if you just killed fish to no end, as Rick had, it's just a waste. Rick lost at least two more full nets of fish this way and maybe more. Even if the net doesn't break under the weight of so many fish, after a long night being held captive underwater, the fish die anyway and begin to decompose. Rick didn't care so long as he could toss them in a brail bag first thing in the morning and motor out to the tender and sell them before anyone caught on.

Rick couldn't bear to miss a fish. So he started fishing all night long and straight through the next day without stopping like a maniac. He was wired, and I wondered whether he was on drugs to stay awake. I didn't know how anyone could maintain such a breakneck schedule for days on end like that without dropping dead or taking methamphetamines.

He continued fishing all day and night even at the expense of taking the odd forty-minute drive out to the tender to sell the fish and come back. As a result, the fish lay in the bottom of his boat in the sun for too long and rotted. But a little thing like rotting, stinking fish wasn't a thing to stop Rick. More than once we saw him ordering his deckhands to move the rotten fish into an empty new brail bag and then cover them up with the fresh fish he kept right on catching, covering up bad with good. The giveaway was that the rotten fish started to stink, and no breath mint or car freshener can wash that stench away.

Chuck watched Rick at it one morning. "Rick, you never did know when to pull out," he said, an allusion to Rick's several children by different women. Rick smirked. He was a rascal in the Errol Flynn mold with a black handlebar mustache, a luxuriant head of bouffant black hair, and a roguish mien. He'd slept with more women than Genghis Khan and with his swashbuckling charisma I could see why.

"I spent half my money on women and booze. I wasted the other half," he said.

Our eyes met.

"I'm a neutron bomb in bed," he said, raising his eyebrows to let me know he was telling me something important.

One of Rick's greenhorns, perhaps tired from being awake all night, threw a fish in frustration and sat down in a huff.

Rick pointed at him. "Sourdough!" he laughed.

"What's a sourdough?" I asked.

"A guy who's soured on Alaska but doesn't have the dough to get out."

Like any of his *Brave New World* predecessors, Rick oozed glib charm and was funny. He cracked me up, and I liked him. But he didn't shy away from reckless or unethical activity. Most of the time Rick came up smelling of roses. He returned from the tender brandishing a receipt and grinning. "Got 'em all!"

"Sheesh," Chuck said, gritting his teeth, disgusted. Fortunately for me, Chuck wasn't interested in grabbing every last dollar and passing rotten fish along to you, trusting consumer. Rick was the boss, so his crewmen had no choice but to go along with his schemes, and it's not possible to leave a job once you're in Smoky Point because you'd die in the wasteland before ever reaching civilization.

The stench of rotten fish is impossible to hide, though, and one day the tender's buyer caught a whiff of it and ordered Rick to remove the fresh fish one by one from the top of his brail bags so he could investigate. From our skiff down below I watched Rick dance and jive up on deck, waving his arms theatrically in an effort to stall, wheedle, divert—leaning on his charisma as he always had. The buyer, a big man with a red face and a sharp nose, was not overcome by Rick's charms.

Rick's fabled luck finally ran out. Perhaps another fisherman had ratted him out to the tender since everyone seemed to know what he was doing. Word had gotten out that Rick was selling bad fish to the Trident Fishing Corp. He received a warning that if it happened again, he'd be blackballed in Bristol Bay and his license would be revoked. From that point on Rick curtailed his seventy-two-hour fishing binges.

I also did a lot of rifle shooting at the ubiquitous seals that were constantly poaching the ready-made fish from our nets. Fishermen lose more fish to seals than any other way. So while it's illegal to kill a seal in Alaska, to the dismay of fishermen everywhere who take a direct hit to their income every time one of these vultures carts off with one of their fish, many fishermen stock their boats with guns anyway.

"Don't tread on me!" Chuck cried out.

We'd be out on the ocean and spot a seal or two feeding on the other end of our net at the farthest distance from us of course, because seals are far from stupid. Chuck tossed me the M48 Liberty rifle, and he grabbed the .22 Colt hand cannon he kept in the gunwale so that he could drive the boat with one hand and fire with the other. Then we started blazing away, lighting up the water in a hail of bullets. It was the only time in my life I've really shot a gun. The rifle kicked into my shoulder hard like a Clydesdale's horseshoe and was really frickin' loud. Chuck hated the seals with such passionate intensity that he was never more animated than when he was shooting at them. His face screaming white hot malice like Emperor Palpatine when he was frying Luke Skywalker, Chuck continued firing at the surface of the water long after the seals had nosedived under the surface and were gone.

Being shot at scares the shit out of seals, though it is probably the only thing that scares them. Seals long ago figured out that many of the things that frighten other wild animals, such as car engines and loud machinery—in this case the outboard motor of the boat—are no threat to them, and thus they ignore them with flamboyant élan. Seals are shameless creatures and will flagrantly flout anything you do to try to protect your turf. A seal will surface just broadside your boat with your largest fish dangling sloppily out of its mouth and stare at you in open, willful defiance to make sure you get a good long look at what it has just stolen from you, taunting expression running up and down its face as it leisurely slurps down your prize, taking three dollars out of your pocket in the process. Chuck was almost crying with hatred every time he saw this. By the time we had thrown down our oars and picked up the heavy artillery and started firing, the seal had nosedived into oblivion and was gone.

Seals are disqualifyingly outrageous, truly maddening creatures. There is no animal innocence here, I assure you, they know exactly what they're doing. The seals were absolutely giddy with mirth and openly laughed at us, their faces almost humanoid in the sophistication of their expressions, as they watched us flail about in frustration. They had the upper flipper and knew it.

Their insistence on poaching the ready-made nets, their protracted indolence and refusal to hone their hunting skills in the oceanic wild, had left them so fat and lazy that it was widely speculated that if all the fishermen pulled their nets from the water and left tomorrow, the entire seal population in Alaska would half itself—die off. That's how dependent these parasitic beasts have become, how greatly their natural hunting skills have eroded thanks to free grazing from the fishermen's nets.

Easy life, moochers!

Chuck confessed to me that over the years, out of millions of shots fired, he had only connected twice, but it was all worth it for those two times when he had the unparalleled pleasure of watching the aquatic bloodsuckers die. As you might suspect, when you're shooting a gun at water and creatures that can submerge themselves in less than a second, you're not going to connect a whole hell of a lot. The seals are experts at their chosen profession of grand piscine larceny. But when Chuck did hit one, he told me, oh, it made up for all the rest of it, to see one of these flashy bastards get its comeuppance, the smug, arrogant expression wiped right off its fat face. The moment the seal realizes it's been shot, you're treated to the exquisite and exceedingly rare look of total shock on its bloated face, the first and last time in its life it's ever been surprised, as it seizes up and petrifies, as if it stopped paying the electric bill on its own nervous system, and sinks down, down, getting its just desserts in a watery grave.

Around halfway through the season, a massive new tender called *Trinity* rolled in. There was a young woman on board—a very curvaceous, pretty blonde from Indiana. Working a six-week stint throwing down tie-up ropes and big smiles at fishermen starved for such a sight, she was more than the boys had seen. She was like a mermaid, a Siren off the coast of Crete luring Odysseus onto the shoals.

For a time everyone couldn't wait to deliver to the tender—fishermen drove in with their brail bags only half-full just to get in a little small talk. Even Rick made the trip more often. Chuck blushed and flirted openly with the nineteen-year-old in a Hoosiers baseball cap and blousy gray sweatshirt that swelled in all the right places. The presence of an attractive female had a calming, mesmerizing effect on the entire bay that, for a minute, countervailed the overload of testosterone, the same testosterone that without a woman around would at some point—perhaps soon—turn psychotic, and eventually murderous with 100 percent certainty, as anyone who has ever worked in an all-male outdoors environment can attest to. It's only a matter of time.

That's how it goes on the high seas. The frontier life is littered with adventurers, drifters, fortune hunters, idealists, misfits, and the certifiably deranged. Every year across Alaska there are deaths, murders, skippers gone mad killing their crew and sometimes themselves.

One case Chuck and I heard about over his radio involved a deckhand doing the final tie-up of the season. He jumped onto the dock to tie up the boat, and his captain just decided to ram him for some reason. He smashed his crewman into hamburger between the ship's hull and the dock. The captain was arrested; the police said he was intoxicated to the tune of .18 percent alcohol in his bloodstream.

Too many backwater people living together on small boats in tight quarters is a sulfurous cauldron of dysfunction, a powder keg ripe to explode. Troubled people with no education, no shore leave, no days off, no privacy, significant financial burdens weighing on both captain and crew, and full-blown careering drug and alcohol habits with no lack of available drugs and booze, all marinate together in a frothy brew of chaos until creeping madness, which is the reality out here, becomes a ticking time bomb.

That summer the Ugashik district saw several deaths not directly related to fishing; you could call them unforced errors. A few arrests were made after the season. The greater number of these deaths, murders really, happened as the season wore on. The more time you spend beside a psychopath, the more comfortable he becomes in your presence and the less obliged he feels to hide it anymore. There comes a point where it's all right out in the open, and by then it's probably too late. Someone is going to die. And by God, if you don't want it to be you, then it has to be him.

"You like sushi?" Chuck asked me one day as we waded back to shore after anchoring the skiff to the beach using the ingenious rope-and-pulley system he'd devised.

"Who doesn't?" I said.

"Good."

Chuck waded back out to the skiff, throttled a fish by its neck, and carried it to shore, still alive and squirming in his fist. He slapped the fish onto the back of the ATV that we drove back to the house each evening. Then he took out a very big knife and slit the fish open. The fish died instantly at the first contact from the knife, and as inured as I had become to the rolling death toll and violence against fish, I grimaced a little.

No one deserves to go out that way.

The fish bled a little, but not as much as when it's freshly caught in the net and gushing blood into your face like a fire hose. The next thing I knew, Chuck was handing me a long thin slice of raw sashimi fish.

"Really?" I asked, circumspect.

He answered by looking me straight in the eye and pushing the entire rest of the fish into his mouth without looking at it.

It took him a full two minutes to chew down that much food before he could swallow it. His eyes watered, and I laughed.

Neither Smoky Point, where we were, nor nearby Pilot Point appear on any map, for good reason—God did not intend for humans to come here. When Chuck and I first touched down by single-propeller biplane in the empty, desolate, treeless, utterly dead region of the Alaskan peninsula known as Smoky Point, one of the first things we noticed was that our neighbors' cabins to the north and south had been razed and thoroughly laid waste to by marauding bears during the winter months when the godless place is completely uninhabitable to human beings. If you were in Smoky Point and faced inland, there was nothing but dirt and a light patina of moss for over a thousand miles in any direction. That and apparently an apocalypse-worthy horde of intelligent bears roaming this wasteland.

"Fuckin' bears," Chuck muttered through clenched teeth. His eyes went glassy and a bead of sweat autogenerated on his brow, and I realized he was scared. Cool Chuck was spooked.

"Strength of bulldozers," he whispered to no one, lost in some internal nightmare.

The fear of being eaten by bears in remote and rural Alaska is intense. Of course I was the greenhorn who had never seen a bear outside of a zoo before. I just wanted to meet one and roll around on the beach with it. It was one of the reasons I had come to Alaska.

We stepped into Rick's house.

"Wow," Chuck said, looking around.

Rick's house had been diligently stripped down to its studs by bears like a professional stripping down of your car. Anything that smelled of food had been torn apart or transported away. The front door of the refrigerator had been ripped off its hinges and flung through the window like a Frisbee. Thor himself could not have ripped that giant stainless steel refrigerator door off its titanium hinges.

But a bear could.

Seeing the thick slab of metal-door ripped off the military-grade steel fridge was awe-inspiring, spellbinding. I looked through the broken window at the clear blue sky outside and felt juiced by the unholy raw strength of the bear. I couldn't believe that bears possessed not only the strength but also the nimble dexterity to separate doors from hinges, like pulling the femur out of the game Operation without the sides buzzing. Perhaps like great white sharks, bears are getting smarter.

The cupboards were gone.

It looked like a bear had slept in the bed.

This had not happened to Chuck's place in the off-season because it had already happened to him once fifteen years earlier. Chuck had arrived in Smoky Point that year with a full heart, brimming with enthusiasm for the season ahead, only to find that his cabin had been decimated during the winter by a troupe of malevolent bears. All that remained of his house was a mountain of driftwood and fragments of porcelain from a toilet that had been viciously ripped apart. Chuck said he'd been wiped out, left with nothing, and had been forced to miss the entire fishing season due to no generator, no oil, no supplies, and no house to live in. He had to live off his savings for a year and, embarrassingly, move back in with his mother at age forty-four.

"Living with your mom seriously affects your ability to get laid," he added ruefully, his eyes narrowing to slits.

I laughed.

Chuck spent the next autumn and spring rebuilding his cabin from scratch and girding it like Superman's Fortress of Solitude, more

Helm's Deep than cabin, he said. He gilded the entire wood exterior with aluminum plating as though he were warehousing plutonium, and sealed the front door with a lock the size of Tyrion Lannister.

The first time I saw Chuck's fortress gleaming in wall-to-wall armor like a bunker—impregnable, invincible—I was impressed. Chuck and I spent most of our first day in Smoky Point unlocking and removing the metal plates one by one from the house's exterior. It took us six hours. Then we animated the house from its dormant winter status—turned on the water supply and removed the dirty blanket covering the generator, the machine that made all this possible.

Chuck's house was a fortress in the truest sense—it was Krull—and quite artfully conceived. An elegant man of sorts, an architect or designer, resided inside Chuck's gruff burly exterior. Chuck had the wherewithal to build his own rather stately two-story house in the middle of absolute nowhere, as nowhere as you can get on the planet outside of the Karakoram Himalayas in northern Burma perhaps, with no natural resources to build from. There wasn't even any wood in Smoky Point, as there wasn't a single tree for a thousand miles in any direction. If you just rolled up here, you wouldn't even be able to make a fire. It was just featureless spongy turf with a few clumps of dry hedge grass, stretching on forever. It's no stretch to say that Smoky Point is among the most inhospitable places on earth, right up there with Siberia and Detroit. It's truly an arctic waste, the kind of place God forgot about. There was nothing, literally *no thing*, around.

In this way, I had been lucky to draw Chuck as my captain. Everyone else's cabin was crappy and ultrabasic, more shack than cabin, providing little more than a roof and four walls. Chuck had built his cabin with a perfectionist's eye for detail and a view toward longevity, befitting someone whose lifetime career is fishing and not just a summer job as it is for many down here. Rick, for example, held another job from September to May. When Chuck wasn't fishing, such as during the king crab-hunting winter months, he didn't work; he traveled around.

There was no electricity grid, no phone lines, no central heating, no cables or services of any kind here. Everything was powered by the generator, a freestanding engine that squatted in the middle of a shed and looked like a nuclear bomb. Chuck woke every morning at dawn to feed the generator gasoline, which it guzzled down like a greedy infant. All our energy—the lights in the house, gas stove, microwave, hot showers, heat—came from barrels of black oil that we poured down the gullet of that rapacious monster each morning. The generator gargled, swished, and belched oil. We bought drums of oil from the same tender we delivered the fish to. Yes, the tender also sold select items fishermen needed to survive in this hostile wasteland.

"Black gold," Chuck purred, grinning like a hyena. He'd been sniffing oil for years now, and the vapors clearly swam in his skull too.

Oil has a complex pungent aroma that is simultaneously attractive and repellant, like sexual organs.

"Oil and water—all one needs to live down here forever," Chuck purred dreamily in a Hamlet-like aside. I realized he was a survivalist like myself; we had more in common than I first thought.

"And what would you do if there was a nuclear apocalypse on the mainland and the tender forgot this place?" I asked him. "Would you die down here without the black gold?"

"Nah ..." Chuck cooed, lost in warm thoughts at the possibility. "After the oil was gone, I'd fish by the rod, no boat, sleep in the cold."

I looked at him. He meant it.

After we sold our fish to the tender, its pincers lowered drums of oil into our boat. The hardest thing we had to do in those months was lift those barrels up over the side of Chuck's skiff and onto the beach. We backed two ATVs into the surf and then used the ocean to float the barrels onto the vehicles' backs, from where we could drive them up to the house. A single drum of oil was so heavy, so very heavy, though, that it took the total of Chuck's and my strength combined to lift a single barrel up over the side of his skiff.

Chuck told me later that he could perform all the tasks of fishing down here himself—he could even set the net by himself, no need for a crewman to do that—but the one thing he indispensably could not do without the help of another person was to lift those drums of oil over the side of his boat. One man simply was not strong enough to lift a full barrel on his own. One drum of oil weighed as much as a building. If not for that, Chuck said he might very well have fished down here alone the last forty years, and I believed him since he didn't seem to need human company. Without oil, though, the generator would starve, and his whole operation would shut down.

One day when the season was a month old, I went out to do a job. I had forgot something back at the house and ran back to get it. I trotted in through the garage and bounded up the stairs to the second floor. I opened the door and was met with the sight of Chuck sweating profusely like a horse and pointing a double-barreled shotgun at my face.

"*Whoa, Chuck, don't shoot! It's me, Tom! Chuck, don't shoot!*" I shouted as Chuck's twitchy finger caressed the trigger.

I had seen enough in my life to know that anyone with a gun is secretly dying to shoot it. Why do you think they bought it in the first place? I tried to halt my forward momentum and lean my body back inside the stairwell. Chuck blinked rapidly like a heroin addict, gripping the trigger white-knuckled, the gun's crosshairs trained on my face.

"Jesus Christ … you scared me," he tittered nervously like a kid caught holding a dirty magazine. "I thought you were a bear … hehe." His sweaty finger still polished the trigger, reluctant to move it away.

I swear there was a part of Chuck that wanted to pull the trigger even after he saw it was me. I watched him making the mental calculations behind his eyes. But the fun of shooting another human being in the face was outweighed, if ever so slightly, by the fact that he needed my help to haul nets and lift drums of oil over the summer if he wanted to make money.

Chuck's shirt was drenched with sweat as though he had just jumped into a swimming pool with his clothes on. When he finally lowered the gun, he was still whispering to himself like a madman, his eyes raving like a lunatic.

I once nearly returned Chuck the favor. I was a greenhorn, remember, so everything we did was new to me. And nearly everything I did, I did badly before I did well.

Sometimes very badly.

There was one complex procedure. When you set a net into the ocean, the aim is to drop the anchors at each end of the net as far apart from one another as possible so that the net is stretched taut. A taut net traps more fish. It was very hard to get this procedure just right, and even when we thought we had dropped the second anchor near its apogee, the net was always slacker than we wanted it to be, and we felt a pang of disappointment. Two perfectionists, Chuck and I always wanted more, and satisfaction remained elusive. A slack net meant we were missing fish—they were bouncing off the curvature of the net or escaping around the sides—a rounded C shape meant we weren't using the whole hundred meters allotted to us under law that we would be if the net was stretched straight.

To set the net taut, after dropping the first anchor, Chuck drove the boat hard away from it toward shore while I teased the net out between my fingers into the water. I had to judge when the rope unspooling out of the boat was as close to its end as possible and then toss the second anchor overboard at the last possible moment to stretch the net taut, but not too late or the anchor would rip clean through the side of the boat before I got it over the side, like an errant cannonball lopping off a bystander's head.

The first time I tried this, I missed the mark badly. We dropped the first anchor, and Chuck drove the boat hard away from it toward shore. I fed the rope smoothly into the water. Chuck's rope was old and ragged, though, and it kept snagging on the feed, and I had to rework the snagged sections quickly to keep the rope flowing into the water in sync with the moving boat.

The rope got snarled in the feed right at the very end, just before it unspooled completely. I untangled the rope, but it was too late. I knew I was a half second late, and I could feel the calamity happen a moment before it did, like being able to see into the future. The heavy metal anchor was in my hands and I was dragging it over to the side of the boat to toss it overboard. But just as I was lifting it, the rope ran completely out and became perfectly taut—*Yay! One hundred percent taut!*—and the anchor ripped clean out of my hands and flew straight at Chuck's face at the speed of sound. Chuck must have glimpsed it out of the corner of his eye because he ducked on pure instinct. The serpent steel tail of the anchor flew an inch and a half to the left of his skull and smashed into the wall of the boat at four hundred miles per hour. The anchor didn't rip clean through the side of his boat, but it embedded itself in the boat's wall like an alien wrapping itself around a human face and plunging its tentacles down its throat. The boat whipped around 360 degrees as though an Iowa twister had picked it up, and the motor killed. Chuck cowered in a corner, his eyeballs white with terror, his face as white as a sheet of A4 paper. Everything went deathly quiet, and the boat drifted aimlessly out to sea.

I couldn't breathe. I was holding my breath. *Oh my God, oh my God, I nearly killed Chuck. Oh my God.* If the anchor had gone through

Chuck's face, which it was about an inch away from doing, he would have been decapitated—the speed and thickness of that black steel mass would have cleaved his head off his body like a warm knife passing through clotted cream—and I would have just killed a man. A homicide.

I looked at Chuck bug-eyed, my face white too, hand over my mouth in total shock. If Chuck hadn't ducked in that .0001 of a second, his face would have been impaled by forty pounds of U.S. steel. There was no one else around. What would I have done? I wouldn't be able to live down here forever. I couldn't lift the barrels of oil over the side of the skiff by myself. I supposed I could just live in Chuck's house and fish by the rod, no boat, and sleep in the cold, as he had said.

In situations like this Chuck usually yelled at me. When I made a mistake, he shook his head and said, "It's so hard to find good help."

With Chuck's usual short temper, I expected he was going to unload on me now. But for once he didn't. Maybe he saw the look of unchecked horror on my face. Maybe he realized that he had nearly checked out of this life for good in the blink of an eye. His greenhorn had nearly taken his fucking head off. Chuck rose slowly, placed one boot against the wall of the boat, and yanked the anchor out with both hands. Then he carried it over to the side of the boat and slowly dropped it overboard, staring at me with a pale face and haunted look in his eyes the whole time. Only after he dropped the anchor into the water did I notice that his hands were shaking.

The season finally ended. Those three months in Smoky Point were the longest of my life, but I did finally escape the place. One quiet, still morning shortly after dawn, Chuck drove me up the coast to Pilot Point, where he had booked the tiniest propeller biplane known to man to fly me the hell out of here. There was only enough room for one passenger inside. I climbed through a diagonal coin slot and leaned back inside a windowed coffin. There are no roads of any kind in or out of the Alaskan Peninsula: you have to fly over a towering rim of mountains called the Aleutian Range to get here from Anchorage.

After I left, Chuck stayed behind in Smoky Point to do God knows what.

"Fish by the rod, chill till the oil runs out," he waxed rapturously, sounding like Cool Hand Luke once again, so long as there were no bears around—the crocodiles to his Captain Hook.

I finally grasped that Smoky Point was Chuck's bliss, his heaven. He truly loved it down here. There was no place in the world he would rather be than this desolate wasteland, this nothingness that's as nothing as nothing can be, living alone in his self-sufficient house.

In the end we had gotten along well. Eight months later he sent me an email, inviting me back for a second season as his crewman. I was glad he invited me back. He offered me a 10 percent increase in the share this time. But by then I was working as a jackeroo on a cattle station in the Australian outback and had to decline.

"Plus, a 10 percent increase of $4,000 is only $4,400," I told him. "The flight alone to Alaska and back would cost more than that."

"Oh," he replied.

It was now early August, and I decided to round out my Alaska experience by working in the infamous processing side of the industry at a fish factory, better known as a cannery. Working in a cannery is the equivalent of working in a coal mine, on an oil rig, on a cattle station, or sifting for blood diamonds in equatorial Africa with a dictator wearing a beret waving a gun at your face. In other words, it's one of the world's worst jobs. Which means, it's exactly where I wanted to be.

I don't think anyone who's worked in a cannery would dispute how bad a job it is. I had heard about the epic drug abuse and the psychopaths who work in these nightmarish hellholes and was eager to get started, with some trepidation for the notorious eighteen-hour workdays on your feet with fish guts and repugnant fish smell permeating everything, even your skin.

The lifers here, middle-aged, were Mexican and Filipino. The young workers, mostly imported unwitting slave labor from Eastern European countries such as Turkey and Slovakia under the misleading title of Travel and Work Program, were mostly well behaved. Travel and Work Program made it sound like fun, or a bit of both. In fact it was 95 percent work and 5 percent travel. It was a program in name only. In reality it was much closer to human trafficking, probably existing in a gray area of legality. You could call it enhanced slavery or indentured servitude without any exaggeration.

The immigrants' visas lasted four months, and they were required to work three months of it in hell—the cannery—in exchange for one month of travel afterward.

Since the fees to some corrupt company in an anonymous strip mall in a former Soviet satellite country and the plane ticket and work visa to get them to Alaska alone cost $3,000 before they ever set foot in America (this number was always the same no matter which country the slave came from), they needed every penny they earned at the cannery just to recoup what they had already spent before leaving their country. Anything earned over three grand went toward one month of onward travel, so they worked feverishly to save up so they could buy a secondhand Volkswagen bus to drive across Canada after the season ended. They returned home flat broke but with huge smiles on their faces. It was definitely one of those predatory programs, like subprime lending, to get workers into the canneries and profit off the backs of the poor. The kids basically handed their wages over to the corrupt company in their failed states that had lured them with dreams of seeing America.

American kids employed by the place, mostly college students out of Washington and Oregon, spent every cent of their seven-dollar-an-hour earnings on weed and whiskey. They were the complete opposite of the Eastern European kids; they made no effort to save so much as a dime. Every night the Americans could be heard retching in the bathroom and TV room. In the morning our living quarters looked like a crime scene—vomit and bodies passed out on the floor, empty cigarette cartons and bottles of Jim Bean lined denuded sofas where cushions had been the night before. The cushions had been ripped apart in a rash of violence; feathers and white sofa stuffing covered the floor like freshly fallen snow.

Trafficking in fish guts is so depressing that every evening people felt compelled to get bombed to the brink of annihilation. Management didn't care. They sometimes came in the middle of the night and banged on our doors with flashlights like the KGB. They bullied the kids they knew had weed into giving it to them. They took the weed back to the manor and smoked it themselves, leaving the potheads with nothing but a hangover. In the morning management was back and kicking the limp, lifeless bodies of kids who'd nearly drunk themselves to death the night before, screaming shrilly for us to put on our fish gloves and aprons and get back on the line—"*Five minutes!*" It was time to spend another grueling ten consecutive hours mindlessly cutting seventy-five thousand pounds of fish.

Much of it stank from sitting on the barges for too many days, roasting and rotting under the hot sun, and cutting it made us dry heave. A lot of the fish had gone bad, but since the tender had already paid for it, the cannery sold it anyway, passing on the poisoned filth to you, trusting consumer, knowing it was bad all along.

We dutifully went along. No one blew the whistle. The place where we were was so remote, and there was no one to listen anyway, no one who cared. The stench of rotten fish was nauseating and intolerable, though. Sometimes a kid abruptly dropped his scalpel in the middle of the job and ran behind the fish grinding machine to puke.

"*Back in line!*" one of our faceless overseers shrieked from the catwalk above.

Another time a Mexican man took his eyes off the fish head-cutting machine for a second to laugh at his friend's insipid joke and the guillotine that cut each fish's head off chopped off his index finger. The blade came down like it was stamping the date on today's newspaper and took off his finger like it was warm butter.

"*Ay dios mío!*" he cried out.

The Mexican man ran around the factory floor screaming with blood spurting from the open stub near his knuckle where his finger had been, like one of the fish in the bottom of Chuck's boat. A lot of the lifers here were missing fingers. A man named Bisque who unloaded the fish off the tender had only his ring and pinky fingers remaining on his right hand.

The cannery was, mostly, a dispiriting place, about on par with a prison.

During my time at the cannery I had the singular experience of being chased, albeit briefly, by a wild bear. Everyone in Naknek, same as all over Alaska, was scared shitless of being chased and eaten alive by a bear. Grizzlies would just rip your limbs off and maul you to death, but black bears would eat you whole like tiramisu.

I met it face-to-face in the tall grass on the bluffs overlooking the cannery's docks and the sea down below. The fecund smell of wet black loam and upturned mulch percolated with sea brine. I had been tipped off to its presence when wild dogs began yelping as though they had just smelled a Terminator. It's the same as in the movie—you know a bear is approaching when dogs start barking. I felt a little like a TV actress in a bad horror movie as I stumbled dumbly in the direction of the dogs' yelping and whining. My heart leapt like crazy, every nerve ending on my epidermis tingled, as I ran forward, eager to meet my bear. At last, my whole purpose for coming here was at hand.

I approached slowly, thinking that I could maintain a safe distance, when, to my great surprise, a medium-sized brown grizzly bear came crashing out of the brush directly in front of me. Its head popped straight up through the tall grass like a prairie dog a mere five feet from me. *Holy shit! A real live bear!*

It was about twice the size of a Great Dane, and it was just as surprised to see me, even more so—clearly it hadn't been expecting me—and it stopped dead in its tracks. The bear looked directly into my eyes in a very humanlike way, reading my character the same way a small child does to an adult, sussing me out. I realized that I might possibly be in my first life-or-death situation of my year of living dangerously (or trying to live dangerously).

For a good five seconds neither the bear nor I moved. We both stood rooted to our spots looking intensely and searchingly into each other's eyes. I had the distinct impression that the bear had the exact same mirror expression I did: curious, innocent, naïve. It occurred to me the bear *was* me, looking back at me from my animal form, and I was looking at it from its human form. I wondered which of us would blink first, and whether this was a game of chicken or a test of *who's the bigger alpha* in the wild. I quickly realized it wouldn't be the bear.

I now understood what people mean when they say an eternity passed in those few seconds. In those five seconds I had all the time in the world to notice that the bear's eyes were melancholy and sweet, and that it was making a very real attempt to communicate with me. I'm sure some bears are vicious and cruel, which I would discern as it was wrapping its jaws around my face. I was just lucky that this bear happened to be sweet. All bears are systematically abandoned by their mothers before age two, as soon as they're capable of surviving on their own. This bear was not yet large and perhaps had only recently been shed by its mother. Its innocent, pure eyes held me fixed as I stared ever deeper into those limpid pools.

The bear broke the trance first. It opened its mouth and a long tongue rolled out like a red carpet. Then it bounded straight at me. It gamboled toward me like a large, playful dog. In Alaska we were taught over and over that all these bears are killers, no matter how young, small, or playful they seem, that it was in their nature, and at the sight of this giant beast lumbering toward me, my heart liquefied. The one thing you're not supposed to do when a bear charges you is to run. This is true for all Alaskan big game except the moose. If a moose charges you, run your ass off or you will end up a moose burger.

I had read plenty on what you're supposed to do if a bear charges. But just as your childhood karate lessons go out the window in a real fight when you're not wearing the pajamas and trying to break a stack of eight wood pallets with your forehead and fantasizing you're the Karate Kid, the same thing happens when you're confronted by a prolific, known killer in the wild.

I wasn't taking any chances. I turned on my heel and booked it. I looked over my shoulder. The bear had upshifted into a gallop and was quickly closing the gap on me. It still had that childish, silly expression on its face, and I had the distinct impression that it was about to tackle me from behind like an older brother. I wasn't sure I wanted to have the bear on top of me.

By some miracle of God an old rusted, junked-up car materialized in the high grass ahead of me like an oasis. I ran toward it as the bear upshifted again into a full run. I looked behind me. The bear was right on my ass now, bearing down on me like an eighteen-wheeler. Shit! I broke out in sweat as I crashed through the tall grass that stung and swatted my face. You don't trip and fall and twist your ankle when you're being hunted by an apex predator in real life; that only happens in the movies. You can be damn sure that in real life you're not going to trip under those circumstances.

Breathless, I reached the rusted car just as the bear nipped my heels. It thrust out its gigantic head to headbutt me in the ass. As it did, I clambered up the crushed hood of the car, which cratered under my boots, and got up onto the roof. I turned around to face my totem. The bear stopped short at the hood. Then it looked up at me with a confused expression, no different than a human child's, as though I had ruined our game by jumping onto the car.

It looked in my eyes again. Why did the bear always look in my eyes? Suddenly it jumped up onto the hood, which made a terrific crashing sound under the bear's weight. I cried out in fright and fell backward on my ass and fell down the back window onto the trunk. I climbed to my feet again and prepared to run. But just then the bear broke our gaze and hopped back down to land. Then, without saying goodbye, in one fluid, graceful motion it turned to the right and flowed over the cliff with no hesitation as though it were roped into a harness, which of course it wasn't. I wondered whether the bear was plummeting through the sky like a stone. Presently I heard panicked screaming from people on the beach down below. The bear seemed to have slid down the cliff to the bottom.

My close brush with being eviscerated—yes, giving death the slip—left me exhilarated, and for a few moments I felt intensely alive. Endorphins lighted up my inner body like first light on Christmas morning. I felt seamlessly interwoven with every living thing around me. I wanted to make love to someone and celebrate the beautiful joy of being alive.

Finally it was over. One morning I shouldered my duffel bag and headed out to the tarmac with all the other fish-processing employees to board a small propeller plane back to Anchorage. The Mexicans and

Filipinos stayed behind; they would move to another cannery where they could eke out another two months of work in the smaller minnow fish-cutting season in September and October before the lucrative king crab season began in November.

The slave laborers from Europe could finally enjoy their much ballyhooed one month of holiday before being deported by Homeland Security. Most of them would peter through the vast nothingness of central Canada in secondhand Volkswagen buses, almost sure to break down in Saskatchewan or Manitoba.

Back in Anchorage my new reality dawned on me. My motorcycle was broken—trashed, destroyed—seven hundred miles away in Whitehorse, Canada. It was the end of August and I would spend the next month dealing with very expensive logistical and repair costs to the bike. The part that had shattered deep inside the bike's soul was obscure—called a stator. No shop had it on hand. It had to be shipped from the factory in Virginia to Anchorage. It would take three weeks for the stator to arrive. It took forever.

I rented a U-Haul and drove seven hundred miles to Whitehorse to pick up my bike with an old German woman named Gretel whom I met at the hostel the night before. Feeling buzzed and excited to finally be retrieving my bike—my one link back to civilization—I was awake after midnight and reading in the hostel lobby when an ancient woman stumbled through the doorway carrying a bicycle with two suitcases lashed to each side with thick yellow rope. Bicycling with two massive suitcases strapped to you like anchors like that must be like Sisyphus pushing that boulder uphill.

She was shivering.

"Jesus," I said, jumping up to help her lift her bicycle across the threshold. "What happened to you?"

The woman was so cold that she struggled to open her mouth.

"You've been riding all night?" I asked helpfully.

It was one in the morning; it had been dark for six hours.

"Ye-s," she croaked in the thickest, most incomprehensible German accent you can imagine. "I rode from Missou-la."

She was shaking like a thrush in the jaws of a cat. She removed the helmet that was strapped to her head like a Berkeley Antifa street fighter. Though she looked cold and miserable, I immediately detected enormous vitality from her, a physical resilience that could outlast eons.

"Missoula, Montana?" I exclaimed, shocked. "That's two thousand miles from here!"

"More, actually," she croaked. "I flew from my home in Bonn, Germany, to Missoula and rode my bicycle over the Rocky Mountains to here."

"Really," I said, my jaw on the floor. "How long did that take?"

"Twenty-eight days." The tent she'd slept in on the side of the road each night was strapped to the front grill of her bicycle like E.T. She had ridden a bicycle clear over the Rocky Mountains from Montana to Alaska carrying an enormous amount of luggage.

She had done it in less than thirty days.

She was seventy-three years old.

Gobsmacked, I asked whether she wanted to get off the bike for a minute and ride in a U-Haul with me fourteen hundred miles—the same distance as halfway across the United States—to Whitehorse, Canada, and back.

She shrugged. A day at the beach for her.

"See you at six a.m. sharp," I said.

The summer fishing season ended a full month ago. Everyone had left Alaska long ago. Everyone except me. It was temperate, dare I say balmy in Anchorage in September, and it never occurred to me that I should buy warmer clothes for the ride south. I had no reason to believe that the temperature inland would be any different than it was here.

After a month of downtime in Anchorage, the motorcycle was finally repaired. Winter was about to come crashing down on my head like a breaking wave and imprison me and my motorcycle in Alaska for the next six months until spring. A feeling of dread pricked over my skin, and suddenly I was seized by a grave urgency to get out of dodge and get south in a hurry. I was not about to waste the next half a year in Anchorage!

I finally set off on the bike for California on September 12, but it was too late. Anchorage was still warm, as it deceptively remains along the coast well into autumn. Coastal cities, beneficiaries of warm ocean currents and low air pressure, are temperate all year round, while landlocked places, still subject to the old powers of earth, receive no such assistance and experience enormous volatility in temperature—hot as the surface of a star in summer, cold as a free swim in the Arctic Ocean in winter.

It never occurred to me that temperatures could be so different inland than they are along the coast, but indeed, no sooner had Anchorage's skyline disappeared in my rearview mirror than the temperature plummeted like a stone. Alaska was going to be colder than anything I had ever experienced.

As soon as I had ridden a mere fifteen minutes outside of the city limits, the temperature plunged in real time as though an invisible thumb were pressing down on the thermostat. I was wearing only jeans, a wifebeater, and a leather jacket—the same thing I would be wearing two thousand miles to the south—and I was getting very cold, very fast. I regretted not buying warmer clothes in the capital where outdoor clothing stores such as Patagonia and North Face were abundant. But now I was so eager to get south that I did not turn around to go back and shop. This was foolish, but the Nothing in *The NeverEnding Story* was coming. I could feel it in my bones. I had to outrun it.

I was not prepared for cold this intense in interior Alaska, and I discovered agony during a long, brutal stretch of four hundred miles before I was finally able to obtain warmer clothes. Extreme cold first flew through my jeans as though I was wearing nothing more than a bathing suit and attacked my joints, the knees specifically. The cold had the effect of extreme arthritis—it froze my joints—so that when I dismounted at gas stations, bending my knees even slightly just to walk was extremely painful. To anyone watching I must have looked like a cripple, unable to shuffle forward more than a step at a time without stopping.

The cold flew through my torso like it was the French army and wrapped itself insidiously around my heart like a black widow's embrace—deathlike, deadly. It gave my heart the odd sensation of liquefying. I felt tiny rivulets of water dripping down inside my heart, and my whole body began to feel falsely warm as though it was thawing out, when in fact the opposite was happening: it was slowly freezing. Later I learned there's a name for this.

It's called hypothermia.

After more than two hundred miles of riding, at last I reached the first motel on the highway. When I finally got out of the cold, I acutely felt everything going on inside my heart all night long, or hallucinated that I did in my hypothermic delirium: all the ticking, clicking, clacking, opening and closing of little valves inside my heart's chambers and ventricles. This scared the shit out of me even more than being chased by the bear because I couldn't see it; I didn't know what was happening to me.

I sat down in the motel's diner to eat something. When the pretty young waitress came over to take my order, she took one look at me and recoiled in horror. When she recoiled, I did too in a mirror reaction of her horror, as though we had both just looked in the same mirror and seen a ghoulish monster staring back at us. Only I was that monster. She said my face was blue like the performers in the Blue Man Group in Las Vegas, blue like the fat kid who eats too much and turns into a blueberry and dies in *Willy Wonka*. I was one foot in the grave, she said, no joke.

"Shit," I croaked. "Really?"

I tried to smile at her, but no smile creased my waxy face. Looking back, I was in the middle stages of hypothermia. Another hour or so exposed on the bike and they might have been scraping my nose off with a spatula in a hospital operating room.

I ordered a hamburger but found I had no appetite, though I hadn't eaten anything since that morning. I picked at it but could only manage a few bites. It was the first and last time in my life I have ever left a hamburger unfinished on my plate. My hands were shaking; I was having difficulty operating a knife and fork. After forcing down a few tasteless bites, I could do no more. I got up and went to look in the bathroom mirror. Indeed my face did have a bluish tint, a ghostly pallor. I looked like Braveheart after he painted his face.

I went back to my room and spent three consecutive hours in the shower with the water turned on maximum hot—scalding—and felt nothing. I couldn't feel the boiling-hot water even though it battered my skin pink like roast beef. My skin was like dragon skin, chainmail … dead, like rubber-chicken skin. My brain was still ticking, but my body was essentially a corpse. I was probably half-dead without knowing it. The hot water continued to patter against my skin, but my inner body remained ice cold, embalmed in mercury. I just could not get warm inside for the life of me.

The icy, arctic air had wormed its way into my bones, where it can be lethal. The cold is not so easy to exorcise once it is inside the marrow, the physical body's last defense, where it was now running wild like kids whose parents have gone on vacation. My bones were cold, and stayed cold.

Only at the end of a full three hours in the shower, the length of a Scorsese film, did the heat finally begin to trickle down into my core, like rivulets of gas dripping down into the motorcycle's engine from the reserve tank. Finally, like a single hot coal that gives off just a shade of heat, a tiny kernel of warmth sprouted somewhere deep inside my bone marrow where the deathly cold had taken hold and started to emanate just a little, as though it were the same magical seed that had given birth to the original stars in the universe. That tiny seed, that lone coal, finally breathed enough heat into my bones to kick the cold back out into my corporeal body, where it ultimately would be easier to expel.

There was still no effect on my overall physical body, but I could feel my bones, my core, my mainframe OS, fighting back. My blood started to flow again and transmute from blue back to red. The reserve power light blinked on, returning the dead Terminator to life. I had turned around and was making the arduous walk back from the lightless land of the dead to the low stone wall that separates the world of the living from the hinterland of death.

I woke early the next morning terrified to leave the motel and venture back out into the arctic cold, but what choice did I have? There was cold both in front and behind me. It didn't matter much which way I went. I couldn't stay in that motel for the next six months until spring. Couldn't stay, couldn't leave. No choice but to go on. So back outside I went.

I was so cold that I was only able to drive the bike at half speed, thirty-five miles per hour. I was just too cold to go any faster. That meant that I was on the road for twice as long as I would normally be at seventy-five miles per hour. My body was shaking at the microrapid rate of a hummingbird's heartbeat and my motor functions were so impaired that I could barely operate the bike's gearshift and brake lever. Every action I took was delayed by at least a second and was often erroneous: I missed turnoffs. I forgot to tip that waitress back at the motel.

Hypothermia left me disoriented. At some point I was giving up hope a bit and sort of surrendered in my mind. Anytime I have been in dire straits, if I reached the point where I completely surrendered resistance to the problem I was facing—*stop trying to fight life*—somehow after that things improved on their own and a solution presented itself. I don't know why or how, but it has always happened so far. Perhaps the lesson is to relax and flow more with life.

I dismounted at a gas station. I was shaking like a wild thing, like a thing in trouble. Like someone with a condition. A stranger approached me. Someone who had been pumping gas. I was half blind—hypothermia causes the world to take on a grayish, ashen discoloration—and I didn't immediately notice the person approaching. The man said that he and his wife had seen me. They saw my face was blue and that I couldn't walk, that I was shuffling toward the gas pumps like a mummy even though I wasn't swaddled in toilet paper. They saw that I was wearing only blue jeans, a leather jacket, and a wifebeater in the arctic in winter.

"Are you crazy?" the man asked me.

"Could be," I wanted to reply, but no sound came out of my mouth.

The man offered me the sweater he was wearing. Dumbfounded, I watched as he pulled his sweater over his head and handed it to me right there in front of the gas pumps. I was stunned, floored by his kindness. I was not used to encountering such kindness in my life. I thanked him feebly; I was too cold to be profuse. I put the sweater on. It didn't help much.

Cotton.

Another hundred miles in, the exact same thing happened again. A stranger walked up to me at a gas station. He said that he and his wife had seen me, seen I was in a bad way. They offered to drive me to their house and give me some clothes. I left the bike at the gas station and climbed into the back of their pickup truck. They drove me the few short miles to their house.

I sat in a brown corduroy armchair in their living room and nursed a cup of hot coffee they had handed me. The elderly couple came back carrying four sweaters and fleeces. I looked at them, looked at the neatly folded stack of clothes in their arms, and broke down and cried in gratitude.

In the end I acquired some sixteen layers of clothing—all given to me by strangers at gas stations who saw my wretched condition, my blue face, and took pity on me. I must have looked pretty bad to inspire that many different strangers to walk up to me unprompted. Maybe I really was one foot in the grave, as the waitress had said—who knows? I have no idea how far gone I actually was. These strangers took me shivering inside their homes and gave me steaming mugs of hot joe and the clothes literally off their backs so that I could continue my journey.

It was the first time in my life I felt that people were on my side, and they were strangers, people I didn't know. They knew they would never see those clothes again. When I offered them money, they said no. Strangers helped me to get across the Arctic, Alaska and the Yukon Territory until the road finally turned south some one thousand miles later. Humans' betrayal, jealousy, and self-interest are truly equaled at times by generosity and deep kindness. I had forgotten that any such kindness still existed in the world. These people in our heartland are truly golden and good. I will never forget you.

Before I could escape from Alaska, I had to drive over a harrowing, intimidating ridge of jagged white teeth—the daunting, much-higher-than-I-expected Alaska Range. I was still suffering from acute cold, but because I was now wearing more layers, I was getting by.

Alaska

When I arrived at the base of the towering sweep of mountains, one body part that I needed to operate the motorcycle was worrisomely becoming colder and colder to the point that I could no longer stand the pain—my hands. While not wearing gloves suitable for Mount Everest, I thought that the gloves I had were adequate. Yet the cold moved effortlessly through them and into my fingers as I puttered up the face of the mountain. My fingers went from numb (okay) to painful (not okay), and the raw fear of hypothermia gripped me once again, the fear of losing my fingers to frostbite. Frostbite attacks the extremities first. People climbing Mount Everest lose their fingers and toes and nose. I knew that if I could just get over these mountains that I would cross into Canada and the road would eventually turn south.

But the Nothing found me first.

I had spent weeks, possibly my entire life, avoiding it. But it was inevitable. The Nothing was always going to find me, no matter where I ran to on the planet. You can't run from what hunts you. The only way to make progress in your life is to turn around and hunt it right back. Hunt what hunts you. Become the hunter yourself.

It overtook a gray sky and came at me low from distance out of the north. A huge roiling black cloud, an immense storm front—the Nothing—bum-rushed me out of goddamn nowhere. It swooped toward me with preternatural, bone-chilling speed. It seemed to be coming just for me. It was a nightmare. I was all alone on the road. The giant black cloud stooped down over my head until it was lower than a four-story building. Lightning crackled inside the black mass, followed by thunder so devastatingly loud that my entire body shook like maracas on Cinco de Mayo. I vibrated so violently that my bike nearly tipped over. I rolled my right wrist down on the throttle to speed up. I had to get over this mountain. I thought I was going to make it.

I didn't make it.

The Nothing opened up its jaws and a maelstrom of snow and hurricane dumped down on my head. It was September 16. Overwhelmed by the blizzard flying into my face like freezing bullets, like being smacked by sea breakers filled with snow instead of water, I had to get off the road.

There was nothing around. Frigid arctic winds howled into my face. I was bitterly cold. I was shivering violently. My fingertips felt like they were falling off, so painful from the cold they were. Desperate, I kept driving, conscious only of the fact I was freezing to death. Suddenly, out of nowhere, something appeared up ahead of me on the left. It looked like a log cabin. I pulled in to the driveway, drove to the front door, and knocked.

Nobody answered.

Frantically I knocked again.

Eventually an old woman with gray, greasy hair opened the door.

I ended up spending three days in the woman's house while the storm raged uncontrollably outside. She was an Evangelical Christian, and she seemed to have lived alone for a long time. I marveled endlessly that the sky was dumping snow in mid-September. It was Indian summer a couple thousand miles to the south. I wondered whether the snow would stop before next June or if I would be stuck in the Alaskan version of Appalachia until spring thaw.

Over the three day storm my motorcycle became buried under an avalanche of snow—literally buried under an actual mountain of snow—and I couldn't see it anymore. I worried about the bike nonstop, as though it were my own child. I didn't know whether the bike's sensitive internal moving organs, I mean parts, could withstand that amount of snow and cold; the bike was frozen solid under that snow pyramid like a cinder block. My motorcycle had seen more abuse than Oliver Twist and Jane Eyre put together.

The snow ended three days later, as the woman said it would.

"First snow of the season ends. Second one don't. Second keeps dumping all winter long till April," she said.

She told me to get the hell out while I still could. There was a very narrow window to escape between the first and second snows of the season. Now that the first had ended, the second could start anytime, making the road impassable for the next six months, barring my way, and that would be game over for me and my motorcycle. There would be no way to drive or hitchhike out with the highway buried under six feet of snow.

I pushed the mountain of snow off my bike. I was prepared for the worst, because the worst was all I had known so far. This time, though, I finally had a little luck. I pulled the choke, and the ignition sparkled to life. Perhaps the bike, like me, was finally getting a little tougher.

And oh yeah—my cookie-dough ass had transmogrified into wood.

I finally got over the fearsome Alaska Range and arrived on the other side of it in a little hamlet called Tok. A tiny backwater at the base of the mountains, Tok consists only of a few log cabins and a gas station. I had never been so happy to see them.

A tiny hardware store was attached to the gas station, and here I was able to buy a survival item that is both gloriously futuristic and reassuringly atavistic—the silver blanket.

This blanket, made of aluminum polyester, is the stuff they use to line the inside of the space shuttle with to keep astronauts warm in space. It's designed for people who are abandoned outdoors in extreme cold to give them an outside chance at survival. You're supposed to strip naked and wrap yourself in this thin tinfoil polymer sheath. It's designed to reflect 80 percent of your body heat back to you and give you a fighting chance against Mother Nature when you're wearing a wifebeater and jeans and riding a motorcycle above the sixty-third parallel in winter.

Of course, whenever you take on Mother Nature she can beat you if she really wants to.

While struggling to get out of Alaska, I wrapped myself in a diaper and metallic dress of this space shuttle shit every morning. I always ended up asking some yokel in the hallway of a motel to scotch tape the shit to my bare back. They usually copped a sneer and looked at me like I was crazy, but they held their noses and taped it to my buck-naked body as I had asked. Asking good ol' boys to tape what looks like a tinfoil diaper onto an adult male's naked body in a motel hallway in silent-majority America is asking quite a lot. In my New Year's Eve opalescent metal-foil dress and cheeks reddened from facial windburn, I looked like Boy George in drag. I'm probably lucky I didn't get my ass kicked and dumped in a ditch somewhere. In fact, everyone I asked did it for me. I'm not so naive as to think this was due only to my charm. Rather, once again, the people in the middle of our country are friendly and loyal.

I slowly worked my way east and finally south over the sinuous, never-ending Alaskan-Canadian Highway to the point where I could lose the dress. One day I stuffed it in a trash can at a gas station, but not before thanking it for saving my life.

During these travels in the north I saw many wild animals: bears (grizzlies and blacks), moose, caribou, wild buffalo, and bald eagles, all naturally out in the wild, not in national parks or enclosures. I saw the northern lights—milky white and lime jello green, they shifted and weaved menacingly across the sky like an interstellar phantom or alien on the cusp of space about to invade. The aurora borealis was bewildering, mystifying, one of the last truly awe-inspiring natural phenomena on earth.

I saw the northern lights in the month while I was waiting for the motorcycle to be repaired. I took a bus from Anchorage to Denali National Park, home to Denali, the highest mountain in North America. Late one night, at one thirty in the morning, a rap came on my door.

"Come out, come out! The lights are *on!*" the British girl said breathlessly.

The lights are on! I will not soon forget that merry, singsong voice on the other side of my door. We had met just briefly earlier that day in a hiking group. Wearing only my pajama bottoms and a beater, I wrapped the bed comforter around my shoulders and slipped outside into breathtaking cold. It was the first weekend of September, Labor Day, and the cold in interior Alaska at night was already blistering, colder than anything I had ever experienced up to that point. The cold was gripping, took on a menacing life of its own, and I figured I could last maybe five minutes, ten at the most, before succumbing to it and rushing back inside. The girl and I stood side by side on a grassy knoll under a vast, starry expanse of luminous Alaskan sky—a cauldron of green, black, and white shifting colors—and stared up into a truly stupendous, mind-stopping aurora borealis. It blanketed the sky immense, and I was spellbound.

I find I can ride forever in the north. When you're riding long distances, hundreds upon hundreds of miles, which become thousands of miles, on a road that snakes on endlessly on a motorcycle in faraway lands in severe climates, your perception, heightened by the cold and the intensity of the climate, turns meditative. You lose yourself in the smooth purr and hypnotic thrum of the moving motorcycle that is like a spaceship ferrying you across the vast glittering cavern of the northern world. The frigid arctic wind slaps your face, scrapes your cheeks, rakes your skin raw. The intense isolation this far north seemed to mirror the isolation in my own heart.

As I wove south through British Columbia to Jasper and Banff, fall was turning the leaves stunningly—fire-engine red, candlewax yellow, and a few like a Japanese garden, all tangerine pink and a rarer deathlike pale blue so ethereal that the leaves were diaphanous and seemed to inhabit some liminal doorway between our world and the next one.

On the bike one has lots of time to think, and not to think. In the meditative state thoughts drift through eerily and wispily, rotating in front of you like spectral faces in a haunted house before turning away again in dreamlike fashion. One has an age to do nothing except look around at the swaying trees, the lilting lakes, the shifting nature, and bear witness to a cascading waterfall of stars that shiver across the heavens in a night basin so majestic that it dwarfs anything in the warmer climes to the south.

The colder the night sky, the brighter the stars gleamed. They twinkle and pulse with greater intensity for those who dare venture near the poles. The closer you come to world's end, the more beautiful that world becomes.

My lodestone as I rode in that black, icy wilderness was a tiny blue icon for the high beams on my bike's dashboard—a bewitching, haunting ice blue. It was an eerie, spectral shade of blue that I had never seen before and had no place in Crayola's crayon box. That unique, singular blue stood out in stark relief against the primitive darkness in one of our planet's more remote quadrants. That lone light, which was like a lighthouse at world's end standing up against the all-drowning darkness, was my solitary companion through many long nights in that dark icy world.

I fixed on the haunting blue light as I rode, gazed at it for hours, unable to tear my eyes away, its ghostly hypnotic hue holding me fast.

I spent hours, nights, wondering where I had seen that particular shade of blue before. It lay somewhere on the deepest recesses of memory—somewhere long ago, like a forgotten smell from childhood that wafts up one day in adulthood twenty years later but dissolves again just as quickly before you can put your finger on it. This elicits a deep sadness because the smell was one from the happiest period of your childhood, perhaps the happiest memory of your entire life, and now it is gone, lost forever, forgotten, and you have never found the smell again. A smell from the kitchen, your mother … if only you could remember. It lies on the deepest vestige of memory … now gone, vanished like a world that was full and complete and will never be that full and complete again. The ice blue was a tiny blue lake in the Swiss Alps that I found once while hiking alone at altitude, or the underbelly of an iceberg just below the surface of the water where it shimmers iridescent.

I became so experienced on the bike that I was able to lean deeply into curves and deliberately brush my knee against the pavement as I curled by—I could time it that closely. During the day the fragrance of asphalt wafted up—an intoxicatingly sweet bouquet of gasoline, oil, and steaming-hot pavement that worked its way up my jeans and into my jacket like a fine leather grease, making the jacket feel supple and lived-in. Pulling on the jacket each morning bequeathed an astonishing amount of comfort that felt almost as much like home as the motorcycle seat. Jumping off the bike at gas stations with the smells of leather, gasoline, and the road swimming in my skull like an addict who snorts asphalt to get high, wide awake and nerves singing, I felt like a man—no one had to remind me I was born free. Footloose, restlessness kept at bay so long as I was on the bike, carrying nothing but a wallet pressed crisply against my thigh in my tight blue jeans, silver chain with an eagle pendant dangling around my neck, and a ring of keys with an Elvis Presley red guitar draped down over the black gas tank—all had an urgent, simplifying appeal. Motorcycle, jeans, flat stomach, eagle pendant on a chain, a few bucks in my pocket … what more does a man need? For me it just felt like home.

This time I murdered my bike myself. In my defense, it was unintentional, though that was cold comfort to my bike, which once again was a corpse. Because I had needlessly been afraid of condensation from the melting snow trickling down the inside wall of the red gas can into the gas and polluting it with water each morning, I kept buying additives at gas stations that supposedly removed the water parts, and pouring them into the gas tank. These additives were killing my bike. Unwittingly I had been feeding my bike cyanide, and it died shortly after I drove south through the gorgeous glacier-studded country of Jasper and Banff, Canada. The ignition would not turn over no matter how far I pulled out the choke. My bike was as dead as, you guessed it, Jacob Marley.

Dammit! What is it this time?

It was an unfortunate error that resulted in thousands of more dollars spent and another month marooned in a foreign capital, this time Vancouver, Canada.

At least it was warm.

I had to get AAA to freight my bike to Vancouver at enormous cost—I could have bought a new Indian motorcycle for the same amount of money I dumped into repairs on this bike—where it took the garage a month to figure out why the bike wouldn't start, since mechanically it was fine.

"Nothing wrong with it," the mechanic said.

"Great!" I said, throwing my hands in the air.

After a month scratching their heads, the mechanics finally emptied the gas tank and refilled it with fresh. They turned the ignition and the bike sparkled to life—it purred lustily like a big cat waking from a long nap. The answer, as usual, was the simplest one—the spurious additives marketed in every gas station across North America to improve your bike's health actually destroy it.

"Don't fall for that marketing shit," the mechanic told me. "The bike is made to run only on gas."

"No shit," I said, holding my hand to my forehead.

I finally returned to San Diego in November and started advertising my bike, hoping to sell it for the same amount I'd bought it for six months earlier.

What happened next was a whole different adventure.

I wish that I was born a thousand years ago
I wish that I'd sailed the darkened seas
On a great big clipper ship
Going from this land here to that
In a sailor's suit and cap
Away from the big city
Where a man cannot be free
Of all the evils of this town
And of himself and those around

—Lou Reed

6

India: Music Box of Wonders

It was like a movie. That's because it *was* a movie. I couldn't contain my glee. I was working with my favorite Indian male movie star, Akshay Kumar. I had seen loads of his movies all over India while on overnight buses, in hotel lobbies, in train station waiting rooms, in cafés, restaurants ... His cheesy mug smoldered from billboards across the country from north to south, east to west. I loved him the way Winston Smith loves Big Brother.

Akshay Kumar is one of India's most prolific film stars, making several movies a year. Indian men are all cheesy, but this actor was my favorite, and is one of India's favorites, because he is *especially* cheesy. The man oozes cheese like a slug oozes a wet skidmark across your driveway. It must have been a big movie because the lead actress, whom I was surprised to see on set, was none other than Aishwarya Rai—the most beautiful, famous actress in the world, and the only Indian actress known outside of Bollywood due to her transcendent, Aphrodite-like beauty. She routinely landed on pop-culture lists of the world's ten most beautiful women, mostly in commonwealth countries with large Indian populations such as England. She was not widely known in America, however topping India, which has three times the population of the United States, qualifies her as the world's most famous actress.

Now she was standing three feet in front of me. Her ethereal, almost celestial beauty was magical to behold.

We were filming a marriage-proposal scene. The set was made up as a living room in an opulent mansion with an ornate winding staircase and tacky paintings adorning the walls of yellow tulips, sheiks in turbans, and jarringly incongruous portraits of colonial Jeffersonian white men in wigs, in an Indian's house. Where, I wondered, were the portraits of Gandhi?

An outrageously large chandelier dripped crystals down nearly to the floor, so low that a six-foot-tall man could easily jump up and swing from it like Tarzan if he wanted to. Which, if I was there again, I would do, since I later learned that the Indians don't give a shit about, well, anything. To the Indians, no ersatz faux luxury is too tacky, no bauble too gaudy, no nouveau riche mansion too gauche.

The Indian actors hugged each other between takes, draping their arms around each other's shoulders and laughing merrily. We were shooting the final scene of the movie, where the protagonist proposes to his girlfriend while their families and hundreds of guests form a circle around them and cheer the couple on, usually by swinging one arm in the air and whooping. Akshay got down on one knee, whispered inaudibly to Aishwarya—the actors' voices would be dubbed in later—Aishwarya accepted with a radiant smile, and the room ignited in ballistic celebration. And when I say ballistic, that's exactly what I mean. An eruption of mania several levels above anything I have ever experienced exploded on the set like human ordnance. The couple's immediate family clasped arms around each other's shoulders and started dancing wildly in a rotating circle around the couple, who were now frozen in a lip-lock at the circle's center like two wax figures in a museum.

Techno music throbbed out of soundstage speakers behind them. The young Indian director, just thirty-one years old, shook his narrow hips and punched the sky with his fist. He danced, spun around in place, and jabbed the air with his fist as though he were trying to knock down a piñata hanging from the ceiling. The pulsating dance music wouldn't be in the final movie—it was just there to lather the actors into the necessary frenzy. We extras in the background had been instructed to go absolutely ape shit at this moment, and we did not shrink from our duties. We erupted in a monkey-bitten, foaming at the mouth, donkey madness more typically associated with rabid diseased dogs. The Indian director flapped his arms like a DJ to rile us up, screaming, "More! Give me more, dammit!" We were expected to go bananas, leaping up and down, high-fiving, doing cartwheels, backflips, whatever we wanted to show the greatest euphoria possible. They'd even brought in a couple ringers. One guy was breakdancing, and two others were doing cheerleading-type moves, jumping and touching both sets of toes in the air. Another guy was spinning on his head like a dreidel. The energy on set was infectious. The mood just kept on soaring. I wondered how high a mood could soar before it plateaued. And yet there was such a kinetic, surging, spilling-over energy in the room that it never plateaued.

Welcome to moviemaking in the subcontinent.

Nearly all Indian movies are themed in the broadest, most simplistic and dumbed-down archetypes. There is no sophisticated fare for the "discerning viewer," that bloviating blowhard who calls himself an "intellectual" and subscribes to the *New Yorker*, the kind of person you can't stand at dinner parties. Rather, Indian films are neatly stupided down as comfort food. It's *cheese* for the masses who adore them—continuous escapism by way of distraction from the grinding poverty just outside the movie house's front door.

Going to a movie in India is quite an experience. It's as if every movie that opens is *Titanic*. The lines at theaters wrap around the block for an average new film, and the crowd will cheer and sometimes stand and clap *throughout the entire movie*, so that you can't see the screen unless you stand too, and then you find yourself watching a whole movie in a language you can't understand, Hindi, while standing in place for two hours. The story lines are so basic, though, that you don't really need dialogue to follow them. Most seem derived from the *Romeo and Juliet* formula—lovers separated by caste or class meet, come apart, and find their way back together at the end when the parents finally accept their child's choice of partner. That actually sounds like most Western movies as well.

In India, movies are inescapable because they are everywhere—on the TV sets of every restaurant, train station waiting room, and hostel lobby, on every channel in your hotel room other than the BBC. The first time you see a Bollywood film, you may be startled by its ludicrous exuberance, so unapologetically effusive that you feel embarrassed for it, the way you feel ashamed after watching a particularly cloying

Valentine's Day film. Indian movies feel no obligation to balance happy and sad emotions like Western comedies do. Laced through every American comedy from *Tootsie* to *The Hangover* is a head-scratching side dish of pathos. Why? No one knows. Because it's worked for a hundred years. *Bullshit!* the Indians say. You only remember the funny parts anyway.

In addition to dismissing our phony need for narrative balance, Indian cinema notably rejects sartorial balance as well, offering instead a full-throated embrace of the primary colors. Bright red, orange, and yellow are the ingrained aesthetic of India and represent the optimism and ebullience of a nation. Modesty, restraint, balance—these are unknown words in India. They were redacted, stricken from the Indian dictionary a thousand years ago. Enough of this cynical black that American girls wear—slimming effect be damned! India, the people and country itself, are awash in color, suffused and steeped in it, paired with a feverish headlong energy that never really lets up, never subsides. Indians know only one direction: up. Crescendo. There is no antidote to the unhinged, galloping madness that animates all aspects of Indian life, and every Indian movie, with the cubic fusion power of the sun.

Which brings us to the next unique feature of Bollywood—the singing and dance numbers that are the backbone of every Indian film and consequently, the entire country. Plot and dialogue take a back seat to these lushly choreographed, narrative-killing dance sequences which stretch on in some cases for half an hour. They go on interminably, tediously to me, but are infectious, ludicrous, hysterical, and indeed, schizophrenic. For example, thirty people dancing in choreographed unison on top of a speeding train with a fake CGI forest streaming by in the background was the centerpiece of the first Bollywood movie I saw. Thirty people dancing on top of a speeding train in a scene that runs continuously without a break in the camera shot for twenty minutes is not cheesy to Indians. It's good stuff. You want to turn it off, but at some point, and this happens to everyone who stays in India too long, the day comes when you can't turn it off anymore. You want to watch it. And God help you, you even kind of like it. You've been seduced by the schlock and their fearless cheesiness, their embrace of a fully euphoric vision that transcends shame or compromise, the kind our Protestant background instinctively recoils from. You watch the absurd dance numbers with the same fascination you would watch a high-speed train derail off the Eiger Mountain and hurtle into the rock-strewn valley floor below—you can't look away, you can't *not* watch anymore.

You're a goner until you leave India.

The most absurd feature of Indian cinema is their penchant for including foreigners in the background of scenes even though, for instance, a Westerner would never be invited to an actual Indian wedding party or marriage-proposal dinner. Sometimes the director gets carried away and gives some random backpacker—no question a backpacker because he has no star quality and is shabby and overweight, a bum essentially—a line or two in the movie. The Westerner delivers his lines in wooden English while everyone else speaks Hindi. You just see this grimy backpacker who hasn't shaved in weeks chatting pointlessly with one of the Indian main characters in the background of what was supposed to be, but no longer is, a crucial scene. It is so visually jarring to see a Caucasian placed so prominently in the frame of a narratively important moment—hovering behind the main characters like a stalker—that you can't focus on what's being said in the foreground. The Indians love this. *Why?* It's just another wonderful thing about India. Where in the developed world we ask, "Why do this?" in India they ask, "Why not?"

It's a liberating view, refreshing, and the Indians never apologize for any of the outrageous things they do. Their puerile clownishness is disarming, even comforting, because it makes you take yourself less seriously. Inserting a random foreigner in the background of a pivotal scene is their pièce de résistance. They love us over there. It's another reason why it's not unusual to have such a special experience traveling through India. It's wonderful to be so adored simply for the color of your skin.

But for every superficial advantage, scratch the surface and you find its dark underbelly—the excrement and gray ooze that make this rat ship tick. The Indians know you're comparatively rich and, with any luck, on your maiden voyage to India. This suggests a much higher chance they can ply you out of some or all of your money. The Indians are better at separating tourists from their money than a Las Vegas casino. If it's your first time in the country, you will probably spend a significant amount of time fending off aggressive touts trying tactics ranging from elaborate scams to boilerplate begging to claw away your money. It can take a while to understand and rise above the first world guilt that is the Indians' most effective weapon in exploiting you. First they pull your heartstrings, and then your purse strings.

However, once you're no longer willing to fall for their guilt baiting, the Indians can see you're no longer vulnerable, and no one will ever hassle you for a handout ever again. Amazing, but true. After passing through this crucible, India's hidden pleasures open up to you like a music box, and they are more abundant and rewarding than you could ever imagine.

India is a genuinely wild place. India is always compelling. There are no weak moments. As you pad up perfumed backstreets and smell the burning incense and sage amid the madcap clatter and din of the bustling marketplace, and the cacophony of traffic weaving around cows standing in the middle of the road, it strikes you and you're either repulsed by it or you fall in love. India is an exotic fantasyland, an infinite feast for the senses with enough depth and texture to span lifetimes, even different worlds. It's a place you'll never forget, never quite figure out, a riddle you'll never solve—a dizzying, dazzling riot of color, chaos, and movement, a grandfather clock of separating and rejoining parts. India is closer to a complex multilayered world dreamed up by a very talented science fiction writer than anything you would recognize on this planet. If countries were novels, India would universally be declared a masterpiece—all the ills and greatness of humanity rolled into one. And still, most places and even difficult situations can be boiled down to just one word if you understand them well enough. India's word might be *intense.*

The Indian hustlers and beggars who pursue young travelers do not pursue affluent middle-aged tourists who actually have a lot of money. Indians are not stupid. They know they will not squeeze one rupee out of these blackhearted Scrooges whom wealth and age have hardened against their fellow man. Instead they target young backpacker types who are just scraping by with very little but who are idealistic, bighearted, naive, and alive with feeling for their fellow man living in poverty whom they don't know but could know.

It's probably not too hard to guess that I was the quintessentially naive, easily duped, nearly broke Western tool when I disembarked in India. I was harassed day and night by Indian scammers. They were often friendly, overly friendly, starting with right inside the airport where they wait in character as ambassadors of India to every grubby gringo who gets off an airplane in New Delhi.

I was beaming when I deplaned. India! I tilted my face back to take in the New Delhi sun, excited to discover a sprawling new country.

An Indian masquerading as a cultural attaché glommed onto me immediately after I passed through customs.

"Excuse me, sir. Where are you staying?"

"Major's Den Hostel," I said.

"Very good, sir. I know the place. I will drive you there."

"Um, okay," I said.

I climbed into his taxi, and we began the long one-hour drive from the airport.

"Sir, it's your first time to India?" he asked.

What a friendly fellow. Delightful fellow! "Why, yes it is! Thanks for asking!" I answered stupidly.

A thin smile crossed his face.

Ten minutes later: "Oh, sir, I forgot to tell you. Major's Den Hostel is closed for renovations. Most inconvenient. But I know a better place. I'll take you there instead."

"Uh, really?" I said. "I just booked Major's Den online this morning. I received an email confirmation. It seems open."

"No, no! Suddenly closed. Don't worry; the place I take you to is very good."

"I don't know …"

"Trust me."

I didn't reply.

He drove on until nightfall, and still longer he drove on. Finally we stopped on a benighted street that had no lamps. "Arrived, sir."

"Finally," I said, exhausted. "What took so long?" It was after nine o'clock.

As I stepped out of the taxi, an Indian in a purple turban descended from steps above like Nathan Lane in the Birdcage and promptly wrapped the cab driver in a bear hug.

"You guys know each other?" I asked, belatedly noticing something was amiss.

"Ha, ha, nooo! Of course not, friend," the taxi driver said, moving to dislodge himself from the other man's embrace. "Krishna, will you please prepare this man's room?" the taxi driver said.

"Of course," the man named Krishna said, and scurried away.

"Wait!" I called after the man. "I want to see the room before the driver leaves."

Krishna froze in the stairwell.

"Ha, ha, no need! Room is fine, friend. No worries! You pay now, okay?" the cab driver said.

"No," I said. "Show me the room first. Or I walk."

I climbed the stairs after Krishna, who frowned. Very reluctantly, he opened the door to the room. Inside was a small dusty space that looked like the janitor's broom closet in your local municipal building, the door you accidentally open thinking it's a bathroom and see mops, bucket-trolleys the mops dunk into, a basketball rack's worth of toilet paper, and long aluminum rods that no one in the world knows what they're for.

A solitary light bulb swung from a wire on the ceiling.

An enormous hostile bug clung to the wall like a poster.

"No way," I said, and turned and walked back down to the street where the taxi was running.

"Wait!" Krishna called after me. "I give you a better room. Stop. Come back!"

The cab driver was behind the wheel, and looked like he was about to drive off with my backpack. I quickly inserted myself between the taxi and the alley. "Hey!" I said, and banged my hand on the hood of his taxi. It was dead dark outside and difficult to see anything on the street.

The driver wouldn't look at me.

"Take me to Major's Den," I said.

"It's closed."

"I'd like to see for myself."

"Fine!"

I pulled the taxi's door handle, but it didn't open. He'd locked it. I banged my hand open-faced hard on his window three times.

Reluctantly he unlocked the door. I climbed inside. When he finally delivered me to Major's Den an hour later, it was a warm and glittering palace.

I stared at the driver.

"My mistake." He shrugged, looking sullen.

I slammed the door shut extra hard when I got out.

Despite this unceremonious parting of ways, astonishingly when I opened my door the next morning to go out for breakfast, the same taxi driver was standing outside my room.

"Jesus!" I recoiled when I saw him.

"Not Jesus, sir. It's me, Sandeep."

"You're the cab driver. What the hell are you doing outside my room?"

"Waiting for you, sir. I'm also your guide. I am here to take you around our beautiful city. I will show you temples and sites not in the guidebook. Very rare and special experience."

"You don't have to drive the taxi today? Pick up tourists from the airport and lie to them that their hotel is closed and then take them to your friend's place instead?"

"No, sir, not today. I am at your disposal."

"I don't know," I said, "How much do you want for it?"

"No charge, sir. Free. I wish to apologize for yesterday's small misunderstanding.

"Free?" I said. "Yeah, right."

"It's the truth. I promise."

"C'mon."

"Don't insult me."

"Fine," I said. "I'm going to breakfast."

"I'll meet you back here in thirty minutes."

"Okay," I said. "Sandeep, right?"

"Yes, sir."

I walked out into New Delhi's dusty main street. Cows walked openly among humans in the street like commuters, almost like humans themselves, just going to work along with everyone else. I wouldn't have been the least bit surprised to see a cow wearing a bad suit and carrying a briefcase.

I found a little café that served an American-style breakfast—eggs on toast—and sat down with a cup of Indian coffee. The coffee was bad—inky and weak, it tasted like instant. Someone had left a New Delhi newspaper on the table. I picked it up and started reading it.

"Excuse me, sir?" said a small voice. I looked up. Sandeep was standing over my breakfast. I flinched backward and banged my head against the wall. The coffee went skittering across the table.

"Jesus!" I said.

"Not Jesus, sir. It's me, Sandeep."

"Didn't we have this conversation already?"

"No."

"Are you my waiter now too?" I asked, reaching for a napkin to wipe up the coffee.

"Would you like me to be?"

"No. Definitely not. What the hell are you doing here? I thought we agreed to meet in front of the hostel in thirty minutes."

"No time, sir. Lots to see and do today. There's no time to sit and read the newspaper. Shall we get going?"

"Sandeep," I said, "that's the first wise thing you've said."

"No, sir, not the first," he replied.

"How much does this cost again?"

"It's free."

"Yeah, right."

"Really."

"C'mon."

"Don't insult me."

"We've had this conversation before."

"No, sir."

I sighed.

His taxi was too wide to fit down New Delhi's narrow main street, so today he was driving a tuk-tuk. A tuk-tuk is a go-kart that's the height of a car—you're basically in a go-kart but sitting higher up off the pavement. The vehicle is as nimble as a centipede—it can squeeze between crowds and drive anywhere except up the side of buildings.

I climbed in, and Sandeep sped off.

True to his word, the first place Sandeep took me to was a temple that wasn't in my *Let's Go* guidebook. Then to a shrine, also not in the guidebook. Then he brought me back to town to the main street and a shop selling rugs.

"Sandeep, I don't want a rug," I said. "Skip this."

"Just a quick peek. You must see. Great store! No need to buy anything, I promise," Sandeep insisted. "Go inside."

So I went inside. The Indians in the store attached themselves to me like flies to a spiked punchbowl.

"Sandeep, I think today's tour is over," I said. I walked out.

Like the Ghost of Christmas Present, he answered, "Just one more stop."

That stop turned out to be a large tent a little off the main street. "Come in for tea," Sandeep said. I ducked inside and was greeted by twelve people sitting in a semicircle on a rug. They were seated around a teapot that was equidistant from each person like an isosceles triangle.

"Come in!" cried an old man, rising up from the floor like a cobra. "Krishna, get him a cup of tea you idiot."

Krishna?

I nearly fell over. The proprietor from the crummy hostel the night before stood up from a corner of the tent and, not looking at me, filled a cup of tea from the pot and, his hand shaking, handed it to me.

"Jesus," I looked at my driver. "Who are these people?"

"Not Jesus, sir. I am Sandeep."

"We've definitely had this conversation before."

"No, sir."

"Yeah, right," I said.

"Sir, this is my family," Sandeep said. "I believe you have already met Krishna, my brother," he said straightforwardly, as though there was nothing strange about this.

The old man piped up, "And here, my daughter!" He pushed a young girl toward me. She giggled and bowed. She appeared not to speak any English.

"Your sister?" I murmured to Sandeep out the side of my mouth.

"Mmhmm."

I sighed. "Thank you but I really must be going. Don't trouble yourself with showing me out. I'll find the way."

"Wait, sir!" Sandeep said. "First you must pay."

"Pay for what?" I said. "I thought you said this was free."

"Don't be ridiculous. The price for today's comprehensive city tour is forty-five hundred rupees."

That's roughly $100 US dollars.

"What?" I exclaimed. "No way. You said it was free. You made that very clear at the beginning. If you had told me there was a charge, I never would have gone with you."

"Exactly."

"So you lied," I said.

"Lied? Never sir. The price is forty-five hundred rupees. I told you that this morning. If you misunderstood or did not hear me, that is not my fault."

"Didn't hear you? Is that your story now?" I said, my voice rising. "I'm leaving."

Suddenly a bony hand, more like the vestigial claw of an ancestral bipedal sea shrimp, gripped my wrist with the confident strength of the undead. A thin voice whined in my ear, "You will not leave until you give me forty-five hundred rupees."

Nervously I looked behind me. The kindly family had all vanished. They had taken the teapot with them.

"Let me go!" I said. "Look, I'll give you ten bucks, okay?"

A horrible shriek emanated from his mouth that matched the Mummy-like death grip he held on my wrist. His face contorted grotesquely. It's not an image I like to remember. It was one of those horribly pained, emotional facial expressions one never wants to see on an adult that remains viscerally burned on your retinas forever. His eyes went milky and blank with self-pity and desperation, and his mouth hung slackly open in a high-pitched scream. I made the mistake of looking at him and saw all the way down his throat to his epiglottis. Gone was my dignified butler, my Jeeves. In his place was who he really was.

An Indian.

"I'll give you twenty bucks. Get off me!"

"Noooooooo!" he screamed, intensely emotional, grief-wracked.

"Here!" I yelled, fumbling through my cash. "There's forty dollars. That's all you get!" He actually swatted it away, turning it down. That genuinely surprised me.

"No! One hundred dollars!" He was crying and whining—far and away the most pathetic behavior I have ever seen in an adult male.

I pushed the forty dollars into his free hand and grabbed his cold fingers and wrapped them around the money. I tried to pry his other hand off my wrist, but it was locked down so tightly, like an alien wrapped around an astronaut's face, that I couldn't move his bony, deathlike fingers at all. Then, in a moment of pure panic, I violently whipped my arm backward with all my strength. The Indian let go rather than go flying across the room with my arm. Released, I turned on my heel and ran out of the tent.

It was like this every day I was in India.

An Indian would wait outside my hostel and offer to take me to a market or shrine the tourist books didn't know about, talk to me at length about India's customs, and at last invite me to his home to introduce me to his daughter and twelve members of his extended family. Like the citizens of all third world countries that forbid premarital sex, Indians breed like rabbits. The longer you allow the Indian to remain in your company, the more money he feels entitled to at the end, regardless of what you agreed to up front, which was usually no money. The meter is running as long as you're with him. Nothing is mentioned up front; the bill only comes due at the end when you try to leave.

In the beginning if you ask the Indian how much he charges, he always insists his patronage is free. He is, after all, your guide purely out of altruism, a volunteer to all dirty backpackers. His overwhelming sense of national pride compels him to a life of service. Above all, he desires cultural exchange between your two great nations.

"No money, no money, friend!" the Indian will cry out. "Come to my house for tea! All free, I promise!"

"Come on, you want money for this," you say. "Don't bullshit me. I know you do."

"*Nooo!* My feelings are hurt you would accuse me so. What do you take me for? My friend, *free!* I promise!"

"Really?"

"*Yes.* I swear. You have my word. I show you temple not in the guidebook. Welcome to India!"

Whatever was said, the Indian considers it null and void the moment you set off with him. At the end when he's demanding payment from you, crying and literally screaming at you, his face twisted in agony, his voice dripping with bitterness as he holds your wrist like it's the last cashmere sweater in the store on Black Friday, try reminding him of what he told you that morning.

"*Noo!*" he'll cry out emotionally, vehemently shaking his head from side to side. In his mind, you spent time with him, you enrolled in his offer and obtained his services. Whatever was said at the beginning is now irrelevant. It wasn't binding. *You're supposed to know it's a lie. If you don't, shame on you. It's an outrage you would try not to pay. Damn American.*

Oddly as I write this now, I see it from the point of view of the Indian, which is truly frightening and disturbing. I see and understand their view quite clearly. They're not honest at all, but in countries like India, Russia, and China, honesty is not a valued precept. It's not the defining article of your character and the measure of your worth as a human being like it is in the West. They value chicanery, lies, deceit. The winner to them is nothing more than the best liar—the man on top by any means necessary.

After falling for this scam, and a few others, I realized that I could no longer accept Indians' invitations anymore. For showing me around a few hours I had given Sandeep forty dollars, like a year's salary in India.

As I padded down the streets of New Delhi and Bombay, ragged, destitute-looking children accosted me continuously. They tugged on my shorts, begging for a few rupees so that they might live out the remainder of the day. Somehow all the kids were adorable. Every single one looked like Oliver Twist. Unless I was overwhelmed by a raft of them at once, I always ended up giving each child a rupee or two.

One little kid who was hounding me like Jacob Marley on Christmas Eve and looked just like Tiny Tim, walking crutch and all, just broke my heart, so much so that I nearly scooped him up right there and took him home and adopted him. He had a cute little Tiny Tim paperboy's hat to go with the heartbreaking walking crutch.

That evening when I was walking home, I saw the *same kid* saunter past me *sans* walking crutch, looking like he could win his junior high school's pole vaulting competition, whistling as he skipped, a bounce in his step like Tigger, wearing a jaunty hat and leather jacket like an Indian Usher. He walked by me in the street without so much as glancing at me. Raggedy Oliver Twist street urchin by day. Hipster by night.

Damn, he's hitting the club!

I couldn't forget that kid's face because it was the same face that broke my heart a couple of hours ago and nearly caused me to adopt him. Now he was off to his best friend's crib with fresh swag bought on my dime, off the clock and heading out for a night on the town.

He don't give a shit about my candy ass.

I found out later that the little kids who accost you in the street are not hungry and are not dying. Anything you give them is taken straight to a ringleader; the kids don't keep a rupee of it. They're fed separately. The kids who are actually starving are not the ones accosting you in the street. The raggedy little urchins tugging your shorts or skirt for handouts are employees punching a time clock.

Varanasi, India, is one of the world's oldest cities and is the most sacred of India's seven sacred cities. Hindus believe that their karma will not be reborn, meaning their lives will not regenerate, if they die in Varanasi, where the banks of the Ganges River forever burn with the bodies of the freshly deceased piled high onto pyres of flame that span both shores of the river for miles on end in a literal wall of fire. It's like a science fiction movie, except it's real. The fires burn day and night, twenty-four hours a day, 365 days a year. The Ganges is gorged with human bodies, both living and dead.

Black and red embers seasoned with charred human flesh flew up my nostrils as I strode down the bank of the Ganges. I was in Varanasi exploring the ghats, or temples, along the riverbank, when a holy man jumped out from behind some scaffolding in an abandoned crypt and asked me for a donation so that holy men—wandering Brahmanic priests called *sadhu*—could buy wood to build the funeral pyres for dead people who were not able to afford the service in life. The holy man told me that the wood is special wood that has to be shipped down the Ganges from the forests in the north and that it costs 150 rupees a kilo, a little less than four dollars a kilo (one dollar was around forty-five rupees).

The *sadhu* priest grinned lecherously, his skin-stretched head a desiccated skull. He reached out and gripped my wrist with thin bony fingers, and as usual in India, he clamped down hard. He then performed a "blessing" where he waved his other hand around in the air, moaned in tongues, and stroked my arm in a creepy manner while telling me I was buying "holy wood."

"You are a saint, foreigner, for sparing our man eternal damnation," he said.

The real price of wood, I learned later, is six rupees a kilo, about one twenty-fifth the 150 rupees a kilo he had quoted me.

I learned later there are hardly any legitimate priests in India anymore; they are all con men now, dressed in rags and face paint and masquerading as Hindu wise men to imitate an image popular with Westerners but really nothing more than a Halloween costume.

In Varanasi it is popular to wake before dawn and watch the sunrise while floating down the Ganges in a small wooden boat. I liked it so much that I did it twice. It was magical and spiritual—watching the light fall rose-colored on the world's holiest river and wash the silent stupas in a soft pink glow was soul-nourishing. The boat operators charged foreigners two hundred rupees for the sunrise boat ride down the Ganges.

Real price: twenty rupees.

You read it here. When you go to Varanasi, don't pay more than twenty rupees for the dawn boat ride. That's what the Indians pay.

Of course, I learned this only after I had paid two hundred rupees for it.

A good rule of thumb is that the real price (the market price) of anything in India is one-tenth or less of what they'll quote a foreigner and is probably more like one-twentieth. This goes for pretty much anything. Of course, unless you are extremely good at negotiating or grew up in India like a human child raised by wolves, you will never get this price. If you can get anything for one-fourth or one-fifth the original asking price, pat yourself on the back, you've done well. Most Westerners are embarrassed to ask for more than one-half off the sticker price because they're afraid of being considered rude. The Indians count on this. They aren't afraid of being considered rude. They'll be rude to you a thousand times before you're rude to them once.

Indians are never insulted by an offer that is "too low." For one, it is not in their culture to be, and two, I can promise you here and now that your offer is not too low. For sure, your offer is still too high. The price you offered is still higher than what they would sell the exact same item to an Indian for. You have no idea what the real price is—it's always far lower than you dreamed it could be.

They may pretend to be insulted by your offer—they are awfully good actors. They know how to act aggrieved, but look back over your shoulder after you've bought an item and watch the shopkeeper hand the exact same piece of crap to another Indian for a small fraction of what you just paid.

I kept getting conned, bilked, robbed, and duped left, right and center.

One night while I was, not uncharacteristically, dining alone in a restaurant in New Delhi, I vowed to myself that I would not get swindled again. I. Would. Not. Pay. For. One. More. Unwanted. Thing.

As I was enjoying my first few mouthfuls of a delicious curry in a darkened room of the restaurant, an Indian emerged from the shadows like a Ringwraith. The restaurant was dark and I couldn't see his face, but he brandished a rather poor watercolor drawing he insisted I buy. I ignored him. He persisted. This was almost too much—the Indian was somehow inside this crowded restaurant, disturbing me while I was trying to eat, and he would not leave. He wouldn't go away no matter how many times I asked him politely, and then forcefully to go. He demanded three hundred rupees for the watercolor drawing. Eventually, because I couldn't enjoy my food with him standing there badgering me, just to get him to leave I blurted out, "I'll give you twelve rupees!" thinking the insult would drive him away. Not wanting the item, I was, for the first time, bargaining effectively. And guess what. The Indian agreed to my ludicrous lowball offer. He asked for three hundred rupees. He wouldn't leave, so I offered him twelve. And the next thing I knew, I looked down and the painting was in my hand. *Tricked again.* I wanted that watercolor like I wanted a finger poked in my eye. Floored, I looked at him. The Indian, over the moon, retreated backward into the shadows, gripping the twelve rupees like a Willy Wonka golden ticket, his head bowed, no thanks given.

Feeling down on myself, that I would never become a good negotiator, one night I was coming back from a day out when I had spent so much money (been duped out of so much money) that I only had a few coins left in my pocket.

An Indian approached wanting to sell me a pornographic T-shirt. Despite being the country that gave us the *kama sutra*, Indian culture is prudish, so I was surprised to see the dirty T-shirt. The Indian was in my face as usual, hounding and harassing me and demanding I buy the T-shirt depicting four graphic sexual acts in silkscreen on the front.

"Oh sure, like I want to buy that." I laughed. I should have known I was likely to end up with the damn thing somehow.

Like a magic trick.

"Only one hundred rupees for you, friend!" he spat in my face.

I ignored him and walked straight through him. It was dark and I was anxious to get back to the hostel.

"Eighty rupees! First time ever to offer such a low price," he said. He circled back around and blocked my path.

I reached in my pocket and took out the coins. "Look," I said, jangling the few loose pieces of copper. "I only have five rupees left."

"No you don't. You have more," he said.

I pulled my pockets out all the way to their white inseams so he could see them. I flapped them around like airplane wings to show him that, nope, I really didn't have any more. "Nothing there."

I shrugged extravagantly.

He looked angry. For once I was having fun. It was the first time I had seen an Indian angry. I thought I might be on to something. I shook the few sad coins in his face, to mock him more than anything else. The Indian was not happy—not happy at all. He looked very grumpy indeed.

Because I had won. I had beaten him.

You got me, you fucking foreigner, he was thinking.

I moved to walk past him, and he grabbed my shoulder. As I turned, he shoved the T-shirt into my face. He grabbed the five rupees out of my hand and left.

That's it.

If you can pull your pockets all the way out to their naked white inseams so that the Indian can see them, you will be able to buy pretty much anything in India with whatever is left in your hand.

Amazing, but true. It works.

Back to the movie I was shooting. We did take after take. The young director shouted, "Action!" Dance music throbbed out of the speakers. Akshay got down on one knee and proposed inaudibly over the techno.

Aishwarya swooned glamorously, true movie star that she is.

She mimed yes, and we all started leaping around in a frenzy, screaming and high-fiving as crazily as we knew how. There was a Caucasian model, or very beautiful girl at least—not a backpacker at any rate—in a strapless party gown and high heels that the producers had installed in front just outside the inner circle of actors playing the leads' families. I stood beside her. She looked like a higher-paid extra, a ringer, an actress, or perhaps an escort of some kind to Bombay's wealthy class—who knows? She didn't really belong there, and yet here she was. I kept finding an excuse to hug her during the celebration part of each take.

A delirious joy-drenched quality saturated in bliss like Christmas morning suffused the movie set. Moviemaking in India is surreal.

The men were all dressed jauntily in brightly colored shirts, ties, suits, and hats from the speakeasy era picked out for us by wardrobe, and ladies wore dresses and jewelry reminiscent of the Roaring Twenties and Depression-era glamour. To be extras for an eleven-hour workday, we were fed lunch and paid five hundred rupees, about ten dollars—fine compensation in India. It was one of the most outlandish and memorable experiences of my entire trip.

The palpable joy of the Indian actors and director was infectious, and I soaked it up, piggybacking on their happiness. It was definitely the sort of fringe, bizarre experience I live for and that gives me so much pleasure. I recommend to anyone traveling in India to go to Bombay, now called Mumbai, a hilarious city where foreigners are in demand as extras on one of hundreds of movies shooting simultaneously across the city at all times. Inquire of your hotel manager about it. If you're a foreigner, the Bollywood machine will happily employ you to destroy otherwise beautiful narrative moments by having you hover over the main actors in the background of crucial scenes.

And since Bombay is the Hollywood of India and all the stars live here, the city has things that are strange to the rest of the country such as fancy hotels with dance clubs where you can rub shoulders with the children of India's wealthy upper class.

Delphine and I had a great time taking a break from the poverty and extreme nature of the rest of India and indulging in something familiar to our lives in the West—a night out on the town. I was reminded how important it is to get dressed up and go out with your partner for a night like this every once in a while, no matter how long you've been together or how different your lives have become.

We each pulled the one nice outfit from our dirty backpacks. Delphine wore a dress and put on makeup for the first time I'd seen since we hooked up in Goa. I wore white pants and a green Hawaiian shirt—my go-to outfit in those years. I had to bribe the doorman because I was wearing tennis shoes instead of dress shoes; having Delphine with me might have helped. And then we broke it down in the five-star Taj Mahal Hotel's ritzy dance club until three in the morning.

Our fellow finely clothed partygoers getting down to the DJ's excellent spin included older British couples staying at the hotel and affluent teenage and twentysomething Indian kids in designer clothes and bling jewelry sipping rum and Cokes ironically while their flash cars peacocked in valet outside. I wondered whether these kids really understood how different their lives were from the other 99.9 percent of their countrymen, including those in the slums of Bombay which were less than half a mile away.

Along with Calcutta, Bombay's slums are the world's most impoverished. I'm talking about the poorest neighborhood in the entire world here. The residences of entire families looked like broken-down porta-potties—they were about the same size—and were stitched together in cardboard tenements like a meaner version of tract housing. Adult men with wasted, emaciated bodies crouched inside normal-sized buckets to bathe as I walked past, and adult women moved behind little makeshift curtains of rag outdoors on the street for a little privacy. A single chicken or pig tethered in front of a cardboard shack was clearly precious tender. Wilbur didn't stand a chance out here.

The women glared at me. They were normal women, their dignity intact. The men looked away, their dignity vacated. They were ashamed, and I felt sorriest for them most of all. I wished I could pull the women, their magnificence undimmed, out of this place, out of these wretched conditions. They looked like queens to me, stripped down to their skin naked and yet dignified, even more so—crazy as it sounds, it's true. But they were not asking me to take them out of here; they did not need me to.

It was fascinating that this area was less than half a mile away from the five-star Taj Mahal Hotel where the privileged danced away. There was an invisible demarcation line like so many cities have that abruptly and starkly separates the rich side of town from the poor side. This invisible boundary was one that people from either side never crossed. There were no street urchins here tugging at my sleeve to beg at the behest of unseen ringleaders. Because no tourists came to these parts, there was no point for them to be here. The children in this poorest area in the world just let me stroll by unmolested, unscathed. They didn't look at me, didn't approach me, *didn't see me.* I noticed that the slums of Bombay were not mentioned in any guidebook. I guess the guidebooks really are just for tourists, not real explorers.

I had come upon the slums quite by accident just in my usual wide amblings of a strange new city. The poor parts are always more interesting than the rich parts. They are stripped of artifice: they're raw, bare, authentic—instead of sophisticated, contrived, manipulated.

In their original state they are stripped down, spare, fused with deep reality, either repulsing you with their abject want or drawing you in closer with their strange beauty. Somehow great wealth is banal compared with great poverty. One is vivid, the other is lifeless. Don't ask me the reason.

Curiouser and curiouser!

—Lewis Carroll, *Alice in Wonderland*

7

Nepalese Days: Leopards of the Moon

We were heading to Nepal to climb in the Himalayas.
As we gravitated toward India's northern border with Nepal, slowly but steadily as though pulled inexorably by a great magnet, whispers of a disturbance, some terrible new conflict, trickled down out of the north. There were rumors of a bombing. Then reports of soldiers opening fire on civilians in the capital city of Kathmandu. Ominous tidings of a new unrest, of war breaking out,

found their way to our ears long before they hit CNN. The restive situation caused most travelers to cancel their plans of entering the country.

My friend Heather backed out of our plan to meet me there. I had met Heather in New Zealand; she had been the one who introduced me to vipassana. Now I was entering Nepal alone. Foreign embassies put out no-travel advisories. The US foreign-travel advisory instructed all Americans in Nepal to leave the country immediately and everyone else not to enter. I refused to change my plans and thumbed my nose at the US foreign-travel advisory by going anyway.

The origin of the war was the long-standing hostilities between the Communist Maoists, a persecuted constituency representing large swaths of Nepali citizens, and the authoritarian government. The conflict had already killed more than seventeen thousand people over the last decade, including gruesome executions such as rebels being hanged from trees while their families were forced to watch. All of this was happening out of view of the world stage but can easily be learned about with a few clicks of a mouse.

The long-festering conflict bubbled over just when I was about to enter Nepal. A full-fledged civil war broke out when the people, having suffered one butchering too many at the hands of the king, finally rose up as an entire nation against him. It was an autocrat's worst nightmare: the people getting united, strategic, and brave all at once. I spent a month in Nepal during the country's shutdown and violent buildup to overthrow its ruler, King Gyanendra, which finally happened the day after I managed to leave the country.

King Gyanendra had dismissed Parliament eight months earlier and seized total power after the globally publicized mass murder of his brother King Birendra, the good king, and almost the entire royal family. Most analysts believe Gyanendra was behind the murder of his brother and his family because he was the only member of the royal family not present at the massacre, and everyone present was wiped out *except Gyanendra's wife and son*, the only other royal survivors, a coincidence that's hard to lie away. Gyanendra's ascension to the throne was only made possible if both of his nephews were eliminated too, and they were. You may vaguely remember hearing about this in the news because, although Nepal is a small country, the Shakespearean bloodbath was so brutal in scope and nature that it had no antecedent in the monarchy since Russia's Romanovs were shot on Lenin's order in 1918. If you type "worst monarchy massacre" in a search engine, nearly every result is about the Nepalese royal massacre.

There had been two public strikes before March to test their efficacy but nothing lasting longer than a week. As news spread that the Nepali people were about to undertake the final strike—one they vowed not to end until either the king was overthrown or the entire nation fell victim to Gyanendra's power-grabbing and the violent bloodshed that would mean—nearly all travelers changed their plans to avoid entering Nepal.

I got in just in the nick of time.

One day before the Nepali people began the final strike, the one they would continue until either the king was deposed or they were killed, high stakes for civilians indeed, I crossed the border into Nepal on a forty-eight-hour bus ride from Varanasi, India. I was lucky to get in because the very next day the border was closed once and for all and no one could enter Nepal overland anymore. I was just one day away from being turned around at the border and sent back to India.

Always good to be early!

The day after I entered Nepal the populace dramatically escalated the strike by shutting down the country's entire public transportation system on the ground. All buses, trains, taxis, rickshaws, bicycles—anything with wheels or a motor or a squawking chicken in the back was grounded and mothballed. Only planes flying out of Kathmandu and Pokhara—Nepal's second-largest city in the country's spartan west—continued to operate.

Massive protests were happening across the country. In response, the government imposed a curfew lasting twenty-four hours a day, all day every day, meaning no one was allowed outside on the street anymore. Since the curfew was now permanent and the Nepalis could no longer go outdoors, Nepal's cities and streets were emptied and laid bare like some tumbleweed-strewn abandoned railroad town. Kathmandu looked like postapocalyptic nuclear winter. Rickshaw drivers were no longer willing to drive tourists anywhere. All shops and storefronts were boarded up and closed. No one in one of the world's poorest countries was going to be making money anytime soon.

In Kathmandu's tourist district of Thamel, guests needed to go outside in the streets to hit the ATM and eat though, so within this tiny corridor only, where nearly all remaining Western tourists were, we were allowed to walk around a tiny warren of alleyways with three or four Western-catering restaurants.

As foreigners we were not part of the conflict, and the government, which relies almost exclusively on tourism for Nepal's entire GDP, had no interest in harming their only industry. Westerners' greatest danger of being bombed, stoned, or shot was if we got caught in crossfire at a protest or violated the strike by bribing a Nepali taxi or rickshaw to drive us somewhere. That would be suicide. If the Maoists saw a driver working during the strike, they would kill him without hesitation. It was very much in their interest to murder any of their own people seen breaking the strike. Nepal is one of those third world countries where human life is cheap. Very quickly there was no amount of money you could offer a Nepali with wheels to take you anywhere.

Many of the Westerners in Kathmandu, far from being scared by the civil war, instead seemed filled with the heightened passion one associates with a Hemingway war novel, where frisson flowers in the air like spores and undergirds day-to-day life with a visceral feeling of aliveness and something approaching euphoria. Westerners were giddy with the sense of being a part of something larger than themselves, larger than living bourgeoisie life with its empty materialism and bland functionality. United by one shared cause of overthrowing an evil usurper who had murdered a beloved monarch, his own brother no less, the whole nation bonded together in outrage to overthrow him at all costs. It was beautiful and inspiring—all the factions united, everyone's priority one and the same. There is nothing more moving than unity.

Political upheaval, potential for heroism, the thrill of risking one's life, and the very real possibility that life could be cut short—all played into the collective tumbling feeling of *feeling alive, being alive.* The intoxication of revolution was what we were swept up in. The tides of history.

Many, particularly hippie types, were especially swept up by the irresistible appeal of a proletariat rising up against a tyrant king, and they threw themselves into aiding the war effort by everything from printing pamphlets fomenting revolution to painting their faces blue in Braveheart fashion and participating in protests along with the fiercest insurgents. It was these protests that were most dangerous and most likely to get a Westerner killed, because after a week of escalating tensions the police started firing into crowds and killing Nepalis by the score. Public executions in town squares, firing squad shootings, and hangings in trees all increased dramatically over the next two weeks. But by then I was high in the Himalayas on Annapurna, the world's tenth-highest peak, in thin air under a liquid blue sky.

I had come to Nepal to hike the famous Annapurna Circuit: a 131-mile-long trail that begins at twenty-five hundred feet and climbs gradually until it eventually crests over the world's highest mountain pass, Thorong La, buried in snow at eighteen thousand feet. The trek takes two to three weeks depending on how fast you walk. Ever since I'd first heard about what is routinely voted the world's best trek, I had wanted to experience the famously pleasurable lifestyle of "teahouse trekking"—hiking over the Himalayas on foot without having to carry any tent, food, or cooking gear. Nights are spent in teahouses that dot the trail: primitive yet charming huts with beds, a fire, and full menu of Nepalese food of dal baht and Western items such as pizza and eggs on toast. It is a deliciously blissful and convenient way to travel in the most beautiful country on earth.

I posted a notice on the public message board at Kathmandu Guest House seeking trekking companions for the Annapurna Circuit. When I checked back the following morning, two slips of paper had been pulled off my ad. Soon after, two notes appeared on my door, and at eleven o'clock that morning I met the two interested parties in the hostel lobby over coffee.

They were Sion, a blond thirty-seven-year-old Welsh home builder who was lean and fit: he had the wiry frame of a free-soloing rock climber, the kind of person you envy because they have the almost mystical ability to eat carbs without getting fat; and Emma, an eighteen-year-old girl from England. Emma had a plump but firm—like springy, spongy turf—creamy-white Rubenesque body, the same body type all young English girls seem to have from *Downton Abbey* to *Pride and Prejudice*. The three of us decided to pull this off together—the complete three-week Annapurna Circuit, the world's highest mountain crossing—without any guide or Sherpas to carry our packs for us. We couldn't afford the expense of hiring Sherpas, but we wouldn't have it any other way. We would do this ourselves.

To hike the three-week-long Annapurna Circuit one begins near Pokhara in a place called Besisahar. Since buses were not running during the strike, travelers were forced to shell out sixty dollars for a short thirty-minute flight from Kathmandu to Pokhara. Getting to the airport became a complicated affair, however, because only designated airport vans—employed by the government so continuing to drive during the strike—were picking up tourists in front of select large hotels and ferrying them to the airport and vice versa. This soon became a dangerous ride, because while the Nepali people did not want to target tourists, they did want to target any Nepalis working during the strike, especially ones driving for the government and thus still earning a paycheck while everyone else had to tighten their belts.

So if it wasn't exactly a deadly ride to the airport, it was definitely fraught with a stimulating amount of tension. Neighborhood militias and roving packs of civilian vigilantes, determined to enforce the strike and attack any vehicles on the road, set up makeshift barricades blockading the arteries to the airport with tires set on fire, ropes of broken glass shards strung across the road, and angry mobs brandishing rocks, crowbars, and other crude implements. Very quickly the government posted an armed guard inside every tourist van driving to and from the airport. When our van reached an obstacle on the road such as a tire set ablaze, we reversed course immediately and traveled by a longer, alternate route instead.

It was spooky. There was never a single human being on the road or anywhere in sight when we saw a burning tire or rope of broken glass stretched across the road ahead. This was taken as an ominous sign, and the guards never allowed the van to approach the obstacle. It was thought to be a trap, with rebels hiding out of view at the site ready to ambush the van when it slowed to go around the obstacle or the driver got out to douse the flames. A deserted street with a wall of fire at one end, like an apocalyptic western, with no human in sight or sound on the air, not a baby's wail, a dog barking, nothing, just eerily quiet … was a faintly pulse-quickening sight. We always backed away from those streets.

Except once.

We turned down a street. Ahead of us an old car was abandoned in the middle of the road. It wasn't set on fire and there were no other outward signs of warfare, but it was a strange object nonetheless. The driver didn't seem to think so, and continued toward it.

Just as we were about to drive around it, out of nowhere the road was suddenly flanked on both sides by a sea of Nepalis—a true mob cocking stones and crowbars at the van. The guard shouted for us to get down. We foreigners dove to the floor. The guard rolled down his window just a slit and pointed the tip of his Uzi out so that the mob could see it. At the sight of it, the mob swooned and took a step back, and for the first time I understood the deterrence of advanced weapons—you cannot necessarily trust people to act in the common good, making some leverage necessary. The mob rocked backward on their heels, then forward again, then backward and forward, as though they were dancing, the zombie apocalypse lurching in lockstep. They didn't want to look cowed but didn't dare approach the van either, trying to decide whether to attack us and push through a hail of bullets, or stand down and let us pass.

The mob stood aside, and we zoomed through the opening just before it puckered shut behind us like a wormhole from another dimension closing a second after a spaceship zooms through it. I watched the angry mob shaking their fists and weapons at us in the van's rearview mirror.

The guard's display of the Uzi semiautomatic machine gun capable of mowing down a row of people as easily as a cane could chop the chaff off a row of wheat was enough to persuade them not to attack us. They also seemed to understand that killing a Western tourist would not be good business. Nepal is the poorest non-African country in the world except for Afghanistan. If only Afghanistan is poorer than you, then you know you've got problems. Nepal is even poorer than Haiti and Burma, which has been looted of its mineral wealth by a corrupt military junta for over seventy years.

I find I'm not afraid of death. I suppose that when no one is depending on you, there is nothing you must urgently live for, and this allows you to run a little faster and freer. But I was very impressed by the poise and lack of fear among the tourists in the airport vans and in Nepal in general at the time.

Sion, Emma, and I passed the streets-on-fire obstacle gauntlet to arrive at the airport. We took the short thirty-minute flight to Pokhara, now the only way to reach the start of the Annapurna Circuit. From here a government bus took us to Besisahar, about half a mile from the trailhead. I felt relieved to be escaping the war in the cities by climbing high into the Himalayas.

I had walked only thirty minutes with my backpack and was already sagging under its weight like Atlas. Since I would have to carry this load by myself for the next three weeks over the world's highest mountain pass, I realized I wouldn't make it unless I lessened my burden.

Climbing upward thousands of meters carrying a heavy pack is a challenge, and there was much discussion among trekkers over the next few weeks about how we would pare down our belongings even further the next time. We resolved that you really only needed to bring one T-shirt, two pairs of underwear, two or three pairs of socks, and the minimal extra layers of expensive but lightweight fleeces.

When a trek includes prolonged exposure to extreme cold at the top, the overall duration of the trek no longer matters. Whether it's one week or five months is irrelevant—the amount of clothing you bring is the same. Truly indispensable items were the goose down jacket and down sleeping bag I'd rented in Kathmandu that could be packed up to the size of an ostrich egg and a log of firewood, respectively. These items were the last line of defense against the frigid cold we would encounter at the upper elevations. There's no way to minimize the weight of your sleeping bag beyond a certain point, nor would you want to sacrifice any warmth for more lightness. But I had brought way too many toiletries. I'd brought hair conditioner, and unfortunately, another trekker on the trail named Dave saw it. We made eye contact—his furtive, mine naive—and he watched me try to palm the bottle of conditioner behind my back and hide it.

Too late.

"Everyone!" he called out, "this man has brought a large bottle of conditioner. Come look!"

Dave waved over Sion, Emma, and a group of people he was trekking with to view the offending item. He waited patiently until everyone had walked over, and then loudly started mocking and berating me until I threw it away. Embarrassed, I impetuously announced that I would shave only by knife blade for the next three weeks to demonstrate my masculinity. I also wouldn't wear deodorant and assured everyone that my natural scent was musky and very manly indeed. Someone said this was more man than anyone wanted or would tolerate. I tried to explain to the laughing hyenas that I was from Los Angeles, where this metrosexual shit actually flies: at the gym at Sony I'd witnessed straight men pinching each other's asses in the shower, coldly appraising one another for body fat. Thankfully I was never close enough to 0 percent body fat to merit this cruel treatment.

I paid a local shopkeeper in Dumre, near Besisahar, to hold my surplus items for the next three weeks until I returned. I didn't know then that in three weeks it would be impossible to reach Dumre. As all the public transportation in the country shut down and the strike curdled into extended war, all these little towns would become like islands cut off from one other, the nation's roads as empty and desolate as an alien planet. The entire country of Nepal was about to become a ghost town.

Dave, the trekker who berated me for bringing conditioner to one of the most rugged mountainous regions on earth, was a British barrister of around fifty who was trekking the Annapurna Circuit with his wife, Shelly, and son, Bruno. They had hired a guide and three Sherpas to carry their packs for them. If you have money, it's easy to hire a whole personal staff in Kathmandu to carry your bags for the whole trek. This caravan of people was traveling on roughly the same daily schedule that Sion, Emma, and I were, and we saw them throughout the day at huts when they stopped to rest and we passed them. Since they weren't carrying their own packs, they moved faster than we did, but they stopped for breaks more often and then we leapfrogged them, the proverbial tortoise and the hare. We passed them with just a greeting at first, but eventually sat down and had a drink with them. There were a limited number of villages on the trail, so we usually ended up staying in the same teahouse at night. After the first few days we started making plans to walk together. There was a strapping young Dutch couple also on the same daily schedule we were, and a few other familiar faces on the trail, but only Dave, Shelly, and Bruno joined us full time.

Similar to the way everyone across Alaska is scared shitless of bears, many first-time trekkers in Nepal are terrified of altitude sickness. It doesn't help that the Lonely Planet and other guidebooks dwell morbidly on how deadly altitude sickness is and the far-ranging symptoms that might mean you have it. These included headaches, shortness of breath, and dizziness—in other words, all things you have at high elevation anyway but don't necessarily mean you have the deadly altitude sickness. The books advised that if you felt any of these symptoms, you should stop climbing and descend immediately. Some people like me were slightly (okay, very) psychosomatic, and I was so concerned about getting altitude sickness that I actually started getting headaches and feeling dizzy *simply because I was afraid of these things happening*. Lame, I know, but as a high-mountain novice, the excessive attention paid to altitude sickness had psyched me out.

Luckily Sion had already been to Nepal and hiked the other major trek—the three-week Everest Base Camp / Gokyo glacier circuit. He told me that I was fine, that if you're sick from altitude, you know it, because you're puking your guts out and can barely walk and your head feels like it's going to explode like a watermelon being shot by a sniper's cannon.

It turned out that the higher I climbed and the more people I met, the more I learned that Sion was right. People who climb Everest for the first time have splitting headaches, nosebleeds, and extreme trouble breathing, necessitating bringing canisters of oxygen, but even this doesn't mean they have the dreaded altitude sickness, merely that they're experiencing the *effects* of altitude. More-serious symptoms include vomiting and intense difficulty moving forward. Then you do need to descend. A pair of young doctors doing voluntary work in the mountains for free room and board for the season told me that only 1 in 330 people experience real altitude sickness trekking in the Himalayas. The guidebooks never mention that only 1 in 330 people get it. They make it sound like *everybody* does. I'm sure I wasn't the only person scared out of my wits that this invisible killer was coming for me too.

Or maybe I was.

As it was, we encountered several people already turning around and going back down the mountain at elevations of only twenty-seven hundred meters. Dave had already trekked Tibet, the entire plateau of which rests at nearly four thousand meters, and I heard him grumbling that these people were lightweights who'd been tricked by their own minds. An elevation of twenty-seven hundred meters is so low that it's physiologically impossible to suffer altitude sickness no matter how vulnerable your constitution is.

One European man in early middle age with long, straggly hair and very expensive gear and clothing was already descending the mountain at this preposterously low elevation. He turned to Dave as he passed and boomed sententiously in his face, *"Climb slowly!"* Dave closed his eyes as the other man's breath washed over his face like a spritz of cologne. It was so annoying that as soon as the man left, Dave scoffed in derision, "Pussy."

I laughed. I liked Dave instantly. You don't become Sheffield's top barrister for nothing.

I had already been experiencing symptoms myself, including the classic inability to breathe enough air into my lungs to sleep at night, meaning that my lungs never felt 100 percent full or inflated when I inhaled. Every time I inhaled, my lungs felt only 75 percent full, never satiated, leaving me always and continuously literally gasping for air.

It's very stressful not being able to draw enough air into your lungs to breathe. There's simply not enough oxygen in the atmosphere up here. It feels like asphyxiation, hypoxia, drowning on dry land—the epitome of unease.

But after listening to Dave shred the guy for thinking he had altitude sickness at such a low elevation, I began to wonder whether I was just psyching myself out. Was I imagining this? At some point over the next few days when we climbed above three thousand meters, I was freaking out to such a degree that Sion pulled me aside and gave me an acid talking-to—he told me to chill out, relax.

"Stop being such a fucking headcase," he said. I guess that's what I needed, because soon after, my headaches and dizziness disappeared. The mind is an evil bastard, isn't it?

Oh, but what a dream Nepal is, especially the Annapurna Circuit. It ranks right at the top of my most indelible experiences. It had a lasting impact on me, and there are reports I'm not the only one. The trail begins near sea level, and for the first several days we climbed through leafy jungle. It felt more like a rainforest than the world's highest mountain range. I didn't even see any mountains for the first week of the trek because they were still so far away. Trees and vegetation at the lower elevations were lush, the soil beneath my boots moist. Gradually the trees became drier—deciduous, conifers, pines—and the earth became drier too.

One day I rounded an innocuous-looking bend in the trail, and all at once the scenery changed dramatically. Gone was the lush vegetation. Before me lay a long, sweeping, grassy plain at high elevation that I couldn't see to the end of. Towering above the deep plain, the upper Himalayan peaks rose over me like Titans, in full view for the very first time. The moment you first glimpse high mountains is spellbinding, and for me, life changing. I had seen the Rockies and Alps before, but never anything like this. The Himalayas are so jaw-droppingly high that they dominate the skyline like a fleet of spaceships hovering above you. That first sight of them was so staggering that it knocked me backward. The effect was as though I were looking up at them from underwater: I was a finger of coral at the bottom of a fishbowl looking up through the water at a much larger, far more miraculous world in the room outside the bowl.

"That's where we're going?" I gulped. Dave looked at me and shook his head in annoyance, not replying. Dave crushed people with his bare hands for breakfast. Such talk to him was nonsense.

The long, grassy plain was a plateau at thirty-four hundred meters, and it's here where the Annapurna trek really begins, really becomes exciting and remains so for the rest of the journey. It was the start of the really exotic scenery: the bleak high plains. Our goal that day was to reach Manang, a picturesque town nestled between two mammoth peaks at thirty-five hundred meters, where we would spend the next two days acclimatizing our bodies to the high altitude.

We didn't make it to Manang that night. Darkness fell, and so we ducked inside two primitive huts that emerged on the beginnings of the long plain. Here we decamped and unfurled our sleeping bags for the night.

I was buzzing, feeling jazzed from reaching the high green plain and seeing the awesome scale of the world's highest peaks for the first time. That night was a magical one. The rudimentary hut's owner cooked hot porridge in a black pot over an ancient blazing fire that was straight out of *Ivanhoe*. When the others went to bed, I stayed up, staring into the fire for a full four hours straight. I couldn't tear my eyes from it. It had been many years since I'd been camping and sat next to a tall, blazing fire. The ancient pleasure of a crackling fire, deeply embedded in the DNA, was satisfying down to my bones, a residual joy left over from our ancestors. The fire danced as I continued feeding it wood deep into the night. Eventually the wood ran out, and I only stopped staring at the flames when my eyes closed on their own.

I awoke in a room that was dead dark and bitingly cold. The fire had burned out. I stood up and fumbled outside into pitch blackness that was so complete and so empty and forbidding under a star-filled sky that it looked as though I had stumbled out onto a foreign planet.

We arrived in Manang before noon the next day. Manang was the last big town on the trail, and it even had a small movie theater. That evening Shelly, Dave and I bought tickets and ducked inside a room that was the size of an outhouse. We were treated to the movie *Everest: Into Thin Air* in which eight people die slow, grisly deaths from high-altitude cerebral edema (HACE), succumbing to hypothermia, hypoxia, and drowning in their own pulmonary fluid on the indifferent face of Mount Everest, which was in the same direction we were heading. Ha, ha, the staffers must have enjoyed their inside joke—give the trekkers a preview of how they'll die a week from now. Before he died luridly of exposure to the cold and a brain aneurysm, the lead guide in the movie kept turning around to his group and whining, "I'm dragging ass today ..."

That rattled around in my head for months, if not to the present day.

"I'm dragging ass today."

Yeah ... Me too, I thought. *I'm dragging ass too.*

I swallowed and the phlegm went hard down my gullet like a stone, leaving my throat sore. We had a long way to go and a lot higher left to climb. It was only going to get harder from here.

The following day we took an acclimatization day. To help our bodies adjust to the altitude, we climbed to a much-higher elevation during the day and then descended back down to Manang to sleep at the same elevation two nights in a row for the first time. Dave and Shelly took a three hundred-meter hike up to Praken Gompa, a small shrine above Manang.

Sion and I did the maximum-elevation hike available, a relentless four hours and one thousand meters straight up to Ice Lake (Kicho Tso) on top of a lonely spire that looked as though it hadn't seen a human visitor in a long time. It was on a windswept face of that dramatic spire that Sion and I had a mystical experience—No, I don't mean of the *Brokeback Mountain* variety.

Sion pointed at the ground.

"Look," he said. Small paw prints dusted the snow. "Snow leopard," he whispered.

Sion was a distinctly cool customer and nonemotional person, but a rare note of mysticism had entered his voice. You may have heard: snow leopards rank right at the top of the world's rarest animals and are even more expert at never being seen than the Loch Ness monster, the yeti, and of course that dinosaur stomping around the center of the earth.

"Let's follow," I said.

The tracks, paw prints printed cleanly in the snow as if they had been stamped by a cookie cutter, were clear proof that snow leopards really do exist. We followed the tracks to the edge of a cliff where the paw prints, and the ground, abruptly disappeared. I gazed out over a cavernous ravine into a gaping sea of space.

"There," Sion said, impressively natural as a mountain man. I followed his finger. On a slope on the next peak over, a furry little yellow animal was streaking alone across the snow. It was a beautiful, indelible image.

"Ah …" said Sion, smiling.

Not only is there no central heating in Nepal's lodges, but at the upper elevations there are no toilets or showers either. They're just primitive huts. In these isolated reaches, after your down jacket, toilet paper is your most precious commodity. Without these two things you are totally fucked. There are no leaves at high elevation to wipe your ass with. It's just dirt and rock and barren moonscape. At high elevation everything alive dies—first the vegetation, then your brain from lack of oxygen, and finally you. Until then, enjoy your stay on planet Pluto, asshole.

At night we took turns boiling a cauldron of water over a wood fire in the lodge kitchen and hauling it fifty meters outside in a black charred cast-iron metal bucket to a tiny windowless room with a cold flagstone floor where we washed out of it. The water was brain-warpingly hot after being cooked in the heart of the kitchen fire, so hot that it took a full thirty minutes before I could even dip a finger into it, let alone bathe out of it. The temperature of the water in the kitchen fire must have been 370 Kelvin, as hot as the surface of a star.

At first I put off washing, not enjoying this little work-filled ritual of carrying the teeming, heavy bucket outside through bone-chilling night air, disrobing in the shivering dark, and standing naked in a tiny freezing room, my toes pressed into the cracks and grooves of the broken stone floor. However, after a while I began to enjoy this austere, medieval method of bathing. There was something anciently satisfying about washing out of a charred metal bucket on a broken flagstone floor.

In Manang we had our first casualties from altitude sickness. The strapping young Dutch couple who had been trekking with us on the same schedule for the past week had to turn around because the man, a robust, healthy-looking blond Dutchman of twenty-six, had suddenly come down with a debilitating case of altitude sickness—splitting headache, nausea, vomiting, inability to stand, the works. We were staying in the same lodge in Manang, and I poked my head into his room to have a look at him.

He lay bedridden, as if he'd been on the front lines in Gallipoli and shot ten times. His girlfriend was hospicing him with a frown on her face. She had been the reluctant first-time trekker, but had gained in confidence as she climbed. Like me she had discovered that *she liked it up here*, and now she was none too thrilled to have to turn around and go back down when we were only three days from the summit.

She dawdled, dithered, dragged her feet, but finally, taking one last look at her boyfriend frothing at the mouth as though someone had smacked him in the face with VX nerve agent, and coughing up blood like a consumptive lunatic in a seventeenth-century French asylum, she admitted he wasn't getting any better and that she had to take him down. She looked disappointed. Short of leaving him here to die, I think she would have done anything to continue. But there is no solution to the problems of altitude other than to descend as quickly as you can.

That night the Dutchman was raving like a mad dog. He was so far gone that he was completely incoherent. When he opened his mouth, foam spittled out like bacon grease flying off the pan and dribbled down his chin like the last dregs of a cashed beer keg. I watched him convulse violently—he looked like he was being fried in the electric chair.

"Should we muzzle him so he doesn't bite his tongue off?" I asked his pretty girlfriend.

She gave me a wry expression, but her eyes said she thought it was funny. The next day I watched her backside with some longing as they left the hut to go down the mountain, her boyfriend humiliated and slung over the saddle of a donkey like luggage. I cringed when I looked at him.

"Take a photo!" I called after her. "You might need it for blackmail later."

She turned around and smirked. She trended down the trail and out of view. I snicked my tongue wistfully, inhaled the sharp, crisp air, and turned around to face ahead to where we were going. The old dread suddenly returned, fear of the altitude sickness that had felled the Dutch. It could happen to anyone from now on, and there was no telling how vulnerable you are to altitude sickness until it clobbers you like a sledgehammer. It's an invisible, indiscriminate killer, a mysterious alchemy.

On Everest the conditions are so severe that they don't even bother to bury the dead. The bodies are left right out in the open like signposts to the underworld. Some two hundred bodies lie in the path in a lurid high-elevation graveyard and you have to step over their ghoulish faces on your way to the top and an uncertain future.

The demise of the Dutch couple, a fixture on the trail with us for over a week, was a grim reminder of the perils we faced as we climbed to ever-higher elevation, sowing a seed of doubt in our minds as to whether we would suffer a similar ignominious fate at the hands of the mountain gods.

We finally reached Thorong Phedi, where we'd spend our highest night at forty-five hundred meters—a very high altitude for anyone to sleep at, with night being the most common and dangerous time to discover how vulnerable one is to altitude. People who die from it usually do so in their sleep. You knock on their door in the morning because they didn't show up for breakfast and find a corpse lying in their bed.

You may have gained a lot in elevation that day, perhaps as much as eight hundred or a thousand meters, when it's officially recommended to only ascend a couple hundred meters a day to ensure your body is acclimatizing safely. Most people climb more than that because their time is limited and they are eager to push to the top. One of the things you can do to counter taking on too much new elevation is, after arriving at the place where you'll be spending the night, drop off your pack and spend the afternoon climbing up to as high a point as you can, hang out there for a few minutes to allow your body to adjust to the even higher elevation, then descend back down to camp where you'll be spending the night, which is at a lower elevation than the one you've just been to. Acclimatization days can save you a lot of misery later, even save your life when the real altitude hits you somewhere near the summit and there's no help to be had.

That afternoon at Thorong Phedi I continued up the trail, hoping to climb two or three hundred meters higher before returning to camp. I had felt a momentary wave of dizziness when I'd entered Thorong Phedi that morning, but I'd attributed it to my reaching the numerical threshold of forty-five hundred meters for the first time in my life. Nothing serious.

As I climbed another hundred meters, I turned to look back at camp and was greeted by the massive vista of the upper Himalayas from an elevation usually reserved for jet airbuses. I stared down into the fathomless depth of the microscopic valley below. The bottom was inconceivably far down, miles down, the floor just barely visible. The scale of the distance of the valley was incomprehensibly deep. Suddenly the sunken floor retreated away from me at an astonishing speed like an arrow loosed from a bow. It yawned away like a 3-D effect, and suddenly I felt like I was perched on the top rung of a ladder teetering high above the earth on the precipice of space. Then I was reeling. The ground reached up from below and smacked me hard in the face like a boxer's punch. The next thing I knew I was lying on the ground and my drool-flecked lips were resting against the cool earth. I had passed out or something—I wasn't sure, since nothing like that had ever happened to me before. I think I had fainted briefly, though I'm not sure for how long.

As I sat up slowly, I had to stare intensely at my shoelaces and at tiny granules of dirt on the ground just to stop the world from spinning. The world was spinning around my head like the walls of a hotel room after drinking a fifth of tequila.

Panic swept into me. I was screwed. I could feel it. The disorientation and fainting had been so swift, so straightforward, that I knew it wasn't mind created and thought that this time I might be in real trouble. I was fucked like the Dutch guy. I was glad my hot Dutch girlfriend hadn't seen me humiliate myself. I had climbed too far, too fast.

Thorong Phedi was the highest night we would spend in the Himalayas, but we still had to climb another thousand meters tomorrow to reach the pass at Thorong La at 5,416 meters before coming down the other side of the towering ring of mountains. Once over the pass, we would descend over a thousand meters the same day to the town of Muktinath at thirty-seven hundred meters in the Tibetan Mustang region of Nepal. Such a spectacularly long day necessitated that we wake up and begin walking at two in the goddamn night. I crawled back down the trail to Thorong Phedi on all fours like an animal, staring at my shoelaces the whole time. If I so much as glanced up at camp, let alone the hulking mountain range and sunken chasm below me, I swooned into nearly passing out again. This sure felt real. I was shit scared.

That night I was freaking out. I wasn't the only one. Several people had symptoms that were alarming them—headaches and shortness of breath. People were swallowing anti–altitude sickness pills like gummy bears. I popped one for the first time. You're not really supposed to take these drugs except in case of emergency because they're said to be quite bad for you. I only needed one tonight to get me over the pass; I wouldn't have to take one again. Unless I couldn't get over the mountain. In that case tomorrow I would take two. Or the whole fucking bottle.

To tell the truth, I would've taken crank that night if it was necessary. I would've shot a horse, drank blood, shoved a needle in my arm, stolen from an old lady, whatever was needed to get over that pass. No way in hell I was going back down the way I'd come.

That night I went to bed scared out of my gourd. I knew by now that other trekkers were also having trouble drawing enough air into their lungs to sleep at night, but tonight my lung capacity was so insufficient that even when I inhaled as mightily as I could, my lungs didn't inflate a millimeter beyond 50 percent. I couldn't breathe, couldn't drag enough air into my lungs. I was literally suffocating—there just wasn't enough oxygen in the atmosphere this high up.

My eyes watered. I began to panic. I felt like crying. Here I was in my down jacket, wool hat, silk undershirt and three fleeces, every single piece of clothing I'd brought with me, stuffed inside my sleeping bag like blue cheese in an olive, gasping for air like a fish mouthing on dry land.

At least my room in Thorong Phedi was pretty, I thought, looking around. The room was spacious. It had a high ceiling. It was full of light. I had a nice Western bed. I wasn't lying in the shit somewhere.

Not a bad way to go …

I knew that part of my extreme trouble breathing was that I was lying flat on my back, so although I needed to sleep, I sat up and got out of bed. I crouched down on the balls of my feet on the cold stone floor and concentrated all my effort on calming myself, trying to ease the strain on the alveoli in my lungs and just take in oxygen. I knew that if I panicked, things would only worsen. I thought perhaps I was like a fat man who thinks he's still hungry because he hasn't had the amount of food he's used to. They say that 75 percent full of food is full; wait another twenty minutes, and you'll feel full. Could it be the same with oxygen?

I was scared that the same thing would happen the next day that had that afternoon—I'd pass out again and wouldn't be able to get over the pass. And then what? I'd climbed ten days to get to Thorong Phedi. I didn't want to go back down the way I'd come, past all the excited trekkers coming up. I would feel awful, ashamed. Dave's plummy Eton accent rang in my ears—*"Tom, you pussy."*

I winced. "No …"

Pussy!

I tried to shut the thought from my mind.

Since I was on the floor already, I decided to pray for the first time in ages. I felt desperate enough to do it. I opened the door and stepped outside into frigid night air. I looked up. The stars were far too numerous to count. There must have been more than one hundred million stars in plain view, easily more than I could count over a lifetime.

The distance of the sky threw me backward. I saw how much deeper the celestial heavens reach than I had previously been aware—layer upon layer, ring upon ring like the rings inside the trunk of an ancient tree—and I saw that we were just one of many worlds. How extraordinary that this many stars could be seen with the naked eye. They were silver ballast slung out from the primordial birthplace, gingerbread crumbs leading one by one back in time to the origin of the universe, some sacred place. I was too scared just then to fully enjoy the stars and the road leading backward to the dawn of time. So I toddled over to Emma's room. I knew she had what I needed.

No, not that. I'm talking about real salvation.

I hoped that Emma hadn't gone to sleep yet. I needed all the help I could get and am not ashamed to admit I was feeling as desperate as I ever have. I was surprised to find her still awake. It was already after eleven o'clock, and we would have to be up at two. I asked if I could borrow the crucifix that hung around her neck.

She did not ask why; she just looked at me a little askance and said, "Don't lose it. It was a gift from my grandmother."

I assured her I would have it back in ten minutes. She unclasped it from her neck and handed it to me, gave me a wry look and disappeared.

I took the cross back to my room, got down on the floor, and prayed to God to get me over the pass tomorrow. I promised I would be a better person, never complain about anything again ...

The usual stuff.

I can understand the power of prayer. Anyone who doesn't has simply never tried it. Prayer does fill you with a warm, cocooning feeling regardless of whether you believe in it or not. You don't even have to believe in it to get those warm womblike feelings from it.

No wonder people do it.

I returned the crucifix to Emma, no questions were asked, and I went back to my room. I glanced at the time and groaned. It was eleven thirty. I would have to be awake in two hours and walk for the next fifteen. I needn't have worried because I never quite made it to sleep. My breathing was slightly better, slightly deeper than before, but still enough of a struggle to keep me from passing entirely into sleep.

I had finally half dozed off when a loud crack split the door. I leaped up and yanked the door open. Bruno was standing outside with a wide smile and a teeming cup of hot tea in his hands. He'd made it for me. I was touched and since I had only just met him, exceptionally moved by this unexpected act of kindness from an all but total stranger.

"Ey, Tom, mornin', mate," Bruno lilted cheerfully, his eyes dancing even at two in the morning on the far side of the world.

Bruno was the apex of enlightenment, the embodiment of how to live. What do you do when you're suffering at two in the morning? Why, you make a cup of tea of course!

Bruno was also wearing a T-shirt and shorts in subzero temperatures, but he didn't appear cold.

Bruno, Dave and Shelly's son, was mentally handicapped and utterly delightful. His heart full of love and his innocent approach to life instantly endeared him to me, and me to him. He did charming things like this—knock on my door in the morning and bring me things I didn't know I needed, like a teeming cup of hot Nepali tea when I couldn't breathe. The tea, and the tenderness, did have restorative powers. Bruno was like the beloved Mr. Dick in *David Copperfield*. With his lack of understanding of universal social norms and self-protecting mechanisms, Bruno had a disarming charm that was incredibly touching and even heartbreaking. I wouldn't be surprised if my eyes misted when he arrived with tea for me that morning.

After a rushed breakfast, everyone fell out of the teahouse onto the parched earth at the same time and started up the trail at three o'clock by flashlight. With a fifteen-hour day of walking ahead of us and the mountain darkness impenetrable, everyone ran ahead pell-mell into the night in a loose scramble, moving as quickly as possible to reach the High Camp before dawn. I hurried after them, struggling to catch up. In all the commotion I temporarily forgot about my fear of altitude and difficulty breathing. I found the chilly darkness strangely bracing. It seemed to support my lungs like an inflatable toy in water.

Our flashlights were so feeble in the inky darkness that I couldn't see a thing beyond a single footstep in front of me. Beyond the tiny sphere of light from my tepid headlamp was nothing less than oblivion—pure darkness, the absolute blackness of the universe before God breathed life into it.

Our group was quickly swallowed by the consummate darkness and separated from one another like runners in a marathon. Before long only Emma and I were shambling along at the back like two pachyderms in an Arabian caravan. Two others fell behind us, and we never saw them again. Emma always walked slower than I did, and I always walked slower than Sion, which usually went down like glass in my throat, but on this particular night I was happy to just inch along at Emma's glacial pace. Simply placing one foot in front of the other, we climbed the steep grade slowly but steadily, wordlessly moving through the chilly night air. It was quieter than usual—quieter, in fact, than anywhere I've ever been my entire life. This was the true primordial darkness—pre-Genesis dark. There was absolutely no light. As I walked, my breathing felt full and fine. Could I thank the darkness for that? I didn't know, but I was too scared to do anything but just keep going.

I knew from climbing this particularly steep stretch the previous afternoon how little space there was between the trail and a sheer drop into oblivion on my left, a chimney with no flue that plummeted five miles straight down to the bottom. You'd fall through space a full minute before you hit the rock-strewn valley floor and your skeleton exploded on impact. I had to trust the narrow strip of path within the tiny sphere of my headlamp to steer me clear of a deadly fall on my left that was nearby but I couldn't see.

However, the velvety darkness proved to be an unexpected boon. Not being able to see anything, even my own hand if I stretched it out in front of my face, did not allow my brain to register the incredible height I found myself in relation to the head-spinning depth of the valley floor below, the sight that had sent me reeling the day before.

The tomblike darkness enveloped me, cocooned me, took my world away, causing me very much to forget where I was. Gradually my fear subsided. What remained in its place was the most amazing feeling of pure bliss I have ever known in all my life as I just kept placing one foot in front of the other within the tiny circle of lamplight that was like the dim glow of a Victorian candle in a second-floor hallway. One step at a time, repeated over and over for hours, was Zen-like—chop wood, carry water.

The curious elixir of blackest universe and unobstructed open space that stretched from that mountain face in the Himalayas to Saturn in a straight line and back, that silent march upward through the night that I had been dreading, instead shifted and slid into something altogether different, melted into one of the most mysterious, purely enjoyable nights of my life. We are distracted, manipulated, controlled, deceived by what we see. Our eyes do not always present the truth of things. When you can't see, darkness becomes like God's hand guiding you. In darkness, the truth reveals itself.

Emma and I floated on in silence, unmoored in this great black ocean. The only thing I was able to make out in the darkness were tiny pinpricks of flashlight from other trekkers who were moving faster high up on the mountain face. They were so high up that they looked like wobbling stars set against the backdrop of the cosmos.

At around six in the morning, after three hours of walking, we reached Thorong Phedi's High Camp at forty-nine hundred meters. We'd completed half the day's elevation already, and I felt fine. More than fine, I felt invigorated.

The steepest section of the ascent now behind us, Emma and I ducked inside High Camp for predawn tea, hot soup, and bread. Bruno, Dave, Shelly, and Sion, who'd already been here thirty minutes, were just finishing as we arrived. The sun was about to rise, and it was necessary for time that we press on. We needed to get over the pass before midday when the sun becomes hot enough to melt the snow and cause avalanches. A troop of thirty Indians was wiped off Thorong La a few years ago by an avalanche.

After High Camp the snow layer began, and for the first time I found myself walking through a fine pewtery dust of snow. It was dark, and Emma and I hurried along inside the fragile halos of our headlamps. Neither of us knew our precise whereabouts. We raced along through the wintry darkness, struggling to catch up with Sion, Bruno and the others who had left camp just a minute or two ahead of us.

It was then that a powerful confluence of forces, quite frightening, literally dawned on us. As the sun edged up between a cleft in the peaks, a powerful beam slashed down through the darkness and suddenly our location was bathed in a spindle of pale orange light.

All was revealed. Emma and I were standing on an extremely narrow pirate plank-wide strip of trail. The mountain face was on our left and a particularly fatal right-angle drop was on our right—a ginormous pit like Jabba's sandpit in *Return of the Jedi*, except with no bottom. We were tight-roping a veritable chasm of death around a bowl that plunged straight down to hell. I was shocked that we were hiking next to something so perilous without any guardrail set up to protect us. I love the lack of protection in developing countries—life is much more exciting.

It can also end a lot sooner.

I was about two meters out on the plank, and I danced back off it to safety. Emma was farther out on the plank than me, and as soon as she saw where she was, she froze, and like a good robot she shut herself down. Rooted to the spot, she began to sob. Emma's loud, mournful wails rose up on the uncaring morning air. She would neither move forward nor back, and I didn't know what to do to help her. If I went out there and tried to pull her backward we might both fall off. I was none too comfortable out there myself, remember; I have a complicated relationship with heights.

Sion, however, was fearless at heights—an experienced Himalayan hiker and a home builder by trade, he was accustomed to walking on rooftops and high beams. But he had gone on ahead of us as usual (bastard). Dave and his family were all carrying hiking poles, which they had used to brace themselves across. They were on four legs basically, like arachnids.

Just when Emma was at her most distraught, her crying reached the ears of Sion and Dave and his family, who all rushed back out onto the ledge from the far side. Dave underhand-tossed one of his hiking poles to Emma like he was pitching an old women's softball game. Then he swanned away from the ledge like an exiting geisha. I realized Dave was no fan of heights himself.

Sion was most impressive. He strode out onto the plank like a cyborg, fearless, like a Saint Bernard on Chamonix. He took Emma by the hand, wrapped his arm around her shoulder, and briskly marched her across the plank. Sion walked side by side with Emma so that he was walking *between her and the abyss*. There wasn't enough room for two people to walk side by side so Sion's right foot inconceivably fell just over the side on the sharp, sheer beginnings of the wall that plunged straight down to hell. Only the inner third of his right shoe made physical contact with the slope, sort of half on, half off it. I was stunned. He did this naturally without even thinking about it, like a goddamn billy goat.

Someone tossed me a ski pole. I caught it heavily with a great show of force as though my life depended on it, and then stiffly began making my way across, leaning heavily into the rock face of the mountain on my left, not daring so much as to glance to my right.

My left cheek grazed against the granite wall, and I didn't care if it bled. I wanted to give myself a tangible touchpoint so that I wouldn't faint and topple into the abyss. When I was about halfway across, I guess Sion thought I was moving too slow, or just looked too pathetic, because he strode back out and grabbed me roughly by my shoulder (a little too roughly, I thought indignantly), and then brusquely marched me across. Insult was added to what was already injury. I opened my mouth to thank him, but no sound came out. He was already long gone anyway, having marched ahead to his usual pole position at the front of the group.

We stopped for hot tea and bread again at the last Nepali outpost before undertaking the final ascent to the pass. We were only a few hours from the top now; the summit was within reach. Gone was fear. We shed our fear like the ones that had been holding us back all our lives. Only anticipation and excitement remained now. Dave sang songs and swung a large mug of tea around jubilantly. It sloshed over the sides onto the table, and Bruno laughed. Everyone sang and laughed; merriment flowed like Christmas. We ate and drank without restraint and made a mess, food flying everywhere. Spirits ran high.

As we left the outpost to start the final leg—a steep three-hour climb to Thorong La—a couple of Nepalis were standing outside the front door like cowboys cooling their heels in front of a saloon. They had four yaks—great yellow, brown, and white-haired beasts with natural-forming dreadlocks like reggae-loving buffalo. Their yellow hair corkscrewed down in hemplike rings, twisting in helixed volutions into cornrows. Yaks are marvelous animals to see. They're not at your local zoo because it's well known that yaks will only screw at high altitude.

As we started out, the Nepalis began to follow us with their yaks. They maintained a respectful distance of about two hundred yards, waiting—hoping—that one of us would fall prey to the altitude and enlist their services to get them up over the pass. For a substantial fee one could ride to the summit bundled across the back of a yak like nuclear payload fitted to the head of a rocket. Perhaps they'd noticed Emma's corpulent frame and thought she might fold like an origami swan under the barometric pressure. If so, they had badly misjudged her deceptive strength. Emma was as slow as grass growing but had more lasting power than Stonehenge. And still the Nepalis stalked us, haunting our footfalls with their beasts, tracking our movements like vultures waiting for us to expire in the desert.

At this altitude, with the exception of Sion, we were all moving extremely slowly, needing to stop every three or four steps just to catch our breath. The steepness of this final stretch, combined with the thinness of the air above five thousand meters, made going even a few meters exhausting, and several hours passed as we slowly wended our way through a now-alien landscape that was completely blanketed in snow. It was a giant whiteout up here. It looked like we were marching across the moon. No birds flew at this elevation; they had given up and were cresting much farther down. We were now nearly eye level with the tops of most of the peaks. There was nothing up here but snow, ice, and a brilliant sapphire blue sky. And still the path climbed relentlessly. I looked up. Shelly's silhouette obscured the bright but weak sun, her coattails gusting hard in the wind. Sion was sprinting to the top like a Jamaican runner at sea level; I shook my head in disbelief. This strange white world was in sharp contrast to the dirt and roaring rivers of Thorong Phedi we had left behind this morning.

And just when some of us thought we couldn't go on much longer, the ordeal was suddenly over and we had reached it. Thorong La, at 5,416 meters supposedly the highest mountain crossing in the world, emerged from behind a rocky outcrop with a huge Tibetan flag-spackled banner greeting us with congratulations and a description of the otherworldly elevation we had reached. We were ecstatic and spontaneously came together in a moment of pure pleasure. David cried out with joy, and so did Shelly and Bruno, Emma, Sion and me. We wrapped our arms around each other and hopped up and down like a basketball team who's just won the title. Then we crested in front of the banner and snapped a few photos. The cold set in quickly the longer we stood still, so we ducked inside a tiny straw-thatched hut perched on the continental divide where a couple of hardy, entrepreneurial Nepalis make a living selling soup, bread, and tea at exorbitant prices to trekkers in search of a hot drink to make a toast with.

We had done it, and now that we would be going down the other side, there would be no more business with that insidious specter that had dominated conversation the last few weeks, altitude sickness. It's not possible to have it when you go down—descending you can only feel better.

"Let's go!" bellowed Dave with the smile of a man who has achieved a goal. We all bundled up as fast as we could and tripped along after the English barrister down the faint slope of the other side. We jogged for a while in ease until the grade steepened and compelled us to descend more gingerly.

After fifteen hours of walking we finally arrived at the far outpost of Muktinath in Nepal's Mustang region at a comfortable thirty-seven hundred meters, far below Thorong Phedi's elevation the night before. In fifteen hours of walking, we had ascended one thousand meters and dropped down another seventeen hundred, a spectacular distance and change of landscapes in one day.

The Mustang region is Tibetan while narrowly falling within the border of Nepal. Tibet itself is difficult to enter without advance planning due to stringent visa restrictions by China, fearful of unflattering news coming out of the annexed country. But Mustang is accessible because it lies just inside Nepal.

Mustang's people are mostly Tibetan. It was my first time to see Tibetan people. Their faces are carved and chiseled, like out of birch wood, exquisite compared to the soft, flat features of other Asian peoples. They have an elegant, regal majesty, and I hope they will be able to preserve their culture. Until this point I had only seen Tibetans in the movies *Seven Years in Tibet* and *Kundun*, both among my favorite movies of all time, probably because the central character is really the mysterious holy city of Lhasa itself. So it was exciting to come close to Lhasa and have my first taste of the real Tibet—the rooftop of the world, gateway to heaven.

The town of Muktinath was filled with prayer wheels—large wooden cylinders engraved with Buddhist prayers. Spin the prayer wheels with your right hand as you pass them, said to bring good luck to the traveler.

Thousands of eye-popping bright orange, yellow, and white prayer flags festooned the upper landscape in long rainbows of brilliant color on strings that whipped and fluttered in the wind. These rainbows of prayer flags, which can stretch more than five hundred meters from a prayer wheel beside you up to a stupa on a mountain face high above you, are visually arresting and intensely, wildly beautiful. The bright popping colors of the flags stand up starkly and harshly against the piercing blue sky of Nepal's upper elevations and go a long way toward creating the magical world up here.

The Mustang landscape is vivid with Martian-red packed clay and red rock. The earth is bloodred, cracked and caked in red dirt like sprinkles on Christmas cookies. Street stalls selling Tibetan wares on the cobbled roads of Muktinath evoked the childhood magical allure of the Arabian marketplace. Perfumed spices, fragrance, and incense, and the bustle of the high-altitude marketplace was like some distant fairytale kingdom in Shangri-La.

Sprawling red mountains swept up above the plain backstopped by the great eight-thousand-plus-meter snowcapped peaks of the upper Himalayas from whence we came. Those towering peaks stretched all the way up to the sun. The challenge we'd faced and overcome, ascended and descended. Behind us in the rearview mirror now, it all felt like a fever dream. The climb was so intense that when it was finally over there was almost the sense it didn't happen—it was too unlikely to have happened, too unreal when you look back at those peaks rising up so high behind you.

"We couldn't possibly have climbed over those mountains, did we?" I asked Dave. "It looks impossible."

This time he didn't shake his head at me. "Yeah," he said, smiling. "I reckon we did."

The Himalayas aren't easy, but they are the perfect escape. They are the ultimate escape, I would say, better than anything or anywhere else. If I were to imagine heaven looks like anything we would recognize, I'd have to say it looks like the Himalayas. I could almost say I've seen it in my dreams.

After we completed the Annapurna Circuit, Sion and I spent an additional four days hiking to the Annapurna Sanctuary, a 360-degree panorama of two of the world's fourteen eight-thousand-plus meter peaks, including Annapurna herself. The sanctuary is situated at a balmy forty-one hundred meters, which would have felt high to me at one time but now frankly feels like a beach since I've been much higher. After we descended from the sanctuary, Sion went on ahead as was his usual wont, and I never saw him again.

Eventually I came all the way down the last three thousand steps until I touched asphalt, the bottom of the highest mountain range on earth.

When I arrived I was starkly reintroduced to reality, which while in heaven I had forgotten is not always a nice place. It's full of war, power-grabbing people, and other horrible things.

There was a solitary guesthouse in Birethanti where the trailhead met the road. I walked in and learned that the strike had not ended during the three weeks I had been in the mountains. In fact, both sides had dug in and the fighting had intensified. After three weeks without income or, in many cases, food, the Nepali people were hungry. I found out that many of them were starving.

No public transportation meant that I would have to walk the forty-one kilometers from the trailhead to Pokhara. That's the length of a full marathon. If I didn't have my backpack, I think I would have run it.

That evening I met a Nepali at the guesthouse and we made a plan to walk to Pokhara together in the morning. Even at the blistering pace he set, walking briskly without ever stopping once, it took us nearly eight hours. Again, with no transportation running, what at any other time would have been a prosaic bus ride from the trailhead into Pokhara, the walk turned into a surprising joy. The joy of travel is foremost the joy of the unknown and the unexpected. In normal life you only get that surprise birthday party where all your friends are hiding in your apartment when you come home from work once a year. In traveling, every day is a surprise. We walked past native villages that received no visitors. They came out and watched as we passed. The air was cool, crisp, fresh, and sunny. Trail-hardened from walking 170 miles the last three weeks, walking one more marathon today was a breeze.

The Nepali walking with me was a professional tour guide who had taken clients around the Annapurna Circuit. His clients had flown back to Kathmandu from Jomson, the only town on the Annapurna Circuit with an airport, but they had declined to buy him a ticket, so now he was returning to Pokhara alone on foot, as I was. From Pokhara we would need to figure out how to get to Kathmandu on our own.

He insisted I walk with him because he said the roads were unsafe at the moment: the Nepali people were hungry from the protracted strike and desperate enough to attack anyone on the roads, perhaps even a fair-skinned tourist, as the lines had blurred on what was considered acceptable. Tension over the struggle to bring down the king had reached a fever pitch, and throughout Nepal now, not only in the cities of Kathmandu and Pokhara, the populace was embroiled in a large-scale civil war against government troops. Protests were happening across the country everyday. Police were firing into crowds when demonstrators failed to disperse and were killing civilians by the score.

As we approached the city outskirts of Pokhara, we were met by heavily armed guards at police checkpoints and cement barricades that had been erected on the roads. Each time I was stopped by the police, my good Nepali companion intervened on my behalf and, speaking the local language, persuaded them to let me pass. And so by his help I arrived safely in Pokhara.

Here I did the only thing I knew to do, which was to go to the Butterfly Inn, recommended to me by someone on the trail as a good place and the name of which had instantly given me a good feeling.

When we arrived at the Butterfly Inn, the proprietor informed us that the airline pilots had joined the strike that day and now there was but one way to fly to Kathmandu—in the army's plane, which flew once per day at a hugely inflated price for people desperate to get back. I said I certainly fit that description. There was one hang-up. The thirty-minute flight cost $120, and I only had $50 left. I had miscalculated how much money I would need in the Himalayas and had nearly run out. I had fifty dollars left in combined US and Nepalese money, with no ATM card and no credit cards on me. It hadn't been smart to leave my ATM card behind in Kathmandu, but I had been warned that Maoists were patrolling the lower trails of the Annapurna Circuit, robbing tourists at gunpoint to finance the rebellion. I was scared that if they found me they would take my cash and my ATM card, the one thing I needed for my onward travels. With fifty dollars left in mixed money, I had just enough to buy a bicycle, but that would leave me with nothing for food or accommodation during the three days of uphill riding it would take me to reach Kathmandu. I had a bigger problem in that I needed to be in Delhi, India, in four days for a flight to Hong Kong that I couldn't change or push back.

I told the proprietor of the Butterfly Inn that I had my credit card details—I'd brought a photocopy with the numbers on it, which the Maoists presumably wouldn't steal if they searched me—and he could punch in the numbers manually—you know, like in Target. The poor man looked at me dumbfounded. He told me that we were in a third world country, that unless I actually had the credit card on me, no numbers could be punched in, no transaction could be processed.

In the end this proprietor who had opened an orphanage in the building next to his inn to take in the hungry, abandoned children of Pokhara, of which there are many, lent me seventy dollars so I could take the army plane back to Kathmandu.

This goodly man of the Butterfly Inn, Govinda was his name, who cares for about a hundred orphans who depend on him completely to eat and have a bed to sleep in at night, gave me seventy US dollars, a not insubstantial sum in Nepal. I promised to pay him back, he said to see that I did, and I thanked him heartily. Almost too much—he even bought me lunch at a restaurant down the street before I left.

As we walked back to the inn together, he strolled hand in hand with his daughter—not actually his daughter, but one of the little orphans he had rescued off the streets of Pokhara. She turned around, looked up at me, and smiled. Govinda bid me farewell, and we parted ways. Since no transportation was operating, he instructed one of his employees to walk me to the airport, as it was a good hour away on foot.

I said goodbye to the Nepali guide, my companion of the last two days who had delivered me unscathed past the tense roadside checkpoints. He had to go to Kathmandu to pick up new clients. He said he would walk because he didn't have the money for the army plane. That's a stunning distance of 120 miles. He said he could do it in four days.

The inn employee deposited me at the airport and left. As I was entering, a Caucasian man came walking down a perpendicular road alone, a strange enough sight these days. He didn't enter the airport. Instead he just kept walking straight down the deserted road heading south toward a towering wall of mountains that looked like a tidal wave approaching in the distance. The ominous black peaks stretched straight up to the sky. He was an Australian tourist. I asked him where he was going. He said he was going to *walk* to India, since no transportation was running. He did not seem to have heard about the danger of being attacked on the roads, but as I suspected this was not truly a danger directed at Western tourists, I did not want to stoke fear where there was none and so said nothing about it.

He told me that the Indian border was about eighty miles south of Pokhara and that he could walk to it in three days. He then set off down the spookily empty road alone. I couldn't imagine how he would cross the jaw-droppingly high rim of Himalayan peaks in his path. The Alps this was not. These mountains were literally twice as high as the Alps. Of one thing I was sure—he would not encounter a single other foreigner on that road. It was decidedly off the beaten track.

Nothing in Nepal happens on time. The trains can be appallingly late—six, eight, ten, twenty-four, even thirty-six hours late. Of a piece with the dilatory trains, the domestic airplanes have yet to implement the basic invention of radar. That means if it is a cloudy day, they literally cannot see and so cannot fly the plane. They actually fly the planes by eyesight still, which is shockingly troubling.

On this day, the army's plane was scheduled to take off at two thirty in the afternoon, but it was late arriving from Kathmandu. The plane had taken off, we were told, was in the air, but by the time it crossed over the mountains that hold Pokhara in the low part of the country, a cloudbank had swooped in with its usual preternatural intelligence to block our escape. A few people in the terminal even claimed they had seen the plane fly over the mountains just before the clouds rolled in. Officials told us that the plane was circling Pokhara and waiting for the clouds to disperse so it could land. That didn't happen, so after another hour we were informed that the plane had returned to Kathmandu because it was running low on gas. We were ordered to leave and come back to the airport at six o'clock the following morning. The guards said that no one was allowed to sleep in the tiny airport. They waited by the door, fingering the triggers of their machine guns, motioning for us all to get out. I was screwed again.

I had not one red cent on me, having given everything of monetary value I had to Govinda for the plane ticket. I reached into my pockets. Zilch. I was really floating now. Govinda's employee and I had walked a long distance from the Butterfly Inn, over an hour, and I had no idea how to get back. It was pitch-black outside—there were absolutely no streetlamps—and it was possibly dangerous on the streets. I had no money to hire someone to show me the way back. I looked around; there was no one to hire anyway. I was fucked.

So I just floated. This was not a lesson I ever had to learn. When I was a teenager, I was surfing during an enormous storm, eager to catch the titanic waves, giant walls of moving water, when a gargantuan wave crashed on top of me and pushed me far below the surface and down into the depths. My surfboard's leash wrapped tightly around my ankles like a tourniquet, binding my legs together so I couldn't move, and I was dragged to the bottom of the ocean as though lashed to a sinking boulder. I felt I was drowning, and didn't know which way was up. So I just relaxed, floated, and seemed to stay that way on the bottom of the ocean for a long time. Then suddenly my head breached the surface of the water without my doing anything—no swimming, no struggling, no frantically searching for the ocean surface. I learned while young that the churning would always stop—that if you do absolutely nothing, the laws of nature will cause your body to rise in water of its own accord.

So I just floated now, waited. Until another miracle arrived.

As it always does. Somehow.

As everyone filed out of the airport, a cute nineteen-year-old Nepali girl noticed I looked lost, I guess, and she asked me whether I had a place to stay for the night. I told her I did not and that I had no money at all, not one cent, literally nothing. Light laughter tinkled from her pretty face. She turned to her mother and asked if I could spend the night with them. The mother gave me a nearly imperceptible scan that was faster than any Deep Blue Watson supercomputer, and promptly agreed. I thanked them profusely in the little of the language I had picked up in the mountains. The mother spoke no English at all, and the girl's was extremely limited. As we walked ... and walked and walked—they turned out to live over an hour away, there are no short distances in the countryside of Nepal—I tried to have a conversation with this cute Nepali girl who had just saved my ass in a big way. But it proved too difficult for either of us after a while, so we stopped trying and just walked in silence.

The scent of her skin, or perhaps it was where her hair parted on top of her head, sent pheromones or some particle of attraction whirling up my nose like a dervish. The aroma emanating from the part in her hair was a medley of skin, a secretion from some interior gland perhaps, and a mysterious hint of cinnamon. Of course, the physical attraction was partly underlaid by the fact she had just saved me.

That night turned out to be, perhaps, the most exhilarating of my entire trip. I loved the town they took me to. There was not the slightest chance, I felt quite sure, that any foreigner had ever set foot here. It was delightful to be somewhere no guidebook, no tourist, no traveler, had ever been. It was colorful and gritty. Colors literally: bright vivid blue, green, and orange lights popped out of windows. Kids played soccer in dirt lots under streetlamps in the dark. Women carried baskets of wash. In the darkness and winding streets singing emanated from untold quarters. It was like where the proles live in *1984*; there was a lot of vitality here.

The mother and daughter took me to their modest but charming apartment. The father worked as a security guard for the United Nations in Africa because the pay was better than anything he could get in Nepal and he sent the money home. The father had leave to visit his family only once a year. Still, like families in third world countries the world over, they were happy.

That evening they fed me dal bhat, the rice-and-lentil dish every Nepali in the country eats every meal of every day. Do you think I'm exaggerating? Ask anyone who has been to Nepal. They really do eat the exact same thing every meal of every day. It was, well, dal bhat, the same thing I'd already had at least forty times. Fortunately dal bhat is pretty good, so I didn't mind eating it, though never eating anything else as the Nepalis do is a little hard to imagine. At the apartment I met the girl's grandmother and little brother who showed me his American rap CDs. We bonded over Coolio and Biggie Smalls. The family generously gave me the boy's bedroom for the night and he slept in his mother's room. As I lay in bed that night, excited by the evening's surprising turn of events and the strange place I found myself, my senses tingled with the feeling that the nineteen-year-old girl would come to my room after a little while. The notion was based on the flirtatious vibes we'd been exchanging.

But she didn't.

I rolled around torturously in bed all night long waiting for a knock on the door that wouldn't come.

Until it did.

The girl woke me at the awful hour of five. Her pretty face leaned in through the doorway, a swoop of black hair falling down to the crest of her well-defined hip. "Good morning," she said, smiling, all brown skin and long hair.

"What? Mornin'," I stammered, sitting up, for just a moment forgetting where I was.

Then it all came rushing back to me.

She wasn't here for nookie but to call me downstairs for breakfast of—you guessed it—dal bhat. The same thing we'd had last night. Yummy. You cannot imagine how one misses pancakes and eggs at times.

Then we headed back to the airport through darkness. The walk turned out to be mystical and beautiful as the sun rose giant, a harvest sun, closer, paler, and larger than usual, sending soft hues of orange and pink light skating across the same streets that had been buzzing so vibrantly the night before, now so still and silent that I could hear every stone crunch beneath my shoes. The street was wide, and after we left the village, the area was completely uninhabited. The sun's first touch prickled the skin on my left forearm, giving me warm goosebumps of pleasure, and the soft dawn light blushed everything in an ambient grace.

Although the army plane was scheduled to depart at seven o'clock, it didn't arrive from Kathmandu until after one in the afternoon. People bum-rushed the plane like the only beer stand at a hooligan soccer game, and the plane took off a mere ten minutes after it landed.

That's how it is in the third world. Nothing happens, and then if it does happen, there's no waiting around. It happens damn quick or not at all.

There was no refuel, no cleaning of the aircraft, no safety check—why would they do that? Just some dictator in a beret and aviators screaming shrilly for everyone to board and to get on damn quick too because the plane would be airborne and gone in less than a minute.

The army plane had no passenger seats, just a single seatbelt–strap that ran the length of each side that people could sort of half sit on. There was a steel bar like a pull-up bar above our heads. I got on the plane last, being the white guy. Nepalis are no different than other Asians—they will elbow and jostle you, maneuver with everything they've got just to get a single place ahead of you in line; there's no such thing as laying back, even onto a plane they already hold a ticket for. Perhaps that is because so many times the transportation has turned out to be oversold.

To this end, somehow there wasn't a seat for me. There were no other foreigners on the army plane; they were all Nepalis flying, I learned, at one-tenth the rate I was paying. Perhaps they had sold me the ticket just to get my $120 (the Nepalis were charged $12), knowing there was no seat left. So I stood the entire time the plane stormed down the runway, took off, was in the air, and landed. I laughed thinking how illegal this would be in America. It's great fun to stand during takeoff, actually. *Woohoo!* It's no problem at all. It made me wonder why we have to sit. I did five pull-ups on the bar above my head during takeoff for the best reason there is—because I could—and generally enjoyed my army plane experience very much. I did feel slightly guilty for essentially being on the wrong side of the conflict by supporting the government instead of the people by flying on the army's plane, but I felt that if the Nepali people knew about the potential loss of my onward ticket to Hong Kong, they would understand.

That's what I told myself anyway.

In Kathmandu I took an airport shuttle back to Thamel and once again had the pleasure of navigating streets terrorized by burning tires and strips of broken glass shards lain across the road. At Kathmandu Guest House I picked up my ATM card and laughed out loud, feeling exhilarated by essentially being homeless, literally penniless, and having my ass saved three times by three extremely kind Nepalis. The girl and her mother I could do nothing for—I had not gotten their address as sensed in some way it was futile—but I would get Govinda his seventy dollars back with plenty of interest. The only problem was that all the banks were closed due to the revolution, and there was no easy way to get money to Pokhara.

In the end I just stuffed cash in an envelope and mailed it to Govinda from the New Delhi post office. When I phoned Govinda to tell him I had simply mailed him the money, he bemoaned my stupidity and complained bitterly that the money would never reach him.

"What are you, stupid?" he said. "Don't you know we are a corrupt people?"

"Yes! I know you are!" I shouted back.

"Fool!" he said. "Either the Indians or the Nepalis will steal it." I heard him snuffling on the other end of the line.

"I have a receipt," I said.

Click. He'd hung up on me in disgust.

I didn't hear from Govinda for a while after that. In typical Indian fashion it took twice as long as the six weeks the post office said it would, but one day Govinda wrote to say that indeed he had received the money. Excitedly he asked me to call him right away.

"Hello!" he cried when he picked up the receiver.

"Hello Govinda! So you got the money?"

"Yes! It's a minor miracle. Listen, do you remember the little girl I introduced you to the day we had lunch? Just before I saw you off?"

"Yes, I remember."

Govinda had walked hand in hand with her. She was three years old, just able to walk, and cute as a button. She had twinkled up the street, a twirl and a skirted step, and looked back around at me and smiled. It touched my heart. Auyshma was her name, and she was unimpeachably adorable.

"I have decided to name you Auyshma's godfather. She will be your goddaughter."

"Thank you!" I gushed. "I've always wanted a daughter."

"Of course, the privilege of having a goddaughter does not come for free," he went on. "You would sponsor her. For a very small amount, just $300 a year, she could be fed, sheltered, educated, and given every opportunity in Nepal until she reaches adulthood. You can speak with her on the phone anytime you like, and I will send you pictures of her throughout the year so you can see her growing up."

"Govinda, you're both a benevolent humanitarian and a shrewd businessman," I said. "You have a good head on your shoulders."

"Of course my head is on my shoulders, where else could it be?" he snapped. "The head must be on the shoulders. Good or bad, I have to carry it around!

"But I'm glad it's a good one," he added with a whimper.

"I would love to sponsor Auyshma," I said, "when I get a job again. But who knows when that will be? I've been traveling the earth for years now."

"Hmm," Govinda grumbled. His mood seemed to have suddenly soured.

The day after I left Nepal for New Delhi, King Gyanendra finally bowed to the pressure of the entire country clamoring for his removal. The killings had begun to be covered by the global news networks, and the international spotlight may have been what really persuaded him to change his mind. Gyanendra agreed to divert some of his power to a council of formerly elected officials he had abolished, but now reinstated. The people at first accepted this olive branch joyfully, but quickly rescinded, saying it was not nearly enough. About a week later amid continuing turmoil the king agreed to reinstate Parliament, and shortly thereafter he was deposed completely when Parliament announced free elections.

The Nepal monarchy ended permanently when Gyanendra, the last king, abdicated the throne to no one. Maoists, in open war with the monarchy for over a decade, were for the first time elected to Parliament in numbers. In government now, the Maoists ended their long-running war. For the first time in seventeen years Nepal was at peace.

Still I felt uncommonly happy at trekking once more behind a string of mules with their bright headbands, gaudy red wool tassels and jingling bells, over a road and country new to me with the promise of sixteen such days ahead. I felt I could go on like this forever, that life had little better to offer than to march day after day in an unknown country to an unattainable goal.

—H. W. Tilman, *Nepal Himalaya*

8

The Escape

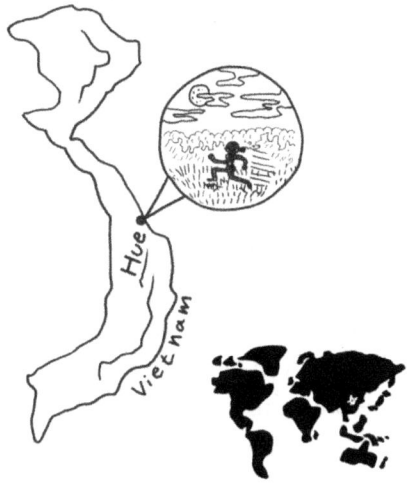

It was November. Linh drove me by motorbike out to a cold, deserted beach in Hue to watch the storm waves crash on the beach. It was raining hard, as it does so often in Vietnam. It rained every day all over the country the entire five weeks I was here.

Linh leaped off the motorbike and ran across the beach to a dilapidated driftwood shack that had been half eaten by the sand. The shack was completely run down and on the verge of collapse. It looked like something Robinson Crusoe had abandoned years ago.

When Linh knocked on the door, I was surprised to see it open from the inside. A middle-aged woman peered out. I was stunned that someone was actually living there—it was a hollowed-out, half-sunken, half-destroyed shack. Linh spoke to the woman a moment and waved me over. The woman led us out to two weather-beaten wood-slat chairs that were buried in the sand. I dug them out and brushed them off. They were falling apart but somehow still held our weight. Half-broken with several slats missing, the chair was surprisingly comfortable, and I eased into it. We sat under a weather-ruined, tattered awning that, despite its rips and holes, provided able shelter from the pelting rain.

In a way, despite the poverty, it was the perfect paradise. This third world experience, which cost nothing, could just as easily have been five-stars thanks to its perfect seclusion, immaculate private beach, and quietude—the very thing rich people pay for in the first place: to wall themselves off from their fellow man. It was no different, only minus the obsequious manservant. Little-known secret: if you vacation in the third world, there is very little difference between poverty and luxury. And poverty has the one thing luxury cannot provide, which paradoxically is the only thing that ultimately matters in creating an indelible, unforgettable experience: authenticity. Luxury offers safety, comfort, anonymity, amenity, and beauty, but struggles to provide the one thing that is the most crucial.

The more authentic the place, the better the food as well.

No starch.

It's the true meaning of organic, as long as you don't die from dysentery.

After a while the woman emerged from the shack carrying an enormous platter of fresh seafood: ten jumbo shrimp, calamari, and two beautiful ocean-fresh lobsters with a tub of hot melted butter to dip them into. It was clear that the seafood had been dragged from the sea very recently, probably that morning. It was the freshest seafood I have ever had, bar none. Being on an uninhabited beach in an impoverished country possibly made it even more delicious. A country being poor renders color, the taste of food, the experience, everything, far more vivid and alive. The memory of it too is more intense, more deeply affecting. Everything is much more brilliant. I don't know how, but our bland pasteurized supermalls with the same chain stores all over the country and anodyne life have stripped suburbia of any magic it might have had.

The rain beat down around us, thundering against the sand like percussion instruments with enormous patter and pace. The harder it deluged, the more relaxed and peaceful I felt. This truly was heaven, and I have never felt more content and at peace than I did at that moment.

There wasn't a soul on the beach. The waves were enormous, at least ten feet high, and only seemed to be getting bigger in the storm, curling and hammering down onto the sand with titanic force very close to us indeed. Thick, curling slabs of liquid blue cement heaved and crashed onto the beach with such raw hydraulic power that they pushed enormous plumes of white spray into the air that fell over us like mist in a rainforest exhibit at the zoo. The weather was turbulent, tumultuous, magic, and all just a foot or two beyond the slender protection afforded us by the flimsy awning.

We ate lobster slowly and sat in silence. Linh was a quiet, unneedy person and I felt comfortable with her, so felt no need to talk. I eased deeper into the driftwood chair and settled into watching the roiling storm. The wild storm was far more entertaining than any movie I've ever watched. Turmoil at sea always silences the turmoil in men's hearts. I suppose that's how Ishmael felt, and why he only felt right on the sea. I breathed in the sharp, tangy brine and felt it strafe the inside of my nostrils. It was atmospheric and redolent of a more ancient time and place. A place with more space and fewer psychological troubles.

It was here that Linh told me an amazing story about being kidnapped to China when she was fifteen years old and sold as a sex slave to a sixty-year-old Chinese man. Linh was a serious, studious girl, and as she began speaking in a low, steady voice, I could scarcely believe what I was hearing. She was a shy, introverted person, and as she continued speaking and her tale took on power, I sat up straighter in my chair and leaned in closer so as not to miss a word.

I was right up close now to the human trafficking world in Southeast Asia. The kidnapping and secreting of teenage girls across the border into China was happening all around me every day in a grisly underworld that was right under my nose but I couldn't see, invisible to me as a tourist yet here all the while, all too bleakly real, proceeding as we sat here, as you read this now, a black commerce, the ugly underbelly of Asia. This lurid world was never farther than the next teenage girl skipping down the path in Vietnam or Laos, no farther than the girl sitting beside me now who, unbeknownst to me, was that rarest of wildflowers—a survivor of sexual slavery.

Linh didn't remember exactly how it had happened, how she had been kidnapped. She only said vaguely that she had been riding a bus, was going home after school … Here she stopped and shook her head. I thought she was dismissing the detail as unimportant, but then she took her head in her hands and held it, and my heart raced out to her. I realized she was in pain at the memory—she blamed herself for getting caught. She was still wondering how she had been kidnapped out of her safe haven.

At some point she had been set up and drugged. She had blacked out, she said. She woke up in a van with her wrists bound tightly behind her. She looked out the window and didn't recognize anything. The van was driving toward a remote village beside a mountain. She was somewhere in rural China, though she didn't know that just yet. If she cried out, one of her captors beat her on her face.

The Escape

When the van arrived at the village, she was brought onto a stage facing a number of old Chinese men. They had come to this place to bid on the stolen girls. It was a "wife" auction. Linh buried her face in her hands and wailed and screamed at the top of her lungs to discourage the men from buying her. Someone hit her hard on the head and ordered her to stop. But she told me she "didn't care." She was "completely ready to die" before being taken as a wife by one of the forty-, fifty-, or sixty-year-old Chinese men. I thought to myself that this was a good thing about being fifteen years old. Being young, I think, helps you in situations like this—you just don't care, so you're less willing to cave to pressure or suck up to your captors.

I read a true story about a young Polish man who was kidnapped by Russians and accused of being a spy. They tortured him in the most horrific ways every day for eighteen months. Every indication said that the torture would last forever. But the man persevered, and he said he thought that being only twenty-four years old helped him. He knew that whatever they did to him, he must not confess to being a spy, that they would surely kill him if he did. The fact he hadn't confessed must be the reason they hadn't killed him so far. As long as he didn't confess, he had a chance. (He was not a spy; he survived.)

Linh succeeded in that no one bought her that day. More men would come the following day to bid on the remaining girls. One of her captors was a large, stout woman who took a sort of liking to Linh and told her that she could sleep in her and her husband's straw-thatched hut instead of the prison where the other kidnapped girls were being held. Linh was told to sleep on a straw mat between the woman and her husband, who had been assigned to watch her.

In the night the man got up to use the bathroom. As soon as he was out of the room, Linh took the opportunity and, barefoot, ran straight out the front door and across a moon-drenched field rutted with rice paddies pool-deep in water soaked in ghostly white hues. She ran away at full speed and never looked back. She climbed up the mountain overlooking the village, relying only on some ancient instinct that she would be safer on higher ground. She had nothing, not even her shoes which she had not wasted valuable seconds for fumbling by the door. No money, identification, sweater, shoes. Nothing.

During the night she climbed up and around the waist of the mountain and on the following morning came down the other side. She glimpsed a road and made her way to it. She waited a long time by the empty road until a blip appeared on the horizon. Soft silver filament steamed off the pavement like dry ice in the far distance as a bus slowly enlarged as it silently approached. Linh moved into the bus' path as it motored past and flagged it down. Just by looking at her face, if she didn't speak, the locals couldn't tell she wasn't Chinese. At the end of the bus route when she was supposed to pay her fare, she gabbled in Vietnamese that she didn't have any money. The bus driver in Central China did not recognize the language and simply thought she was crazy and ejected her from the bus. Linh took three more buses in this manner. Not knowing her direction or whereabouts, she had gone further afield into China.

In Dickensian fashion, on the streets of some unknown strange city, she was befriended by an older Vietnamese woman who said that she herself had been kidnapped when she was young; only unlike Linh she had not had the courage to run, as most girls don't, and so she had been consigned to her fate: married to an older Chinese man who forced her to spend her entire life working in his rice fields and bearing his children.

The woman appeared to be sympathetic to Linh and invited her to stay at her house for a few days. But Linh wanted to get to the border and get home, so she rejected this offer and left the woman. She managed to find her way to a police station.

The Escape

The police welcomed her by throwing her in jail for eight days. They interrogated her again and again, trying to determine whether she was lying or telling the truth. If she admitted that she had already been married to a Chinese man, she would be considered his property, and they would force her to return to her Chinese husband. She kept saying that she had been lucky and escaped, but the Chinese policemen found her story fanciful and unlikely. They said that not one in a hundred girls escaped sexual enslavement once they were kidnapped into China, and Linh did not look exceptional by the sight of her. Linh said that most girls don't have the nerve to run when they get a sliver of opportunity—they hesitate because they don't know their surroundings, don't know where they are, even what country they're in, and they're afraid of getting lost in some strange forest or foreign capital if they run for it.

"This was not a problem for me because I would rather die, starve in the forest, anything, than be forced to marry an old Chinese man," Linh, now nineteen, looking straight ahead, said calmly.

After spending eight long days in a Chinese jail cell, the police suddenly cleared her to go home to Vietnam. She was transferred overnight to the border. As she described it, she was to walk from the Chinese police station at the border to the Vietnam entry point down the road. But as she was walking the sixth of a mile or so through no-man's-land, she was approached by two Chinese women in a car who spoke kindly to her and told her to get in the car—they would drive her the rest of the short distance to the border. Linh said they spoke Vietnamese and seemed kind, so she got in. Once Linh was in the car, they kidnapped her and brought her back into China all over again to be sold into marriage.

They took her to an office where hundreds of photographs of other kidnapped teenage girls from around Southeast Asia were thumbtacked to the walls. The office was a hub of human trafficking, a sex trafficking syndicate, a sophisticated criminal network. The sight of all four walls plastered with hundreds, if not thousands, of eight-by-ten photographs of young girls, with each girl's age scrawled across the photo in red felt marker—the only data point that mattered apparently—sent a sickening lurch through Linh's stomach.

Another woman arrived at the office, picked Linh up and drove her to a house. She locked Linh in a bedroom upstairs. The woman's ten-year-old daughter was assigned to watch her. The daughter tied Linh's hands to a chair and beat her viciously on her face.

The woman holding Linh told her that she liked her—"quiet girl, pretty and mild"—and would give her "a young husband." One was quickly secured. Linh was told that the man was on his way to the house to procure her.

The woman was downstairs preparing breakfast; she said she would give Linh "a good breakfast before she was to be married." The upstairs bedroom door was unlocked because the woman's ten-year-old daughter was watching Linh before she was to be handed over to the buyer. Finally something broke Linh's way. In a mighty stroke of luck, the sadistic daughter exhausted herself and with heavy eyelids nodded off to sleep. Linh, spying her chance, loosed the poorly tied bindings and slipped past the girl. She ran downstairs to the foot of the kitchen where her captor was cooking her breakfast. Linh fled past the woman and out of the house. She hid under a stairwell outside for forty-five minutes.

Finally she worked her way back to the police. Another four days in jail. One of the policemen offered to put her up in a fancy guesthouse instead of the jail. In exchange, he said he would help himself to her body each night. She rejected the proposal, but the policeman installed her in the guesthouse anyway. Linh lived in terror all night long waiting for the sound of tumblers turning in the keyhole that would be the policeman coming to force himself on her. The night passed torturously, but he did not come. At the police station, where at first they seemed not to want to believe her again, they finally telephoned her father. He answered and was permitted to come retrieve his daughter.

I told Linh I was amazed at the close shave with the man who was en route to the house to buy her. He couldn't have been more than a few minutes away when she escaped. Linh just shrugged and said she would have run away later, whenever, as soon as she had a chance, married or not. She was soft-spoken and shy, but she had more resilience and inner strength than the rest of us.

Feathery rain drizzled against my cheek. I looked out at the storm waves ahead.

I realized I hadn't noticed the powerful waves exploding on the beach for the last hour while she had been talking. I had been completely transfixed and lost in her story. Linh was a true survivor, a genuine hero. As soon as she stopped talking, she shuddered, and a shiver emanated off her slender frame. Whether from shuffling off the horror of what had happened to her or merely from the drizzly cold, I did not know. I took another blanket from the back of the chair and wrapped it around her shoulders.

I care for myself. The more solitary, the more friendless, the more unsustained I am, the more I will respect myself.

—Charlotte Brontë, Jane Eyre

9

Outback Cowboy

On my watch, 742 cows slaughtered. RIP. (Sorry …)

All of the backpackers in Brisbane were headed to the Gold Coast to hang out at the beach, drink, get laid—you know, normal stuff.

Fun stuff.

I was the only one taking a hard-left turn into hell.

I woke early before dawn to catch the seven o'clock bus to Numil Downs, an unknown place deep in the Australian outback. The bus drove for three days out of Brisbane, moving ever further from the populous eastern seaboard into the heartless interior of the outback, the Australian desert that dominates over 90 percent of the country. At nightfall on the third day I was thrown out at the terminus, a tiny backwater called Julia Creek. Even the bus seemed to reject the place—as soon as I got off, it instantly recoiled and whipped around and hurried back in the direction it had come.

I should've taken the hint.

I scanned the bus timetables: no bus was scheduled to arrive for another four days. I walked into the town's only diner and waited for three hours, too nervous to eat or read anything. I was terrified. I was filled with absolute dread, consumed by all-out fear, more so than I have ever been in my life. The quest to conquer fear can feel like a lifelong journey.

I closed my eyes for a moment and just swam in the fear. It flooded my body, occupying every molecule. It felt like drowning in water. I found I could stand it, but just barely.

Finally Coby Cranston entered through the screen door. Bells jangled from the top of the door, as they do in small towns. He saw the one person sitting there who didn't belong. After a laconic introduction, I climbed in the cab of his truck, and he drove us two and a half hours on to Numil Downs.

After the first ten minutes the asphalt gave way to dirt, and that is how the road would remain until it petered out somewhere deep in the Nullarbor Desert. Coby was driving an enormous metal truck, like a meat truck, with double sets of giant tires, each the size of a lifeboat, on all four corners, eight tires in total, the same giant tires long-distance eighteen-wheelers use.

Perfect for the apocalypse.

I sat high up in the passenger cab of the truck behind a large flat, broad window like a school bus' that gave us full panoramic visibility over the sweeping desolation. I asked Coby why the truck needed two pairs of tires on each axle.

"You'll see," he whispered, his eyes stapled open like *A Clockwork Orange*.

Coby pushed his foot down on the accelerator, increasing the speed of the truck until it was caroming along at a bracingly fast clip considering its lumbering size. Drifting along the edge of vision I felt, before I saw, a flutter of movement. Ghosting through the desert along the horizon, flickering and translucent, part solid, part invisible, the very first kangaroo I had ever seen materialized in the desert. It was like a vision, something from a dream. The kangaroo hopped right up alongside the truck and started jumping parallel with us. Incredibly, it kept pace with the truck.

"Kangaroo!" I cried out, like a child.

Coby looked startled. He shook his head as though he had been slapped, like he wasn't sure whether I was joking or not. Then he shot me an annoyed look and sighed out his window.

We were getting along great already.

I was astonished at how fast the kangaroo could move. It was keeping pace with our truck which was rocketing along at an impressive eighty miles per hour over rutted dirt road. *Damn, those rats can move.* At that speed a kangaroo is jumping so many times per second that it looks like it's running like a roadrunner, but if you look closely you can see it's jumping at the hyperfast rate of a hummingbird's heartbeat. After all, a kangaroo can only jump.

Suddenly one kangaroo was five. More roos emerged out of the ether and surrounded the truck on all sides, all hopping at microrapid repetitions and maintaining our speed. Five kangaroos soon became fifteen, and then fifty, and then all at once our truck was surrounded by more than a hundred kangaroos. We were barreling along inside a fluctuating net of hopping critters that all seemed controlled by one nonlocal brain. Coby looked relaxed, not the least bit concerned by the steadily massing army of beasts that was tightening around us like a noose.

Suddenly Coby sat up straight, stretched, cracked his neck, yawned, cleared his throat, and then leaned forward over the wheel. He visibly checked out behind his eyes, which turned milky and unfocused, as his human side disappeared and something else, something horrible, rose to the surface and took over. He pressed the gas pedal all the way down to the floor, and the meat truck surged forward as though a bomb had detonated in the trunk. The truck spit up whorls of dust as it rocketed ahead like nuclear-tipped ordnance.

Irrationally, the kangaroos began to make hard right ninety-degree turns directly into the path of the oncoming truck, committing suicide in a kind of losing game of chicken. I had never seen anything like it. I had never seen anything like *any of this*.

As the roos darted in front of the truck, Coby made no effort to swerve around them. Instead, as though the Terminator were driving the truck, he just plowed straight into them. If anything, he turned the wheel slightly so he could hit them. It was like a live video game—Bam! *Crack!* Kangaroos were being crunched beneath our giant wheels like crabs on the beach. The truck rocked, bounced, and galloped over marsupials the size of basketball players. As soon as we ran over one kangaroo, three more appeared to take its place. The deaths only seemed to energize the other kangaroos.

Splat! A roo smashed into our windshield like a missile and exploded like a water balloon. Its blood splattered all over the windshield like red paint. I felt relieved the roo hadn't punched straight through the glass and impaled me—its body was enormous. Coby throttled the windshield wiper-fluid lever like he was strangling a chicken, squirting it nonstop, the wipers on high to wash away a lake's worth of blood. It was like driving through an abattoir, a kangaroo genocide.

There was a sickening *crunch* sound as our wheels broke a kangaroo's back, ripping its spine apart like the wishbone of a Thanksgiving turkey. A large kangaroo moved right up beside our front left wheel. It glanced casually at me. Then the roo looked down at our tire and laid its body directly in front of the wheel, turning its body into a launching ramp that propelled our front wheels up in the air, one step higher on the stairway to heaven, and suddenly our whole truck was airborne.

"*Wooooo!*" screamed Coby.

"*Shit!*" I yelled. I grabbed the handlebar as our truck sailed through the air like the bus in the movie *Speed*.

Coby cackled with glee as the truck fell back to earth and landed on its front tires with a giant thud. The truck lurched grotesquely as the bounce sent our rear wheels up into the air and our cab's front nose downward until we hit the ground and started plowing through the earth like a shovel.

"*Shiiit!*" I glanced at the odometer. The cab was plowing the ground like a hoe through a field and should have acted as a brake, but despite the drag, the truck was still rocketing along at an incredible ninety miles per hour over road that had more pockmarks than a teenager's face. Dead kangaroo bodies were piling up faster than a serial killer's freezer. The stomach-wrenching, audible *crunching* sound of the animals' spines and necks being torn apart beneath our giant wheels and their blood splattering our windshield would have been nauseating if I wasn't just trying to stay alive. As we trucked over roo after roo, it occurred to me that this was *Mad Max*—this was Australia's imagery of a car running hellfire over a desert fleeing maniacs on motorbikes. Except in real life the maniacs are suicidal kangaroos.

One particularly large kangaroo that was nearly twice the size of a normal one, their champion apparently, emerged from the pack and rotated its beastly head to look directly inside Coby's driver-side window. The kangaroo didn't look very impressed with what it saw.

It chortled. Then it looked down at our front left wheel. It snapped its head back straight again to stay on course, then turned and looked down at our front left wheel again, teeing it up. The animal was planning something. *My God, it was thinking!*

Suddenly, with a deft movement, the beast lowered its full body inside our front left wheel shaft as though it were leaning down to sip a full cocktail on a bar, and casually committed suicide. As our truck's wheel shaft tried to absorb the addition of a massive kangaroo, I heard, or rather felt, an explosion—one of the giant front tires, each one the size of a Zodiac, blew up as though we'd driven over an IED. Jolted by the explosion, the truck belted skyward, as though the ground beneath us had punched the eject button, and the whole truck burst through the sky like a rainbow. The dead kangaroo had taken one of our tires with it to the afterlife.

The truck landed with a gallop like an exuberant foal. It buckled and wheezed from the shockwaves as it absorbed the explosion of the giant tire. Then the truck seemed to find its footing because it rocketed ahead anew, surging forward like a bat out of hell, faster than ever, blasting ahead on V8 cylinders, now on just one tire on our front left side instead of two.

Then another kangaroo emerged from the pack where the last had been. This one looked even smarter. It launched its body sideways through the air like a Chinese martial arts actor and its whole body curved inside the same front left wheel shaft like a perfectly thrown dart. It flapped around in our axle like a stuffed animal being whipped around in windmills by a demonic child, and jammed up our wheel boot but good. All at once the truck locked up as if the kangaroo had snipped our gas line while it was under there, and I felt Coby lose cortical control of the steering. The mammoth truck launched airborne on top of the dead kangaroo's back and this time the truck tilted sideways as it flew through the air.

Coby gnashed his teeth and shouted, "Fuck! Fuck! Fuck!"

The truck hurtled sideways through the air at ninety miles per hour and came crashing down on a forty-five-degree angle as our right wheels lifted clean into the air, spinning madly into the abyss, and I stared sideways through the windshield into the setting sun. For a second we hovered on a near-perfect axis, suspended in midair. I thought the truck was going to roll all the way over and we would turn upside down. But at its zenith, the truck finally found its equilibrium, gravity wrested it back in its tug of war with momentum, and we came crashing down to earth. The truck scudded, groaned, and shuddered to a halt. Our rampaging monster spaceship-truck had been felled, taken down by the one billion kangaroos of the outback. If this scene sounds surreal, let me assure you it was every bit as surreal as it sounds.

Coby was all whipped up into a lather. "Yeeeeeeee!" he shouted. He flapped his lips like a horse, and a spit thread ejected from his mouth, one end of the spit rainbow clinging to his lower lip while the other end drifted around the cab like a gossamer cobweb.

Coby kicked open his door and jumped down to the ground. He hawked a loogie in the dirt and started cursing at the mangled carcass of the dead kangaroo that had proved our better.

"Fucking shitworm!" Coby screamed at the lifeless body. He started kicking it violently.

The dead carcass was wedged tightly inside the wheel shaft like a broken key inside a lock, with half its body being dragged out in front of the tire. The combination of it being both stuck in the axle and dragged out in front without being completely crushed by our tires or thrown clear was the reason we'd been beached. This kangaroo would receive the kangaroos' Congressional Medal of Honor and a Purple Heart.

Mission accomplished, you human assholes.

Somewhere its leaders were cheering, smoking skinny cigarettes and sipping cognac. *La kangaroo résistance* lived to fight another day. Luckily I was brand new, so Coby didn't ask me to pick the dead roo out of the wheel shaft. He produced a rather large knife from inside his jacket, leaned down on his belly, and pried out the dead animal. He tossed the body aside with no more compassion than a sociopath. I was surprised he didn't saw its head off to keep as a trophy. Coby didn't say another word until we arrived at the farm.

During the daytime at Numil Downs I never saw a single kangaroo. Though they breed at a rate that would make maggots blush, the open savannahs were always empty of the giant critters as far as I could see. But when day gave way to night, the one billion kangaroos that were out there somewhere descended on Numil like locusts and blanketed the farm like a plague of Egypt.

Exhausted from my dawn-to-dark daily Sisyphean treadmill of physical labor, each night after dinner I padded back to my guestroom that was about five hundred meters from the main house, trudging through slate darkness carrying a flashlight. As soon as I left the farmhouse, the Cranstons cut the lights behind me and I was unmoored in utter blackness. The darkness in the outback is so extreme, so dense, and the location so remote, that it felt like I was on the surface of another planet. I didn't feel like I was on earth anymore. The wind-spit terrain felt wildly foreign and as alien as the smooth, windy face of a rock in outer space.

When the lights went out behind me, I was estranged in blind dark. I sat in it for a moment, just feeling the estrangement, the slight terror at being exposed, so isolated, abandoned. When I clicked on the flashlight, suddenly millions of kangaroos were standing all around me in the dark like Easter Island statues for as far as I could see in any direction. Every night when I turned on my flashlight and it revealed an army of giant beasts arrayed against me like pawns on a life-sized chessboard, a spike of horror pricked down my spine. I never got used to this. It was creepy, eerie, and not a little threatening.

There were so many beasts, and all of them staring directly into my eyes, that I felt overwhelmed. It's weird how an animal looks straight into your eyes and nowhere else. It's as if they see into your soul. I have no doubt that they do. Imagine hundreds, if not thousands, of kangaroos all standing motionless in your path, staring into your eyes simultaneously. They could easily have torn me to ribbons with their talons if they wanted to. There were far too many of them to resist if they attacked me.

Oh, who am I kidding? I couldn't even have taken one.

They stood just a couple of feet from wherever I stood, in front and all around me in the darkness. That means wherever I walked, I was walking straight into them, into a sea of zombies. They must have been shuffling soundlessly from side to side in the darkness to avoid hitting me and then freezing the moment I clicked on the flashlight.

The kangaroo shuffle.

I never bumped into one—thank God for that! They were always standing right there, though, just an inch or two beyond the full extension of my arm, a thick forest of giant rodents. They towered over me, well over six feet, the size of moose. They were immense, like sentinels of the underworld staring down at their lesser creation.

They never flinched or batted an eyelash when I shined the flashlight into their faces. The fact that light shined directly into their eyes didn't faze them was proof enough of the horror they were capable of. Their eyes—large, brown glistening opals—never blinked. It was like a wax museum or some deserted castle where medieval knights in armor suits watch you through the slits in their facemasks as you walk down the corridor at night before suddenly coming to life and attacking you.

It's a good thing the kangaroos were seemingly neutral gods, because they could easily have trampled me and then swamped the main house and overrun all of Australia if they wanted to, wiping out the human invaders with immaculate ease and returning the country to its marsupial bosom. There were far too many of them for twenty million Australians and me to take on. There are probably two hundred billion kangaroos in the Outback. Fit them in Kevlar, hand them guns, control them with a joystick, and you'd have the greatest fighting force on earth. If we could just find the nonlocal brain that controls them all and directs them to work in unison to overthrow our truck.

Kangaroos are deemed pests in Australia. Let's just say they will not appear on endangered species lists anytime soon.

Searching for more intense feeling, something lower to the ground, at a more elemental frequency, something where I could once again feel the frisson of life that I had growing up and find a way to increase the richness of my heart, I had come at last to work on cattle stations, mostly because the mere idea of it scared the hell out of me. If something scares me, I pretty much feel compelled to do it, just to rid myself of the fear. Startled by the fear, awakened by it, I treated it as a beacon, a Siren call. The fear was intense feeling. At last I could feel something again, feel fully alive. Though it was terror and fear, it was far preferable to feeling *nothing*. To feel nothing is the worst thing of all for any human being. I had wandered for several years with my strangely insolvent heart, a spiritual soul wound, a malady I didn't understand at all. I treated the fear I felt at the thought of working on the cattle stations like the last lifeboat off a sinking ship, like the last life preserver dangling above the black water.

Strobe lights pulsed around the room, flashing down brilliant purple, yellow and green beams of light as if from the underbelly of a landing spaceship. A chintzy disco ball rotated slowly on the ceiling. I walked away from a mouthwateringly gorgeous, six feet tall, nineteen-year-old Swedish blonde in a miniskirt who spent nights dancing with me in the nightclubs of Byron Bay, looking up at me with milky eyes that were both innocent and wanton, both unknowing and depraved. I left behind this young blue star whom I had not really gotten to know yet, and instead waded into an apocalyptic, male-only nightmare that was much worse than anything you could possibly imagine.

It was a cool May day when I arrived at Numil Downs, Bob and Lorraine Cranston's property. To this day the name Bob Cranston sends a rivulet of icy mercury sliding down my spine. Evil cunt, to use Carlton's parlance. Numil Downs was a cattle ranch like we have in America, only in Australia they're not called ranches, they're called cattle stations. Which is fine by me because a ranch sounds friendly, the kind of place with a grandparent in a rocking chair on the front porch. But there was nothing friendly about this place.

The nearest town was Julia Creek where Coby Cranston, Bob and Lorraine's Quasimodo-lookalike son, had picked me up from the diner. The nearest town that would show up on a map is Cloncurry. A little farther out is Mount Isa. All of this was in Queensland State.

Queensland is best known for its famous Gold and Sunshine Coasts with their seemingly infinite pristine white sand beaches, such as the Whitsunday Islands, that stretch all the way up the country's glamorous east coast and include hall-of-fame spots like Brisbane, Surfers Paradise, Cairns, and Australia's most popular attraction, the Great Barrier Reef.

But I was far away from all that. For some unknown reason I had chosen to turn my back on all that goodness, that glamor-studded paradise, and rush straight into hell instead.

Queensland is a vast state that stretches from the east coast of Australia halfway across the whole continent toward the rugged west coast, Perth, and the Indian Ocean. The isolated west coast—bleak, beautiful, barren—is more my cup of tea than the crowded tourist trap of the east coast. I was in far western Queensland, deep in Australia's interior in the very center of the country, its nadir, its low point, the real fucking outback, mate. The outback is Australia's heart of darkness, a forlorn lawless place, a giant desert that was never meant to be inhabited by man. The outback is like some inhospitable, lifeless rock in space that will be humankind's future home after we ruin this beautiful planet. Shunned and rejected by all normal people and by society at large, the few hardbitten, eccentric souls who call this place home are left to stew in their own dysfunction, kill people whenever they see fit without any repercussions and, in the meantime, groom cattle for the slaughterhouse.

When I arrived at the station, I was dismayed to find that I was the only worker. They were in low season, and it would be weeks before any cattle were to be rounded up and sold. Until there was cattle work to do, there was hard labor to do. I mostly did fences. The Cranstons were replacing a lot of their old fencing—metal posts replacing rotted-out wood posts, new wire replacing old sagging wire, flashy new metal gates with a bull's head emblem to replace decrepit wood gates.

I left the house at sunrise each morning with a chainsaw, cut down all the trees in the path of the fence line, hauled away the felled trees, took all the old wire bindings out of the fence and tossed them in a bucket, pulled the old wire out of the posts and rolled it up—barbed wire first, then straight (barbed wire would catch on itself and roll up, but straight wire flopped out every which way and wouldn't roll)—and finally, straining by hand, pulled the old posts out of the ground, which required Thor's strength. Most times I couldn't budge the posts, let alone yank them out of the ground. It was as if their roots stretched down to the center of the earth. I loaded the few posts I had been able to pull out and the old wire onto the bed of a pickup truck and drove it out to a remote location where I doused it in gasoline, lit a match, and burned it all in a massive, toxic metal bonfire. Can metal wire catch fire and burn? Oh yes … it can. Can you imagine anything worse for the environment? No wonder there's a hole the size of Lithuania in the ozone layer above Australia.

I did all this so you wouldn't have to.

I imagine this work was not too different from that in one of Stalin's concentration camps. As I pulled up wood posts, the fence line stretched on in front of me forever, as far as the eye could see, disappearing in the horizon but continuing on unabated. The fence had no end, none that I ever saw or knew.

It was hot as hell out here too. Farmers in the outback frequently get skin cancer because the sun is somehow more potent in Australia than it is at an equal distance from the equator in the Northern Hemisphere. Some say this is due to that hole in the ozone, but I think that's horseshit. While it's no hotter than, say, Vegas or Phoenix in summer, the sun is stronger, and it will singe the hell out of you. Even sunscreen is powerless against it after thirty minutes or so. The farmers who live here don't even bother to put it on anymore, having tired of slapping on the wet stuff long ago. Everyone just wears a hat and hopes for the best. People look terrible because the sun has ravaged their faces and turned them into leather. All the men look five to ten years older than their age. But this is man country, so no one says shit about it. An early death is not unusual out here. To many it may be secretly welcome.

I had never worked from dark to dark like that before. Up in the dark, quick breakfast with the Cranstons in the main house, then out to the fields at first light. And I mean *at first light*—it was dawn when I exited the house each morning. I'd shoulder an equipment bag and walk straight into the desert as the sun crept over the horizon. There was no bank of trees or hill on the wide open plain to obstruct my unfettered view of the rising sun, creating the illusion that it was rising right in front of me and that the plain stretched on forever, which it did. The landscape was bleak and unforgiving and felt vaguely unreal.

I worked all day, came home at night only when it was too dark to see, and was in bed at nine thirty so I could rise at four thirty and do the same thing all over again. It was a continuous, unflagging nightmare. I cursed at the sun, begging it to arc down faster so that the day would end and I could return to the farmhouse. But the sun refused to budge and stubbornly held its position aloft in the sky. Time stood still. The day just would not end.

There was no letting up on the job either. Coby Cranston, who was about my age and would one day inherit the farm from his father, was a dour killjoy and a sadist—one of those types who no matter how hard you work always demands you work harder, faster, letting you know you're not doing a good job no matter how hard you're busting your ass. Types like that never breathe a word of praise or say "good job" when a task is done well. In fact, they're careful not to. Which is fine by me. I don't want praise from those kind of people.

I could see where he'd learned it from. His father, Bob Cranston, was about as evil as a rancher gets. He reminded me of Gene Hackman's character in *The Quick and the Dead*. Looked a bit like him too. He gave me long assignments—"Tom, open this gate with this combination, push the cattle through, walk around back and open this other gate, then go west and unlock that gate and pull out that post. And if you don't get it all right or come back without it done properly, then fuck you! What good are you?"

I bit hard into my lower lip. I felt my head tilt down, my fists wrapping themselves into balls. A small part of me wanted to deck him. But then that's what he wants, isn't it? He's trying to get a rise out of me. He wants my reaction. I'm disinclined to give him what he wants. It's funny when people you hardly know speak to you so personally just because you're in their employ. Bob's insults didn't matter much to me, so I turned around without replying and went off to do the job. In another life, Bob, I would bury you. Maybe I'll bury you in this life. But then how the hell would I get out of here?

When Coby gave me orders, I was sometimes confused what he wanted due to his Australian English. Instead of saying, "Give the cow some hay," he'd look at me and whisper, "*Feed the beast*," as though he wanted me to go feed virgins to a monster. When I returned, he'd ask in a grim whisper, "*Did the beast like its food?*" which means, "Did the cow eat the hay you gave it?"

Instead of saying, "It's time to eat," he'd hiss, "*It's time for a feed*" or "*Have you fed today?*" as though we were vampires who'd learned how to be courteous in Victorian England. On the Sunshine Coast, an Aussie girl or *sheila*, their word for a chick, asked me where I had gotten my slice of cheese pizza. I pointed her the way.

"*Champion...*" she breathed in my ear, before vanishing around a corner. For a moment I was taken aback by such lavish praise. Being knighted a beautiful woman's champion just for showing her where the pizza joint is—wow, what a compliment. Later I realized it's just more of their goofy slang.

I did learn a lot on the farm. Such as how to wield a chainsaw. If I ever have to mow down a home invader in self-defense, I will be well prepared. I learned how to weld and cut steel and drive a tractor. I chopped down a lot of trees with an old ax George Washington–style when there weren't enough trees along the fence line to merit bringing the chainsaw. If Coby was watching, I'd have to wail on those trees like an ax murderer or else he was likely to make some demeaning comment. As with the ceaseless work on the fishing boat in Alaska, I felt myself becoming stronger and leaner. My body was sore at night, but it was that good kind of muscle sore. I was as brown as a Mexican from that fierce sun. I kept dropping weight too, no matter how much I ate.

My bungalow didn't have a shower, so every morning I padded across a dusty field in the dark and showered in an outdoor stone alcove. This was the most pleasurable part in an otherwise unpleasant day. I felt the fissures in the stone, the grooves in the broken rock, massage the places between my toes that had long been neglected as I showered outside in the primitive desert darkness and stared across an empty pale continent until the horizon cracked open like an egg and a splotch of yellow shone through. I pressed my bare toes deeper into the crags of the stone floor of the alcove as the first honeyed light of dawn bled out down the plain.

One morning as I washed myself in the predawn darkness, I noticed that all superfluous weight had even dropped from my thighs and forearms. I had the body of a twelve-year-old boy. I must have weighed less than 150 pounds. I should have auditioned for an underwear commercial immediately after leaving here. It was bizarre to see not a single ounce of fat on my body anywhere. I was either a model or a refugee from a third world country. Could one be both at the same time, a refugee model? Instead of starving ourselves to look like models, why don't we just hire refugees instead?

I could eat whatever I wanted without gaining weight, and at first did so—triple helpings of ice cream, huge refined white flour, sugar-napalm yellow-frostinged cakes—the most poisonous foods on earth, basically—until one day eating a lot simply lost its point. I started eating small meals without noticing it and felt full almost immediately, after just ten bites or so, and found myself passing on dessert. Somehow farm work had weaned me off my craving for sugar, like a heroin addict weaned off his addiction to opium.

Of course, just one day back in the city and I was already reaching for the first ice cream I saw. I noticed, as with many nervous habits in urban life, this was done primarily out of boredom rather than any real craving for the ice cream itself. Compulsively checking our phones, buying a cake at the café, smoking—all are done mostly out of boredom, a persistent low-grade undertow of static anxiety that seems married to city life, to doing highly paid but weak-as-shit desk work. This vague, dimly felt yet ubiquitous undercurrent of anxiety in the background of urban life is our modern affliction.

At least we were just working too damn hard out here to have any anxiety.

In the early days, other than sleep, stuffing my face with food was my only real pleasure on the farm. I noticed that when you're in a horrible joyless situation, your mental architecture, your neural scaffolding, the electrical lattices in your brain software, adjust on their own and create new pleasure pathways that didn't previously exist during your more comfortable existence. Accordingly, depression adapts to any luxury. It's probably worse in luxury because you have more leisure time. My few basic pleasures, what people in ordinary life take for granted—sleeping, eating, going to the bathroom, even shuffling through the dirt at night from the main house back to my room—took on an enhanced sensual glow, a heightened beauty in an orphaned world. Sleep became a voluptuous thing, as if my bed—hard and fit for a convict if seen with sane eyes—and pillow were a woman with large breasts that I was wrapping my arms around and burying my face between each night. Eating food was tantamount to orgasm. Sad as all this sounds, in the moment you're just grateful for such small pleasures. It's okay. Well, no, it's not okay, is it? These are the things that can happen to a man when he's working in the outback, on a fishing boat, or in prison. Life is terrible when there are no women around.

Three weeks after I started, a woman from South Africa named Alison arrived on the farm. She had been hired by Lorraine to do domestic work around the house. By that point any small boon was a blessing, and I felt a wave of relief when Alison, someone normal, arrived. I had only been here three weeks but it already felt like I'd spent half my life here—indeed, it already felt longer than my entire childhood. I was miserable at Numil and starved for another backpacker—anyone I could remotely relate to—to talk with. There's a word for that. It's called loneliness. Alison was thirty-two, and quite quickly, she hated Numil too. When the people at the top are no good, the whole organization is corrupt all the way down.

Once a week Alison and I stole away for a rare walk and roamed as far away from the farm as we could, elapsing enormous distances over wild, virgin landscape. I think we walked the distance of an entire marathon some days—thirteen miles out and thirteen miles back. Like great explorers we lighted out for the territory at first dawn before the sun breached the horizon. To begin a day at dawn is a glorious thing. The world feels always fresh and redolent with possibility at this hour. You can smell dawn in the air, the dew, the newness and cleanness of it. Wherever I travel, I always endeavor to get out of the hostel as early as possible in the morning. The earlier you are out on the cobblestoned piazza for breakfast, when the townsfolk are still washing the stones, the better the breakfast tastes and the more beautiful that morning is. I always try to arrive just as the café opens. The food tastes better, and the silence is golden.

Shouldering small packs containing lunch and a water bottle, Alison and I took off down the fence line until we reached a river that bisected Numil Downs, where wild boars and pigs congregated to drink. We waded across the river, holding our shoes above our heads, and the boars and pigs scattered as we approached. Lucky for us, because the boars were large with long tusks. If they attacked us, they would have won. Fortunately no one had told them that.

Then we set off into unknown terrain, keeping track of landmarks so as not to get lost but still with some trepidation for the possibility of it since we were walking in uncharted, uninhabited landscape. If we got turned around and lost, it was very plausible no one would ever find us. I knew Bob Cranston would shed no tear if we were swallowed up by the outback.

We trod ever deeper into the Australian bush, each time pressing farther afield, all our instincts urging us further away from the farmhouse, until one day we arrived at an area where wild horses ran free. The magnificent, loping animals stopped to congregate beneath the shade of a single, stand-alone tree that stooped over a small watering hole, as if God had felicitously set them both down there together so that neither the tree nor the watering hole would ever be lonely.

It was a beautiful, isolated place. We sat among untamed stallions who knew no master, no bridle, no hand on them. With our backs resting against the trunk of the tree, looking up at the majestic animals as they drank from the cool pool in our secret oasis in the desert, we discussed the unfortunate circumstances of our unusual confinement and began to hatch a plan to escape.

I finally got to work with cattle. It was what I had come for. Mustering, which means herding the cattle; drafting, which means separating the cattle out by type so that the calves go into one pen, cows in another, bulls in another; and branding and castrating them are where the action is, and I loved it.

Your hand glides across the smooth, glistening skin of these massive beasts that jostle and collide against you like tectonic plates, and you can feel the enormous life pulsing inside them. You know you're really doing something when you're working on a cattle station branding calves and they're fighting you and kicking you with their powerful legs, braying and looking up at you with frightened eyes as you struggle to pin them down so you can push the red hot poker into their skin. I did love it. At first. Spending all day wrestling animals, pushing them through swinging gates into narrow chutes called "the races," screaming at the top of your lungs while being buffeted, battered, kicked, and rammed by these monsters, is quite a thing. If a cow or horse pushes you, you don't hold your ground. You fly backward as though a bullet train slammed into you.

Bob Cranston continued to harass me from atop a postapocalyptic wooden tower—the perfect perch for a megalomaniac—where he shouted down instructions and directed traffic. At the time I did nothing because he was my boss and I was in the middle of nowhere, in a way at his mercy. Today I might have turned the shotgun on him and just shot him. The cattle certainly would have thanked me if I had. If ever there was a place where you could dispose of a body and get clean away with it, it was here. I doubt there was any law enforcement around for a thousand miles.

After a month and a half suffering at the hands of the Cranstons, Alison and I finally caught a break. Bob Cranston had to take a trip to Brisbane to pick up new animal feed to fatten up his cows for the slaughter. Lorraine never missed an opportunity to visit her sister in the city, and Coby was going too. Bob, paranoid miser that he was, didn't trust Alison and me in his house alone. He was convinced we would steal something. Or maybe burn down his whole fucking farm. In some way he must have known he was a bastard. Abuse the help and they may turn on you if given the chance. Bob resolved that the only way to protect his farmstead from the mistreated help was to get rid of us wholesale and move us off his property.

But how to do it?

Lorraine got on the horn with some ranches around the area and got us transferred to another cattle station called Taldora, under the direction of the charismatic Carlton Curr. Lorraine warned us that Taldora was going to be far more intense, much gnarlier than Numil.

"Ten times tougher," she said. "Balls to the wall." Alison and I didn't care. We were just so happy to hear we'd be leaving.

But not without a few parting words from Bob Cranston first. Instead of giving us a bonus or even saying thank you, he took the opportunity to rain down abuse on me one last time. Bob tried to make me feel guilty for taking a few sandwiches Lorraine had made us to the roundup.

"Now you're taking my food? Unbelievable, you have no shame," he said, glaring at me through his gray, creased face.

Right. Unbelievable, I thought. *Prick.*

The farmers down here were pretty wealthy because beef sold at a premium—the Cranstons' cars, farm machinery, and tractors, a few of which were as large as aircraft carriers, were leased and replaced every three years with state-of-the-art new ones that cost between $100,000 and $300,000 each; the monthly payments on them couldn't have been cheap—but they paid Alison and me mere sustenance wages. There was no handshake or even a goodbye from Bob. No surprise. That was fine with me because at least we were getting off Numil Downs, a place that had largely made me miserable.

"Y'all like the roundup?" Lorraine Cranston asked us.

"What?" Alison and I asked in unison.

The beginning of the end was really the rodeo. Only don't call it a rodeo in Australia; it's called a roundup. But a rodeo is what it was. Our new ranch boss, Carlton Curr of Taldora, wasn't immediately available to pick us up, but by pure chance there happened to be a local rodeo on, affording us a place to go for three days until Carlton could come and collect us.

Sandwiched between the two stints working at Numil Downs and Taldora, the three-day roundup was a reprieve from darkness. The linchpin of the rodeo was a large party on Saturday night. The music was all country, all the time—a live hoedown with rail-thin men in ginormous cowboy hats swiveling their narrow hips and kicking their boot tips up into the air. I had never seen anything like it outside of the movie *Thelma & Louise*.

When Alison and I rolled up, we exchanged a look of pure shock when we both realized the same thing: the music was pretty damn good! This was initially alarming because no hip young person likes country music. What was the matter, were we getting old? But I quickly realized that wasn't it. We liked the music because we had been living on the cattle station for months. Anyone leading the cow herding life is going to like country music, period. The country hit "Save a Horse (Ride a Cowboy)" is as good as anything going and should be backing up the clubs of Surfers Paradise.

I looked around at everyone singing and dancing. The place was jumping. The party startled up distant, dormant memories of what normal life used to look like. I had thrown it away for this—a spare, wandering existence as a homeless traveler of oceans. I wanted to jump in and dance with the vivacious, pretty women in tight-fitting blue jeans and swelling white shirts trellised with frills and lace. Cowboys undulated rhythmically like sea grass as the girls turned around and backed their asses into the men's pelvises like pickup trucks thirsty for gas. As fireworks boomed in the distance, the girls bent over, leaned down, grinding against the men's crotches, their blonde hair tossing wildly in the night sky, wide smiles breaking their faces radiantly.

Intellectually I knew it was sexy, but the torture on the cattle station had been too much. I'd been scarred by it and felt too numb to party.

So I just watched. As I sipped a beer and the shock of the last couple of months edged off a bit, a little spleen returned to me, as Melville might have said. My wrist betrayed a pulse, my modem hawked up a dial tone, and I too felt excited when the crowd roared as "Save a Horse (Ride a Cowboy)" came blasting out over the loudspeakers. I hadn't heard any music for the last eight weeks. But I didn't have a cowboy hat, the one thing a man irretrievably cannot be without at a rodeo. In a lawless country with no rules, it is the one rule, the one sacrament. If you are not wearing a hat that is about six times too big for your head, you will not get laid that night. It's as simple as that. No ten-gallon hat at a rodeo is like showing up at a gay apartment party without ecstasy and assless pants.

There was no motel or shelter at the rodeo. Other than the bullring, only a few stands selling hot dogs and beer dotted the bleak landscape. The event was pitched out in the vast nothingness of the desert like a sanctuary city, Area 51 alien holding pen, swingers retreat, rendition site, or safe zone from the zombie apocalypse—in other words any place you don't want found. You couldn't get here any other way than driving, and everyone slept in their trailers in the car park at night, car park being the whole desert in this case. No one was going to charge you twenty bucks for a parking place out here.

Alison and I had no trailer or tent, so we waded into the dark woods like Hansel and Gretel. I built a fire, and we crawled inside sleeping bags set down under the stars.

The fire burned out and I passed into sleep. At some point during the night a disturbance prodded me awake. I bolted upright. I scanned the darkness and saw … nothing. It was pitch-black except for a sea of stars that glimmered high in the firmament. I gazed up at the stars, grateful that they were there. They cast down just enough light to create a few shadows.

Suddenly the scene turned hostile, and I felt afraid. A clot of darkness darted in front of me. I felt it before I saw it; it was what had awoken me. The fear in the pit of my stomach was real gut fear and I knew I hadn't dreamed or imagined it; something was really there. It felt ugly, cruel, and close, perhaps just a few feet from me. Though the night air was warm, a terrible cold gripped me, and I shivered. My ears pricked up like an animal rounding the watering hole at midnight, listening for any sound in the primitive darkness. I tensed. I was barely breathing now. I pawed the dirt for the only weapon I could think of, an empty beer bottle from the night before. I gripped the bottle's neck and held it tightly in my lap.

Then the thing approached. A black shadow loomed over me like Malachi in *Children of the Corn*. It blackened out the stars. Heavy boots slid firmly into place in front of me. The shadow reached down and grabbed me roughly by my hair. A strong hand yanked my head backward. It was a man. It dawned on me that he could easily have murdered us in our sleep a few minutes ago had the impulse occurred to him; there was nothing I could've done to prevent it while we were asleep. We had no employer, no guardian, no shelter, and no law enforcement here to protect us. We were totally exposed in the forest at the mercy of the horror that was standing above me and gripping my hair. Alison sensed the disturbance and roused.

"What is it?" her voice quavered, thick with fear.

It was a drunk, homeless quarter-caste (one-fourth) aboriginal, and he was clearly mentally unstable. He rasped out something in a slurred, rattling voice, and it took me a moment to realize he was asking for liquor.

I slapped his hand away and told him we didn't have any alcohol and we were sleeping, so please go away. Engaging him turned out to be a mistake, though, because it only energized him. I got out of my sleeping bag, stood up and shoved him, but the confrontation only thrilled him, as though it was the thing he desired most, even more than liquor, and he laughed and wheezed at the feeling of my hands pressing against his chest. Like an inflatable doll, he bounced back. He slouched and leered toward me, talking louder and more confidently now. I had forgotten a cardinal rule: never fight down, only fight up. The aboriginal was viciously drunk, and I wasn't sure how to handle him. He stayed with us the rest of the night and harassed me straight through till dawn. I didn't dare go back to sleep because I thought there was a very real chance he might slit our throats if I did.

Later I found out that this aboriginal had, not surprisingly, been abandoned by his ride, and the day after our encounter he literally walked across the desert with nothing but the clothes on his back. He was even freer than I was. He eventually walked over forty miles to Taldora, where Carlton found him and put him to work alongside us because he didn't know what else to do with him.

I was shocked when I walked into breakfast one morning to find this same maniac who had come close to slitting our throats in our sleep now sitting beside me at the kitchen table asking me to pass him the cheerios. It was like coming upstairs one night to find Hannibal Lector reading in your bed. This crazy bastard who had terrorized us all night long was now working side by side with me in Carlton's drafting pen, still harassing me in his insane way. All these little things started to add up, and I realized only belatedly that this was not the sort of place where one wanted to spend their time.

At Taldora, Alison joined a girl named Mojito as domestic help in the house. Mojito was an English nurse of Barbados descent who could work in any commonwealth country with her UK citizenship. Mojito wasn't pretty, but she was built like a brick shithouse. She was so quiet that I wondered if she could speak.

The day after Carlton Curr picked us up from the rodeo, on my very first morning at Taldora, he took me out to do some mustering with his best jackeroo, a capable aboriginal named Josh.

After we'd finished loading horses onto the truck, apropos of nothing, Carlton, this giant of a man whom I didn't know from Adam, turned to me and said, "You want to fight me? Because I want to fight you."

My instinctual response was, "I can box." I set my right foot back and got ready. Josh looked up, taking interest.

Carlton lowered his eyes to the right and murmured, "I always did want to fight an American."

"Okay ... fair enough," I said. It had been a strange summer already.

I moved in to look for an opening. Carlton looked into my eyes, and I guess he saw what he was looking for—that I was ready to go—because suddenly he threw down his arms and began laughing hysterically. He clapped Josh on the shoulder and then rushed in and hugged me, swinging a massive arm around in a heavy clap across my chest that was meant in affection but was so hard it stung. One of Carlton's hands was the size of a porterhouse steak for two. One of his hands was the size of a world map.

After that, Carlton really seemed to like me, and when he passed me in the courtyard or hallway, he always put up his dukes for play-fighting. I'd do the same, and then he'd howl with laughter like a little kid. He had taken my measure and found me worthy.

Carlton Curr was a genuine cowboy. He was a real ranch boss, and I got to do everything at Taldora that I've ever seen in westerns, other than have a romance with a Native American girl who doesn't speak English. But this was no movie. Shit was real. At Taldora there was nothing but work. Lorraine wasn't lying. There were no days off. There were no hours off. The good part was that I was launched into mustering work right away—I was in full cowboy world. It was dawn-to-dusk mustering, roping cattle, and drafting them.

I was mustering on horseback, something I didn't do at Numil Downs where we rode quads, or four-wheel ATVs. Riding horses is far more authentic and glamorous than driving ATVs and it was one of the reasons I signed up to work on cattle stations in the first place—learning how to ride a horse in the wild had been a lifelong dream of mine ever since I'd watched *The Princess Bride* as a wide-eyed child.

But I had a bad horse who wanted to hurt me, and did so. I quickly discovered that this was real life, not a Disney movie where just anyone can jump on a horse and make it do what you want. It's not that easy. My horse was hell-bent on killing me. From the first time I crawled up into its saddle—indeed from the first time it laid eyes on me, I'm sure—the horse knew on a native level that I had no experience riding horses.

The horse was passive-aggressive. When I kicked its flanks with the razor-sharp, star-spiked spurs on the heels of my boots to giddy up, the horse walked forward only three paces and stopped. When I kicked it again, it ignored me outright, a small smile curling on its lips.

It was toying with me.

When Carlton or the other ranch hands bestrode the exact same horse and lightly grazed its flanks with their boots, the horse shot forward like a ball loosed from a catapult. The horse moved even before their boots kissed its flesh. A horse's ability to read the competence, stature, and inborn character of a human being is astounding. Horses always know when a human is lying.

Dirty humans.

To show its disdain for me (I wanted to tell the horse this really wasn't necessary, I know my place) and its resentment at being tasked with ferrying around a novice, the horse simply ignored my commands. When everyone else kicked off at five in the morning to start the workday, leaving me behind in humiliating fashion, I had no choice but to kick the horse in its ribs as hard as I could so that I wouldn't miss the workday entirely. I didn't know where the others were going and wouldn't be able to catch up if they rode out of sight.

The Australian morning was bleak, frosty and cold; the sun had not yet risen to bathe it in the Venus-like inferno it would become by midmorning. Though it was cold, perspiration broke out on my forehead as the others pounded out of sight, leaving me on the verge of missing the workday completely. Frustration welled up in me and I kicked the horse again, this time with all my weight behind the spurs, and I felt the metal spikes sink into its skin, piercing its flesh like a fish knife.

That had to have hurt. That kind of pain could not easily be ignored unless the horse was completely psychotic, which I was beginning to think was a distinct possibility. The horse lifted its head up proudly, trotted forward a few paces, and then broke into a bumpy canter. I kicked it again, but it declined to move into a full run. I limped along after the others. That day my horse cooperated with my instructions up to a point—always half-heartedly, never fully—and wouldn't run no matter how hard I kicked it. A canter is a bumpy, disjointed, uncomfortable ride, whereas a run is smooth, and the horse knows this, so it deliberately kept me in a canter all day. I didn't know then that it was merely biding its time, patiently waiting for the moment it had preselected to fuck me over.

That happened late in the day. The sun was sagging low in the sky and had just touched down to the horizon when we arrived at a large clearing where we had rustled a great mass of cattle. They were milling about, grazing on dry grass.

The day was nearly over. I began to dismount when, just as my right foot came free of the stirrup, the horse all at once bolted forward from zero to sixty in a flat dead run. I never knew a horse could accelerate from a standstill to full speed faster than a Lamborghini. It shot forward like a greyhound loosed from a box, tearing ahead with mind-boggling speed, and headed straight toward a ridge of trees on the far edge of the clearing. I couldn't get my right foot back inside the stirrup because we were going so fast that I was literally twisting in the wind like laundry flapping from a single clothespin in a hurricane, just barely hanging on for dear life. I screamed and ducked as the horse, without breaking speed, launched itself full-bore into a thicket of leaves, trunks, and branches.

Now I was crashing through stinging tree branches in thickening darkness. We must have been hurtling along at fifty miles per hour or more. My left leg was still locked in its stirrup as my right leg flailed wildly out into space. I desperately clutched the reins with my right hand and grabbed a clump of the horse's mane with my left hand, which probably enraged it further. I just barely ducked under a particularly thick branch, then twisted willy-nilly and lost my balance completely. I went reeling out of the stirrup, hit my head hard on a heavy branch as I fell, and crash-landed on top of a large log on my left arm. I felt like I'd fallen from a great height. I *had* fallen from a great height. My body hurt so bad, at such a blinding pitch, that I had to wait thirty seconds, lying perfectly still, before I could tell whether any bones were broken.

I looked up through dull vision struck glassy by pain and saw the horse standing above me. It had circled back and was standing directly over me. It looked down at me, grinning from ear to ear just like a human. I groaned and rolled away from it, rolling on top of my damaged left arm, which caused me to cry out in pain. The horse had been fucking with me from the start, and now its revenge was as complete as Monte Cristo's.

It gave a bravura, delighted whinny and then pranced off into the forest, free, leaving me alone. Finally the pain in my arm subsided just enough for me to know that no bones were broken. I crossed myself—having no medical insurance will do that to you—and lying there across the log, cradling my damaged arm, I realized I was never going to be a cowboy. Because I couldn't ride a horse—something my tormentor never let me forget. For how could you be a cowboy when you couldn't ride a horse?

When I arrived at breakfast the next morning, Alison was gone.
"Where's Alison?" I asked Carlton.
"Who?" Carlton said.
"The South African."
Carlton raised his eyebrows.
"You picked us up at the rodeo together—I mean the roundup."
Carlton turned and called to his petite wife, Trish, who was my age, "Honey, what happened to that girl we hired?"
But Trish disappeared into the kitchen carrying two armloads of plates.
The insane aboriginal who had tormented me in the forest, his eyes forever on me, shook the box of cheerios in my face. I backed my chair away. He reached down and scratched his butt with his hand and pushed his palm into my face. I ignored him.
Mojito leaned down and deposited a fresh pot of coffee and a plate of burnt white toast on the table. Carlton picked up a piece of blackened toast and examined it.
"Mojito, have you seen Alison?" I asked.
As she bent over the table Mojito's prodigious chest strained against the confines of her shirt, the fabric getting no relief from the pressure and appearing in danger of splitting open. Alison had been mannish, but for the first time I noticed that Mojito was pretty, despite my original impression that she was not. In fact, she was red-hot.

The aboriginal scratched his ass again and reached across the table and stuck his first two fingers up my nostrils. Angrily I slapped his hand away.

Our job most days was to draft the cattle, drafting meaning separating them into three types: steer, cow, and calf. Or male, female, and baby. We had to separate each category into separate pens. We were breaking up cattle families because the buyer purchased cattle by type. Cattle ranching is cruel.

In the beginning the herd all clings together in the main pen, no different than humans, none of them wishing to be apart from one another. Our job was to provoke them, shake the center loose, and get the cattle running helter-skelter so that we could pick them off one by one and funnel them into the small drafting pen in more manageable numbers of ten to twenty. From here we could more easily draft this smaller group, funneling them one at a time into the different pens of their type.

To kickstart the process of breaking up the main herd, we ran at the mass of cows, waving our arms and shouting and banging pans and drum cymbals to scare them into motion. Jangling, metallic sounds and machine noises scare most animals into running. Except seals and horses because they're too damn smart—they're smarter than humans actually. The trick, since you have to be inside the herd with the cows to scare them, is not to get trampled when they start running. Frightened cows are like frightened humans—when feeling threatened, some of them spontaneously attack. Humans are really no more evolved on the primal level than animals. Not enough eons have elapsed for us to evolve beyond animals on an emotional level. A skittish cow can turn on you and ram and headbutt you and then just start full-on kicking your head in and stamping the living shit out of you. Cattle have personalities the same as humans do. Some are docile; some are vicious. Some are sweet, and some hate you with an unquenchable desire to kill you for no apparent reason at all. I was kicked and gored several times during these days of heavy mustering, and my body still bears nicks and scars from those injuries today. Running with the bulls in Pamplona is a social media update for pussies compared with what I was doing.

We made jangling noise to frighten the tangle of cows in the main herd and then picked off the ones that ran, just as a predator picks off the weakest animal of a group in the wild. Only humans reward the weakest humans with a desk job. After I nudged ten or twenty cattle into the smaller drafting pen, it was easier to manipulate this smaller number. From here I nudged them one at a time through an onward gate, where Carlton was waiting atop a wooden tower, as Bob Cranston had done. Carlton identified each animal by sight and called out, "Cow!" "Push!" (for steers) or "Calf!" Three ranch hands stood in front of three pens and coaxed each animal inside the appropriate gate for their type. Because the animals were running, we had to move quickly or a cow might run through the wrong gate. This was miscategorization. Carlton was furious when this happened—the buyer could complain because he's paying for one type of cow and not another.

    Once we had all the males, females, and babies in their respective pens, next up was branding them. We branded the cattle so that the buyer and other ranchers knew they were ours, preventing theft, accidental or otherwise. From the pens, we had to push the cattle through the races. The races are a single-lane corridor of fence that are too narrow for the cattle to move from side to side so they can only move forward in a single-file line. At that point we have unimpeded access to the cow in the front of the line, and it has no means of escape. Then you can grab the cow by its legs and get your whole body underneath it and, using your back, flip the whole cow upside down like a wrestler performing a cheap shot against an opponent. *Hey, that's below the belt, asshole,* the cow would say if it could talk.

And then with the cow lying helplessly on its back you can hogtie its legs in the air and press the red hot poker into its skin. When the cow feels the brand that's as hot as the surface of a star sink into its flesh, its eyes open up wide and it screams in pain like the lambs Clarice Starling heard in Montana as a child.

It's pretty awful to watch.

Kind of sick actually.

Unless you're a sadist like Coby Cranston, who licked his dry lips and panted excitedly, "Do it, Tom, oh yeah, do it …" when I pressed the pulsing hot poker into the animal's flesh. Coby reminded me a lot of Zed in *Pulp Fiction*.

Finally we sold the cattle. The buyer sent up a huge truck that was the size of a tender called a roadtrain to come and collect them. On the last day of their life, before a giant mallet the size of Colossus at Rhodes slams down on their head, instantly removing the life from their body, we pushed the cows into the races one final time. One by one they boarded the roadtrain or "barge of death" in a grim single-file line, the same way you board the economy section of an airplane. The barge of death then porters the suddenly pale-faced animals to the abattoir. A week later they are on your backyard grill and in your mouth.

You're welcome. For your barbecue.

I didn't know when I woke that morning that it was going to be such a traumatic day. I was out at five in the morning as usual, working harder than perhaps I have ever worked in my entire life. We were drafting cows into separate pens of steer, cow, and calf. As soon as one clutch of cattle was drafted, I jumped back over the races into the big pen where the main herd still loitered. Then I jumped up and down like a scarecrow on fire to scare more cows into the smaller drafting pen, moved them into their category pens, and then repeated the process over and over for the rest of the day.

After running nonstop for many hours in unforgiving heat without taking a break, I began to get very dehydrated without noticing it. We were so busy that I only had a couple mouthfuls of water from a small canteen we'd brought that was nearly empty. Carlton, like the Cranstons, was not one for taking many breaks. The aboriginal ranch hands didn't seem as dehydrated as I was; perhaps they were more acclimated to the desert because they had been born into it. They also weren't running around as much as I was. Carlton had given them just one job to do, while I was assigned to bang cymbals in the main pen, then run over to the drafting pen to move the cows into the category pens, and run back, and I was constantly running back and forth between the pens. Perhaps I'd gotten the worst job because I was the greenhorn. Or perhaps because I'm too nice.

In the early afternoon Trish brought us some cake and soda during a five-minute break, the first one we'd had all day. I vacuumed down both, and apparently the intake of sugar, instead of the water I really needed, combined with the few minutes of sitting, caused my dehydrated muscles to tighten. After that break, any abrupt movement I made caused some or all of the muscles in my legs to suddenly seize up in a massive, ultra-painful cramp that completely immobilized me. I'd had a charley horse before, but this was a full-body cramp, every muscle clenching and locking down forcefully on itself, with no chance of moving while under lockdown.

I tried to jump over the races and run to the pens, but my body would seize from the sudden jerking movement of jumping or lifting my leg. The muscle seizures were so intense and the pain from them so blinding that it was momentarily intolerable. I cursed, grimaced, and ground my teeth. Forced to stop whatever I was doing and kneel to the ground like a priest before a banker, I could do nothing but wait until my muscles unclenched in their own time. But there was no letting up in the work and Carlton and the others were so immersed that I'm not sure anyone noticed I was struggling. I tried to keep up, but I simply could not move when one of the spasms struck. If a cow charged or kicked me while I was locked down, I wouldn't be able to do a thing, and if the cow hit me in the right place, it could break my bones or even kill me, I suppose. Cattle are immensely physically strong creatures—they could put the Terminator in a shallow grave with lightning ease. There's no man that could beat a cow in a fair fight. Only intelligence and tools make us their masters. If these beasts ever evolved and became as smart as we are, they could kill us with their superior strength (and, one presumes, the guns they would start holding).

While herding a gaggle of cattle from the big pen into the drafting pen, a flutter of movement on my periphery notified me that something bad was about to happen. In a surprise blitzkrieg maneuver, a cow jumped on top of the back of a smaller cow in front of it and springboarded off its ass with its back hooves, launching itself fully airborne. This is not an exaggeration: I saw this—it was surreal. The cow pushed off the smaller animal like a swimmer pushing off the deep end of a pool and it sailed through the air and kicked me square in the chest with its two front hooves like two pistons. I flew backward ten feet as though Superman had shoved me, and crashed to the ground in a dirty heap, whorls of dust coiling around my wrists like handcuffs.

When I hit the ground, my body convulsed in a massive spasm, every single muscle collapsing back to zero, and my wrists and ankles were yanked to the ground as though pulled by magnets. I was as crippled as if a New Orleans witchdoctor were pushing pins into my voodoo doll at ever-deeper increments of pain.

A large cow saw me lying helpless on the ground and attacked. It had identified an opportunity to take out one of the human oppressors, and it did not hesitate to act. If only I could achieve such boldness in my life. The cow wheeled, locked me in its crosshairs, and charged. I screamed as I watched it building speed and barrel down on me. I was pinned to the ground by the muscle lockdown, unable to move. Instinctually, like a wild thing that comes into contact with a stronger creature, I simply extended my two hands out in front of my face to absorb the impact, and placed them against the cow's forehead in the fraction of a second before it ran over me like a freight train. Somehow—I don't know how—the animal spooked at the touch of my hands against its forehead (*Eww, gross, human hands...*) and it lurched violently to one side. One of the beast's great hooves thundered down beside my left ear as it abruptly changed directions at the last possible moment like a train averted onto another track just before running over a body tied to the tracks. With this amazing stroke of luck, barely spared being trampled to death by this one-ton monster, I crawled over to a fence and pulled myself up it to avoid malevolent cows.

And that's when it happened. A small cry tore the air. A keen of fear. A tremor on the earth. A huge white bull charged the worker who was doing the herding with me—Josh, the aboriginal who was very experienced, but was taken by surprise by this bull, which shows it can happen to anyone. This poor aboriginal got absolutely *rolled* by this bull like nothing I've ever seen. The bull's eyes raged murder as it trampled the kid in a decidedly one-sided affair, stamping his face with its hooves and battering him again and again with its massive dinosaur head.

Bone white, the bull was a creature from the abyss, from your nightmares. As I looked on, I really thought the bull was going to take this kid's life right here. I'd already seen someone die in New Zealand; I thought this was going to be the second time. It was bloody and violent and bad. I stood frozen almost directly on top of the carnage as this immense animal—this great white hoofed Moby Dick, this Jaws with feet—was going absolutely medieval on this ranch hand.

Josh gripped the bull's head, his arm crooked at the elbow, trying to pull the beast's head into his breast to mitigate the gigantic hydraulic force the bull was ramming him with. He cried out, "What are you doing?" as if the monster was capable of mercy, and understanding English.

Then I heard Carlton's voice ring out, high and clear on the air like a bell, *"Tom, goddammit, help him, man!"*

I snapped out of my reverie. I was standing right in front of the mauling. The rampaging animal hadn't noticed me yet and I wasn't sure how to attack it. It occurred to me that the only thing I could really do was to swing my steel-toed boot around and roundhouse the animal in the skull. I wondered whether kicking an animal in the head would give me some dark thrill, or whether I could even do it at all. I'm not a violent person and had never physically abused an animal before. But I had to do it, because Carlton had ordered me to. Because this kid was going to die if I didn't.

As I pulled my leg back to kick, I tensed to give it everything I had, and just as I was about to kick, the tensing caused my body to seize and contract in a massive muscle spasm. Every corpuscle from my neck to my toes shuddered and pulled back to a singularity, and my leg wouldn't swing. I was so dehydrated that my body was rebelling on a massive scale. I stood frozen in place like a statue, unable to move.

Since I had made this motion to attack it, the beast finally noticed me. It looked at me reluctantly, like someone in a bar who has been ignoring you but has finally decided you're a nuisance that has to be dealt with before he can return to more important matters. The bull's eyes were scarlet and it issued a war cry at me. The beast was furious. Its white body and terrifying red eyes made it look like a poltergeist, and only when I looked into its eyes filled with rage did I wonder, *Why is an animal that's supposed to be dumb so angry?*

It charged me. To save my life, I was forced to rip myself out of a deep muscle lockdown. The pain from this was indescribable, like a billion tiny needles being pushed into the interior walls of my arteries where I couldn't stop or reach them. Writhing in excruciating pain, I threw myself onto the fence as every muscle in my body sang out in white-hot pain leaving me gasping in agony. Jesus wouldn't have traded places with me during the Passion at that moment. He would have said, "I'll take my chances here."

When I flung myself onto the fence, I hoped that the diversion had provided Josh an opening to escape, but he was still lying on the ground in a crumpled heap and the bull, intent on finishing the job it had started, had not gone for my bluff, which in all fairness was pretty weak, and was still ravaging him.

A high, sonorous note filled the air—*"Fuck you, you white cunt!"*

And there was Carlton Curr, my boss, an enormous man at six foot four, forty years of age, a man's man through and through, charming in a Southern style, tough, rich, and handsome to boot, running straight at the monster like Ahab himself. He was charging the beast, very much as Ahab would have charged the whale running over water if he could. The bull, its interest aroused by a more worthy opponent, left Josh, and rounded with surprising humanlike agility. It charged Carlton.

The beast had both the monstrous strength of a Tyrannosaurus Rex and the nimble grace of a ballerina. An unholy chimera, it was the perfect killing machine. Somewhere the great white shark was nodding in respect. As the bull charged, it was like the last scene in the movie *Legends of the Fall*. I thought, *Carlton, you're my hero, but this is one battle you're not going to win. Just look at that goddamn thing.*

Carlton ran straight at the monster. The bull's flanks rippled in huge, fluttering spasms of muscle as it exploded off the turf with tremendous power, accelerating, revealing the physical perfection God had given the animal, its symmetrical beauty and pure evil. Carlton had nothing in his hands, no weapon to speak of. I thought, *Who is this guy? What does he intend to do?* The bull collided with the giant of a man right in the chest. Carlton crumpled like an origami swan and disappeared under the bull's hooves. The monster trucked over him like the iceberg ran over the *Titanic*, and it was over.

Suddenly Carlton sprang up as though nothing had happened and jogged cheerfully over to me like a high school quarterback after completing a particularly easy touchdown. He leaped up onto the fence beside me while the bull did a perfect three-point turn that would have earned it a driver's license.

The bull zoomed over to us like a racecar, again with surprising speed. It snapped its jaws at my feet and bit my ankles with its teeth, furious, jumping up and down and headbutting me in the ass with its gargantuan head, this monster that made the Balrog look like a Chihuahua. It was trying to bite my shoe and pull me down off the fence as we kicked at its blunt face from above.

Carlton was screaming, *"My ribs! My ribs! You broke my ribs you miserable cunt! Goddamn unmanageable cunt!"*

Carlton looked freaked out and a little pale—I had never seen him look haunted like that before. He was breathing in sharp labored gasps and clutching his rib cage.

He looked at me, both of us standing side by side on the fence, his eyes wet from the pain of a few broken ribs, and he said, "What are you doing? I only have one leg."

It was true. About sixteen months earlier, Carlton had been mustering cattle from a plane, and the plane had crashed to earth from eighty meters up in the sky. What would have killed any other man, Carlton walked away from.

Ranchers have so much cattle spread over their land that some cattle stations, like Taldora, are literally the size of a small country. Rich ranchers buy a plane or hire a helicopter to muster their cattle from above, especially wayward gaggles that have wandered to remote corners of the property, diffused over vast distances, that would otherwise be impossible to bring back. The cows are afraid of loud machine noises, so a low-flying airplane or helicopter can nudge them back in the right direction.

I had the chance to ride around in a helicopter.

The pilot bumped the joystick, and the helicopter dipped down to earth and skimmed along the ground of a vast open plain with a ridge of forest at the end of it. The pilot skillfully maneuvered the chopper *right alongside a solitary running horse.* The magnificent animal's hind muscles rippled as it ran flat out across the plain at full speed. The pilot angled the chopper beside the graceful animal. Instead of changing directions under duress, the horse continued pounding straight ahead in an overwhelming effort to outrun the helicopter.

"Go for it," the Aussie pilot grinned to me, his aviators glinting in the sunlight.

I reached out the open pod, which was windowless on both sides, and laid my hand on the velvety-smooth hide of the running horse as it screamed ahead in real time. Both the helicopter and the horse were tearing across the plain at a hundred miles per hour, and yet I touched the animal's glistening skin as it ran, as though we were both standing still. It was magic. It was so surreal that afterward I wondered if it had really happened.

The pilot tapped the joystick and the chopper leaned back and shot skyward again, the glorious horse receding backward from view like an airplane falling backward into the sky after you've skydived out of it. The flyboy grinned, loving what he did for a living, delighted at his ability to catch a horse out of the sky.

Carlton only survived the fall to earth from eighty meters up because he's such a tough son of a bitch and has a tough guy's name like Carlton Curr. Really, could you pick a better name for a cowboy? The crash shattered one of his legs and put him in the hospital for a year, but he was walking around fine when I was here. Trish told me that he had special instruments inserted in his shoe to keep his leg from collapsing, but I wouldn't have known it other than a slight limp that he carried. Carlton also spoke with a lisp because the crash had shredded his tongue as though it had been pushed through a cheese grater, and the area around his mouth was marked up with little red inflections like it had been whipped with the cat o' nine tails.

But if anything, all this only enhanced Carlton's magnetic presence, made him even more larger-than-life. He was a mighty man who had that special quality called leadership so few men have—one in a thousand. He had a gravitational pull that rivaled the sun's: everything around him was attracted into his orbit, me included. He was the kind of person you only encounter a few times across a lifetime. He was burning bright, like a blue flame against a dead background, had an aura, and he could have been a successful politician, movie actor, or Supreme Allied Commander of Europe. He had that compelling quality that rivets the attention. And he was strong as Achilles. Taking his life would not be easy, for the white bull, for man, for nature, even for fate. He could fall from the sky in a broken airplane, smash into the ground at four hundred miles per hour, and walk away from it under his own power. The man was indestructible, goddamn invincible. Carlton was somehow stronger than anyone or anything around him. And he was humble. Most importantly, he had a big heart. In a way he was the father I always wanted. I could admire him.

I couldn't tell Carlton about my body seizing up in muscle spasms because it sounded ridiculous, like an excuse. Carlton thought I felt bad about not doing more to help Josh, and he was a nice guy, so he said, "Nah, you did good, kid." And the ruse had worked—Carlton had sufficiently drawn the bull's attention away so that Josh had been able to crawl to safety. Josh was unresponsive and bloodied, but not fatally. He would live.

There were still four more days before my Australian work visa expired, but Carlton was going to Julia Creek the next day to pick up supplies. I asked him if he could take me with him then.

He said no.

Carlton was a good guy. I had lucked out getting him after the bad experience at Numil. Carlton was always complimenting me on my work and giving me free beers—his way of showing that he approved of my work, or just approved of me. I was surprised when one day he offered me extended work on his brother Marcus' ranch down the way. The Cranstons had been cheap and tightfisted, but Carlton was the opposite. He was kind and generous. Tough. Strong. Routinely shrugged off death. He'd put himself in harm's way, thrown his life in the balance, to save that aboriginal employee as if it were his own son. I thought if there was a war on, or he did something I was actually interested in, I would follow this man.

As it was, that night in the dark hours before Carlton would rise to drive to Julia Creek for supplies, I had a lucid dream where I wanted to leave because my body was wracked, but Carlton had me pinned down on a wrestling mat and was laughing maniacally while I frantically tried to tap out. "Carlton! Carlton!" I screamed as he laughed and slowly bent my arm backward at the elbow until it snapped like a twig. Then all of a sudden the horse—a goddamn genius with an IQ of 250—was standing over me, looking down at me and laughing. It lowered one horseshoed hoof onto my face and slowly mashed it into hamburger. I felt my face being pulverized into the floor by a hoof so strong that I couldn't stop it. I was still conscious when my skull started to crack ...

I sat up in a cold sweat, Dracula-like from the coffin. I can never remember my dreams upon waking, but that was the rare instance when I remembered every detail. Disturbed, knowing I had no chance of falling back asleep after that nightmare, I looked at the clock and saw it was one o'clock, three hours ahead of my daily wakeup at four.

I was becoming a real farmer.

Filled with a rare conviction that I shouldn't be here anymore, I lay awake in the darkness for hours. I was wide awake, as awake as it's possible to be. The feeling of dread and sheer panic that had consumed me every single day since I'd arrived in this country dissipated with the decision to leave.

I rose before four and went to the kitchen, where Carlton was already roasting coffee beans and frying eggs alone in the predawn hour. Accustomed to solitude at this hour, he didn't hear me come in, and I saw him first. He wore a content smile and was humming merrily. He was in his element. He truly loved his life, and it's easy to love anyone who loves their life that much. He was in his bliss—that golden, sacrosanct hour before dawn—cooking breakfast in his quiet, warm, well-lighted kitchen. He looked up and our eyes met, his expression more like a father's than an employer's, and maybe I felt the same way. A wellspring of love for him bubbled up inside of me.

I told him I wanted to leave, and this time he said okay, though he mocked me a little. He called me a pussy and a cunt. He cried out loudly in his empty kitchen, "You have no heart! You bleeding cunt!"

He didn't hold back. An emotional man, he never attempted to mask his feelings. He taunted me and challenged me to stay. But I detected the trace of a smile behind the fusillade and as always, the kindness in his eyes. He was a good man inside and that part rises to the surface. Honest, open heart. I think he was a little disappointed I was leaving because I think he liked me too.

I was sorry to disappoint Carlton, but I was messed up to the point where I was having difficulty walking, and more importantly, I was really over it. The horse had crushed me, had broken me physically, psychologically, and emotionally. But I didn't tell Carlton any of that. In that culture men keep their injuries to themselves. I was also very careful never to cross my legs while seated and never to stand with my body weight shifted onto one leg to rest the other like the cosmopolitan city dweller I really am. Rather, I always stood with both legs ramrod straight, hands on hips, scarcely breathing, glowering at some point in the middle distance. This pseudomasculine posture mostly kept people from fucking with me, until a situation arose where it was obvious I didn't know what I was doing, which was often. Then people either fucked with me or were nice to me depending on who they were—much like all people and all life everywhere.

The question begged at me for just a moment, *Why am I here?*

Then the question dissolved in a rich and buttery happiness. I knew why. I lived for this stuff—to visit every nook and cranny of our wide, beautiful world. There's nothing like it—exploring strange lands. At times I would see a towering range of mountains far off in the distance and thrilled by the high dark peaks, just set out running toward them. Or I would see lights twinkling on some high steep strange hillside and impelled, would change course and just set out for them, drawn by their mystery and the wide, open space. The great love is just traveling overland, or on a ship, with nothing but a bag on your back, no map. Traveling as you go, from place to place, driven always by the desire to go further … to, if you could, go further than anyone has ever been.

Three days after Carlton dropped me off in Julia Creek, a local bus dumped me in a small coastal fishing village somewhere near Brisbane, like a kidnapping victim whose ransom had been paid. I sniffed the ocean air and smiled as I inhaled the vastly appealing bouquet of salt and brine. Evil's hold is weak near the sea. The sea is life itself. I looked around at the unfamiliar terrain—civilization.

That first day back I wandered the cobblestoned backstreets of the obscure fishing village like a zombie half-dead, half-alive, thinking how bizarre it was to see people eating in restaurants.

Why eat in a restaurant? *That's so weird.*

To be honest, many things yuppies do are a complete waste of time. Eating in restaurants is one of them. You watch them—what the hell are they doing? Anything to try and kill off or paper over their extreme boredom.

After a couple of days I was able to rejoin the Oz Experience, the prepaid backpacker bus service that circles the country with pickup points in every major Australian city. As I sat on the little bus, the driver put on Green Day. Everyone else started bopping their heads and singing along. They knew all the words and obviously liked the music, but I kept thinking how boring it was. I didn't understand why the driver didn't play "Save a Horse (Ride a Cowboy)." It was so much better than Green Day. Alternative rock doesn't have jack shit on country.

He who has felt the deepest grief is best able to experience supreme happiness. We must have felt what it is to die, Morrel, that we may appreciate the enjoyments of life.

—Alexandre Dumas, The Count of Monte Cristo

10

The Best Years of Our Lives

I wandered through the Christmas party at Sony Pictures. I had already quit one year ago, but I felt like going to the annual Christmas party, so I went.

Actually I broke in.

It was a party I had attended five Christmases in five years working here, but because I no longer worked at the studio it felt more special this time, tinged with nostalgia for what was and what might have been. The party was always well funded and splashed out in a large circus tent pitched on the middle of the studio lot. It was filled with old amusement park games and curios—shooting gallery, apple bobbing, dunk tank, strong-man hammer throw, Skee-Ball, Pac-Man arcade, ring toss, basketball shooting—all the games we loved as kids. They had everything except the bearded lady and man on stilts. Chinese lanterns floated on the ceiling like lanterns twinkling down the bayou. It was enchanting.

Suddenly a pair of strong arms looped around my waist. I was grabbed roughly from behind and yanked backward into someone's pelvis. I craned my neck around. It was Janine, my boss of the last five years.

"*Whaaat!*" she said. "*Oh my God! What are you doing here?*"

To my enormous surprise, since she was the one who had tried to push me out of Sony, she threw her arms around my neck and hugged me. She pressed her chest against mine and our faces mashed together. Our lips even pressed together for a couple of seconds. I couldn't believe it: I was kissing her. It occurred to me that if I hadn't worked for her but had just met her out somewhere, like a bar, or even here, we might very well have ended up in bed together.

I opened my mouth to say, "I thought you hated me," but was stymied by her large breasts resting on my chest like two German beer steins resting on a shelf in the garage.

We stood locked in a febrile embrace. Her breath fell hot on my face.

"Oh my God, you're heeere! How did you get in?" she said.

"I know the security guard, Darnell," I said, nodding toward the entrance.

Darnell, the buff black guard in charge of the guest list, also guarded the movie sets, and I had gotten to know him during my wide wanderings on the lot in search of films in production over the years.

Janine's eyes dilated. Her pupils were the size of saucers. *"No you didn't!"* she squealed.

"Janine, just let it be," I said.

An old fear welled up in me that she would call security and have me thrown out. She was that kind of person—Sigourney Weaver in *Working Girl*, Dolores Umbridge in *Harry Potter*, Salieri, Nurse Ratched—the bad guy in office movies, basically. Like her forebears—small-minded people of limited talent and likability who resort to corruption and sabotage to stop people with more of both—Janine fit the mold to a tee.

She stared into my eyes. Her pupils were now the size of kittens. I stared back, horrified.

She burst out laughing.

She was drunk.

She didn't call security. She was still holding on to me like the last lifeboat off the *Titanic*. Her breasts heaved against my chest like water breaking against a brick dam. I could feel the tidal currents of those formidable orbs, and I suppose she was enjoying the brick dam. The woman who had power harassed me was now sexually harassing me … Well, when an attractive woman decides to prop her rack on your chest you can't really call it sexual harassment. You just have to decide whether you're going to take her home or not.

Not.

I hadn't forgotten what eventually made me leave Sony. I broke away. She stood smiling foolishly at me, both eyebrows raised, mouth open, a drink in her hand.

"Merry Christmas, Janine," I said, and moved on.

There were only a few other people I recognized. Most of the other junior people hadn't even stayed this long. It was a bunch of doe-eyed freshmen. Maybe I had stayed long enough. Time to try something new. The people who clung to their jobs were mostly directors and above who were making good bread already.

The oriental red lanterns dancing along the ceiling drew my eye until they tapered off in a dead end at a far wall of the tent. To my surprise, a person edged out of a hidden flap in the wall, a flap I otherwise never would have seen. For a brief moment the room behind the flap was illuminated and I glimpsed men in white robes in a séance-type setting. Intrigued, I walked over and ducked inside the clandestine room. A handful of people—partygoers and robed fortune-tellers—were seated and standing, talking.

Three tables stood side by side. The room was like an 1890 belle epoque Parisian party room. Dimly lighted with antique furniture and lamps, it shimmered in an antebellum glow. An elegant young black man with finely hewn bone structure and a kingly cast to his face stood near me, and I sat down with him to have my fortune read. I had done this once before at my high school prom's after-party. That fortune-teller had been a total hack: she told me I would meet the love of my life at age twenty-three. Hadn't happened. So I didn't really believe in it but was game for some fun, and not a little taken with the beautiful anachronistic ambience of the room that was not unlike one of our movie sets.

The regal black man looked at my palm. "Hmm," he said.

He frowned. His brow furrowed.

He laid out five tarot cards on a table face up and asked me to pick one. The cards were ornate in the manner of gothic tarot—serpents entwined with a bearded Neptune, sword and trident, that sort of thing. All had roughly the same mythic quality, so I chose one. The sage sighed.

"You're going to go overseas for a long time," he said.

"How did you know?" I asked.

My own answer startled me. Up until that point I had not planned on taking a trip around the world, but it was almost as if some deeper part of me—the part that's timeless and has already lived your own past-present-future—already knew it was going to happen. Maybe it was his saying it that planted the idea in my mind in the first place. Who knows?

He frowned again. "You're going to struggle," he said, looking a bit sad. "You're going to have a hard time."

I swallowed. "Um, that's not really necessary. I'm quite all right. I don't need to struggle. Thank you but no—"

"It'll take a while," he continued, "but ... you'll be okay ... finally." A long pause. He shut his eyes and seemed to commune deeply. "Yeah," he said.

"What?" I cried out. "I'll be okay?" I asked desperately, my voice rising.

He paused as if waiting for instructions. "Yes," he said, nodding infinitesimally. He stood perfectly still, as if the communing had left him spent.

"Thank you," I said. "What's your name?"

"Justin," he said.

As this room was an antechamber apart from the main party, I asked whether I was supposed to pay for the reading.

"No," he said.

"Would you accept a tip?" I asked.

He hesitated. He looked as though he was going to say no but then seemed to change his mind. "Okay," he said.

I handed him ten dollars, then turned and left the room. When I reentered the main party, I suddenly quite strongly missed the fey chamber I had just left. Compared with the large party, the fin de siècle room was so much more exciting. I turned around and walked straight back inside. Immediately the room appeared different. It was still there, but Justin was gone. I looked around for two minutes but he didn't reappear. The antebellum shimmer was also gone; the room was well-lighted now. I asked another fortune-teller where Justin was.

"Justin? He left an hour ago."

"No," I said. "I was with him just a minute ago. He just read my palm. Did you see?" I pointed at the empty chair. "I left the room for a second and came right back, and now he's gone."

The guy shrugged. "I'm telling you, Justin went home an hour ago when his shift ended. He hasn't been here since. He left through that back flap there." He pointed to a different flap at the back of the tent.

"Justin—the black guy, right?" I asked.

"Yeah, that's him. He left an hour ago." There were only five people in the room; it was a small room, about twenty-five square feet. You couldn't miss the only black fortune-teller.

"You saw me here a minute ago?" I pressed.

"Yeah," he said. "You were sitting there. But Justin wasn't there."

"Is there another black fortune-teller?"

"No," he said.

I shook my head.

I strode to the back wall of the tent and pushed through the heavy flap. It led out onto the empty lot. As the flap fell down behind me, all the sound from the party was sucked up and suddenly I was engulfed in total darkness. There was nothing there but blacktop and the silent night.

I had no idea who had just taken my fortune.

I joined Sony Pictures when I was twenty-two after a year working at a smaller movie studio that was acquired by Paramount Pictures. At Sony the years went by with a few promotions and raises. One day I woke up and realized I was twenty-seven. *Shit, that went fast.* I had been at Sony almost five years and was stuck in a marketing job that had gradually become more clerical and less satisfying. I'd enjoyed it the first three years, but now it had become routine.

It had always been my dream to work at a movie studio, and I felt blessed to be at Sony—its Columbia Pictures lot had once been MGM, Hollywood's first studio, and our lot was easily Hollywood's grandest, the jewel of Tinseltown. My job—creating DVD release schedules as head of Worldwide DVD Programming for Sony's international territories—was good. Most importantly, I was working at one of Hollywood's five major studios, which delighted me to no end. It had been my dream job since college, and I had worked hard, and been lucky, to get here. I was working in Hollywood, where I wanted to be, around creative people, which was thrilling, though not yet making a living as a creative myself, which was my real goal.

I had the joy of being around major movie stars strolling leisurely across the lot like Cary Grant and Katharine Hepburn in cinema's heyday. Don't let anyone tell you the heyday was any time other than the 1940s—the storytelling and quality of the screenplays reached an apex that decade. The 1980s also sparkled with creative verve and a seismic leap in originality as auteurs like John Hughes brought their visions to bear, and the 1990s had a few inventive, vastly influential films such as *Pulp Fiction*, *Forrest Gump*, and *The Matrix*.

When I worked at Sony, we made more garbage than a family of four on a weekend camping trip. We made enough bad movies to landfill a new borough in the ocean off of Manhattan. They could really use some good leadership over there (mine) instead of making awful *Ghostbusters* remakes of out-of-date properties. They need fresh stories that have the potential to become franchises—not remake their old library. I could help them with that.

Because I did once before.

Working on the lot was a dream. I walked around looking for stars descending from trailers onto movie sets. I saw someone nearly every time I went out. There's Harrison Ford on the set of *What Lies Beneath*. There's Tom Hanks in the flesh! He's super skinny—how'd he do that?—and walking around the wave pool set (really the size of a Jacuzzi) of *Castaway*. There's the *Planet of the Apes* set, an entire jungle milieu built inside a warehouse, and the New York City Hall set of *Spider-Man*.

One day Darnell stopped me on the lot.

"Hey Tom, Madonna is outside warehouse 23."

"Thanks brother." I clasped his hand, and hugged him.

Aspiring to an autograph, I grabbed the only thing connected with Madonna I could find—a CD of the soundtrack to her then-husband Guy Ritchie's movie *Snatch,* which Sony produced—and set off for warehouse 23. I curved around the side of the soundstage, and there she was: Madonna was reposing alone on asphalt—no bodyguards, nothing—taking a break from rehearsing for her Blond Ambition Tour. I walked up to her with a huge smile on my face.

"Madonna," I said, "I'm not gay, but I'm still a huge fan."

I thought it was funny, just enough of a slight, I hoped, to attract the attention of a supernova megastar like Madonna. It's always best to treat everyone as an equal, never higher, never lower.

Like most celebrities, Madonna looks normal on screen, but in reality she's quite petite. She was bottle blonde for her tour, and she and her husband had recently filmed the Sony mega-bomb *Swept Away*, a remake of the revered 1974 Italian movie that was one of the ten best films of that decade. This was during the period when Madonna had muscled out her biceps, and I got to see them up close. She took the CD from me, ignoring my proffered pen.

She looked at the CD case and frowned.

"*Snatch* is your husband's movie," I said helpfully, hoping that spousal love would entice her. "Would you sign it?"

Madonna looked at me with the exact same expression she wears throughout her Sony movie *A League of Their Own*. "It's not my movie. Ask him to sign it," she said, and slapped the case back in my hand as I stood mouthing the air like a fish out of water.

"But, Madonna …" I sputtered.

She spun around and sashayed off, swinging her ass from left to right in exaggerated motions.

Yes, Madonna, I see you've still got it.
Dammit!

After making *Snatch* and marrying Madonna, Guy Ritchie didn't make another good movie for the ten years they were married, if ever again, and I could now understand why.

On another occasion I happened to spy Tobey Maguire and Kirsten Dunst strolling across the lot together. I decided to follow them. They had been making *Spider-Man*, and the press were saying they were an item. I had my doubts. He's a fussy, nebbish, vegetarian introvert, not much taller than a midget, and I figured Kirsten, being of German descent, would be into more masculine guys. What meat eater could ever be happy with a vegetarian? It's just not a match.

As they walked in the quiet privacy of the lot, they weren't holding hands, and I knew I was right. Soon, Sam Raimi, the director of *Spider-Man*, always dressed in a frumpy black suit and tie, joined them in front of an unmarked building. I knew something was up. I got right up behind Tobey as a security guard used a turnstile key to let them into the nondescript building.

The top of Tobey's head came up to my nipple. I peered down on the crown of his head. He looked no more than fifteen years old, though he must have been nearly twice that. He craned his neck around like a puffin bird and looked up at me with large wet eyes. He held the door for me.

"Thank you, Tobey," I said.

He blinked rapidly twice but said nothing. Polite kid making $15 million a picture. Someone he had never seen before was following his inner circle inside a secret building, and he wore a confused look that said, *Who are you?*

No acting there, I thought. That's real.

But celebrities live in a bubble, not the real world, and he had no ability to say no or start screaming at the top of his lungs, "*Imposter! Stranger who has nothing to do with our one-billion-dollar franchise cornerstone film behind me!*" It was a private screening room, one of countless number on the studio lot.

Tobey and Kirsten flopped down into two seats in the front row and Sam took a seat in the back. I sat directly behind Tobey and Kirsten so I could see whether they were holding hands or not. Incredibly, my primary interest was still of a tabloid nature—*are they fucking or not?* I'd had a crush on Kirsten ever since seeing her in *Bring It On*.

As I leaned forward, my breath fell hot on the back of Tobey's neck. For the second time in less than a minute he craned his neck around to see who was breathing on the nape of his neck. He looked straight in my eyes. I met his gaze and very, very slowly shook my head from side to side, indicating he should turn around and mind his own business. He did, and then, giraffe-like, I thrust my neck between them and looked down at their armrest. Nope, not holding hands.

I knew it!

The lights dimmed, and the projector made that famous clicking sound beloved by movie fans all around the world as the reel started turning, and suddenly an unfinished version of Sony's first *Spider-Man* movie flapped up onto the screen. All the acting scenes had been shot, but no special effects had been added yet. During the action scenes where there would be flying and fighting, the screen went black, and the words POW! and BAM!, like in the old *Batman* serial, appeared on the screen. Sam's inside joke. He would CGI in the special effects later.

All the actors' scenes were finished straight through to the end, though, and when the movie was over, I had a terrific realization: other than Sam, Tobey, Kirsten, and possibly the producer, I was the first person on earth to see *Spider-Man*. I was the fifth person in the world to see the first *Spider-Man* movie, which went on to have the largest opening weekend of all time, $114 million, and became Sony's most profitable movie ever.

On Monday morning after the opening weekend, I saw Sony's CEO and top brass embrace and hug each other in Columbia's courtyard, ebullient over achieving the all-time record. Little did they know I had seen the movie before they did.

When the lights came up, we stood and walked out. I was behind Kirsten Dunst, who carelessly held the door ajar for me but disappointingly didn't look back as Tobey had done. Kirsten was silly and carefree, not at all serious, and I envied her freedom. I nearly pulled her around and kissed her, so attracted to her I was. She seems smart and sexy on screen, but in real life she's much more *normal*. She was hot as hell, though—that much is the same. Though, again, much shorter than I expected.

Once we left the screening room, unable to pull myself away, I kept walking behind them, part of their posse now. Sam Raimi, Kirsten Dunst, Tobey Maguire, and me. Again, no hand holding between the two stars. Kirsten was single! I wanted to ask her out, but didn't quite have the mud to do it. What would a girl making $15 million a picture want with me? Now I could do it. They walked inside an unmarked office on the lot and I followed them in. Sam nodded to a woman sitting behind a desk close to the door.

"Good?" she asked him.

Sam, eccentric introvert himself, smiled idiosyncratically and didn't reply but simply shuffled forward, his feet not lifting off the ground as he walked, his too-baggy suit legs dragging across the floor as though exercise weights were strapped to his ankles. Sam always wore a rumpled suit no matter what.

The stars disappeared somewhere, and I found myself standing in front of the woman at the desk. She looked up at me with a wan expression, the same way Madonna looked at me. The woman opened her mouth to speak.

I jumped in first to make sure a friendly rapport was established. "Hi," I said, pumping out all my warmth and charm. "The movie was … wow—just terrific."

"Excuse me?" she said. "What are you talking about?"

"We just saw a rough cut of *Spider-Man*. It was amazing. Amazing like the amazing Spider-Man. It's going to do gangbuster business. We have a huge hit on our hands." I was rocking back and forth on my heels, enjoying myself.

The woman dropped her pen and sat up. "Who are you?"

"A fan," I said vaguely. "A fan of yours … I work here."

"Which department are you in? What's your name?"

I gulped. But to my mind I wasn't doing anything wrong. I'm not a sneaky person; I don't do anything I'm ashamed of, and I certainly don't lie. "I'm Tom. I work in home entertainment in Maxine's department." The woman reached for a phone and started dialing a number.

"And you are?" I asked cheerfully, still rocking back and forth on my heels.

"I'm Laura Ziskin. The producer of *Spider-Man*. That was a private screening you just saw. Do you have any idea how many millions of dollars are involved here?"

"Oh good," I said. "I'm glad they gave you a big budget to work with. It's going to pay off huge."

She stared at me.

"Don't worry; my lips are sealed. This conversation never happened."

"Get out."

"Yes, Ms. Ziskin."

I padded back to my office whistling, clueless and oblivious as ever, in love with the lot as always.

The lot was a menagerie. It was like the Serengeti, teeming with exotic wildlife. But the sun was setting now, and the lot was completely empty. Where was Darnell? Would he be able to secret me onto any more sets today? Where's Tom Hanks? Where's Leo? Can't get too greedy—it had been a good day already. I was still whistling when I entered the office.

"Where were you?" my coworker José asked.

"I just saw *Spider-Man*. Little bit disappointing, I have to say. I was hoping for a script with more teeth. CGI's not done yet, but all the acting scenes are." I yawned.

"Whaaaaat? You saw *Spider-Man*?" he said. "Hey, everybody, Tom saw *Spider-Man*!"

"Umm, yeah, like I said, it's not bad, but I was hoping for something a little sharper—"

Suddenly there was pandemonium as José spread the word around the department in a little over a second. A phone was ringing. Maxine, the head of our department, picked it up in her office. "Hello? ... Mmm ... Mhmm ... Mhmm, okay, thanks."

Maxine came out. "I got a call from Laura Ziskin. She says you saw a rough cut of *Spider-Man*. She's concerned about security. I told her, 'Oh, don't worry. It's just Tom—he's harmless.'"

"That's right!" I cried out. "I'm harmless!"

Maxine laughed and waved it away.

Janine was in a corner, growling like a cornered wolf.

Everyone else was buzzing now. I had injected a little excitement into a stale, boring afternoon at the office, and the cube rats were grateful. Maxine, laughing, turned around and went back inside her office.

My job more or less was sending a few Excel charts out to Sony's offices in countries around the world. The international aspect of the job was what I liked most of all. I bought *National Geographic's* largest world map, a monster at sixty-three inches across. It spanned the entire back wall of my office, nicely underscoring my position as head of worldwide DVD programming.

I stared at all those countries on earth and dreamed of visiting them. Part of my job was to phone our offices in random countries around the world three times a week just to check on them, remind them who's boss. With relish, I phoned Jakarta, Indonesia; Stockholm, Sweden; Bucharest, Romania; and Tokyo, Japan—all places I would one day visit on foot.

My emails and charts were like witty diplomatic cables from low-ranking officers in the field that no one reads or cares about. The territories all wanted to do their own thing, and at the end of the day, other than not renewing their contract or withholding the shipment of DVD masters, we had limited control over our satellite offices, wayward as they sometimes were. They knew their local markets better than we did, so while Peru might release *Soccer Dog* because Latin America is soccer crazy, they would refuse to release an urban comedy starring Ice Cube no matter how much we demanded it because they knew there's no audience for it in their country.

Sometimes we insisted the territory release a movie because it was a "Ben favorite." Ben was our president. For example, all the territories had to release *Frankenfish*, about a giant man-eating piranha on the loose, because Ben loved it. The subsidiaries added it to their schedules at our behest and pretended to release it but didn't, because they didn't want to take a bath on the marketing costs, which were theirs locally. Like most businesses, these sins could be overlooked as long as they turned a profit and the Incan gold hit Sony's coffers. Not turning a profit was the real sin. In that case we cut the licensee as soon as their contract was up and went with their competitor instead.

I was fortunate to be at Sony Pictures for DVD's beginnings and subsequent boom around the world. Sony was the first Hollywood studio to release DVD since no other studio had the stones to gamble on the new format. Sony first experimented with selling DVD in Japan in 1997 and based on that trial success, greenlit it for America. Ben shrewdly signed a lucrative deal with Universal Pictures to release their DVDs in exchange for 50 percent of their profits after our production costs. Universal was risk-averse and inked an onerous deal with us, showing once again that making money is for the bold.

Ben was raised to superstar status when home entertainment receipts eclipsed TV and theatrical receipts for the first time. A torrent of money, hundreds of millions of dollars, poured in with minimal spend on our side. Our DVD production facility was humming twenty-four hours a day to produce and release as many Universal titles as we could within the three-year term of the contract. The DVD format took off like a monster, as you know, and Universal watched with chagrin as it was forced to fork over half its profits to us on movies we ordinarily held no rights to such as *Back to the Future* and *Jurassic Park*.

I had been lucky to get into Sony at the beginning of a new format, no different than when television or VHS were first invented. It was a windfall for the studio, for the whole industry. We looked like rainmakers, but the reality was that DVD was a winning innovation, a product consumers were willing to shell out north of $30 for if we added a little piffle like "director's commentary," which we called "added value." Ben, a former finance whiz, openly marveled that consumers were willing to pay $30 for a disc that cost us less than a refill of coffee to make. He attributed it to people's desire for ownership, to own the movie in their home, though they might never watch it more than once, if that. We were in the right place at the right time.

The most important chart I had to make, and the only one that ultimately mattered, told us when we would release the DVD of a new movie such as *Spider-Man* in each territory, taking care that larger countries like Germany released before small countries like Italy if both languages were on the same disc. If the Italian disc flooded Germany's market before Germany's release date, it would cannibalize our sales in Germany, which was a much larger market. In the end these parallel imports became a big enough problem that we produced own-language discs for every major country. Then the primary enemy became piracy—illegal copies made in places like Eastern Europe and Southeast Asia that were sold for three dollars instead of twenty or thirty. Of course the quality of pirated copies was much lower, but nonetheless it made a huge dent in our sales. To combat this, we feverishly sped up the production timeline so that we could release on DVD as soon after the theatrical release as possible. In the beginning we had to adhere to a six month waiting-period "window" following the theatrical release before we could go out on DVD to allow theatrical to maximize its profits, but we persistently started pushing this window down to four months, then three, and finally, for titles that bombed in theaters, which were many while I was at Sony, just two months.

When I eventually left Sony, Maxine told me, "You were a key member of DVD." I thanked her for that.

When I joined the company, I was a rising star, promoted twice before even being there a year. But there was one problem. Like many people who have had an office job, there are one or two dickheads, though most of the time you can ignore them—unless that dickhead is your boss.

Around my third year, my boss Janine became obsessed with creating a new database to store the exact same information that was already being ably stored in the database we were using. Janine's real reason for building a new database was to leverage it to get a promotion for herself. The problem was that her database was worse than the one we were already using, which worked fine. In short, there was no compelling need for a new database. Her new one didn't function properly and was worse in every respect than the existing one, but nevertheless she forced us to enter all the release dates twice, in both databases. Because hers didn't work, she soon began work on a *third* database, all to perform the exact same function of storing DVD release dates. In the end, every time a release date changed, which was constantly—Ben changed dates while sitting on the throne in the morning—we had to update five separate databases for the change. It was mindlessly repetitive.

Janine didn't know anything about movies. She looked at the schedule of upcoming movies as though it was the Dead Sea Scrolls—she had no idea who was starring in what or who the writer or director were.

In one meeting with senior executives, one of them looked at the upcoming releases and asked "What is *Secret Window*?"

"It's the directorial debut of the writer of *Panic Room*," I answered. (He had directed before but this was his first major picture.)

The executives smiled, always appreciating my deep knowledge of movies. But over their shoulders, I noticed Janine glaring at me with what can only be described as a deep reservoir of hate.

Janine happily admitted to being a "control freak" with chronic "anxiety" who was terrified to fly on airplanes because she wasn't flying the plane and therefore "couldn't control it." She said she would only feel comfortable if she was flying the airplane, though she wasn't a pilot and had never flown one of course.

Janine would have been just as happy selling bars of soap or widgets; it literally made no difference to her that we worked at a movie studio. She nearly left us once early on to go manage a 7-Eleven franchise. She actually resigned from Sony, but unfortunately Maxine offered her the director title she coveted to retain her. After getting the director title, Janine became a menace. She started power-tripping like no other director at the company. She quickly fired her own assistant, and then set her sights on a large guy named Robbie who was in charge of obtaining the physical metal used in the DVDs; these metal shipments were chronically late. Janine went after him with real gusto until Robbie's nice boss, a tall drink of water named Mitch, stood up and politely told her to go to hell. Realizing she couldn't fire other people's employees, Janine set her sights on a Texan who reported to her and forced him out instead.

One day she stood in my office demanding I sign a phony review she'd trumped up with outright falsehoods. There was a small box at the bottom of the review where employees could leave a comment, and I fired back.

"This review is unnecessarily harsh and unfair. I've made no mistakes. I sent all the release schedules on time. DVD profits are soaring. This review is a joke," I wrote.

I held my nose and dropped it on her desk. When I stepped back in my office, my phone was ringing. I picked it up. Janine whined in my ear, "You left a comment …"

Her voice sounded wounded, scared.

"Uh, yeah …" I said.

"Maxine will see it!" she burst out.

I was confused. I didn't think Maxine would care about Janine's bullshit review or my comment. A minute later Janine strolled into my office feigning nonchalance. I could feel her insanity bristling off her.

She dropped the review on my desk and said, "I printed it again. I changed some of your scores back. Just sign it. And don't leave a comment."

Janine told me not to write a comment in the employee space of the review because her boss would see it. The entire purpose of that employee box being there was to prevent exactly this kind of power abuse. She had perverted the review into a weapon to bully unsuspecting innocent subordinates. She had achieved the complete separation of review from performance. I was ambushed, but I wish my instincts had been more alive. When a person demands you sign something, of course you don't sign it. Just a flat no and show them your middle finger instead.

But I did.

She was my boss, and I was twenty-four years old. I wanted to get over to the production side and was trying to preserve my chance of doing something great at the studio. Her harassment didn't stop with just that one review, though, and each time I swallowed it down, hoping I was doing the right thing.

I hadn't always been such a doormat.

In high school, I had a problem with someone egging my house on Friday and Saturday nights when I was working as a waiter (illegally because I was too young to be serving tequila) at El Torito restaurant in San Diego. I would come home late at night, and find my house's garage door covered in egg. In retrospect it wasn't as big a deal as it seemed at the time, and my mother wasn't as scared as I thought she was, but I was furious. It was kids from high school, but I had no idea who.

So I sprinkled some chum in the water. That week in homeroom class, I said loudly to the guy sitting next to me that some kids were egging my house at night. An Asian kid smirked in the row next to mine. *Fucker's in on it,* I thought.

I waited outside the classroom as the other kids filed out. When the Asian kid—the one in school who wears a visor and dresses like a golfer and tries to hang out with the popular kids—came out of the classroom, I was waiting for him behind the bungalow. In Southern California the schools are all open-air, with classes held in separate bungalows. His name was Terry. As he walked down the ramp, I stepped out in front of him and grabbed him by his throat. I started squeezing the life out of him. I slammed him up against the wall of the bungalow.

"Who's egging my house, Terry?"

"I don't know! I swear! I don't know!"

"Bullshit!"

Just one sixteen-year-old throttling another in broad daylight.

"Terry, if you don't tell me who it is right now, so help me God I will rip out your voice box."

I was hoping I wouldn't have to, but, you know, Nixon's madman theory always works to great effect.

"It's Bryan and …" He rattled off a few names.

"See, now that wasn't so hard, was it?"

I dropped him.

Interesting. The names made perfect sense, but they were all people I hardly knew and never would have guessed. Bryan was a short blond kid two grades below me—I was a senior, he was a sophomore—who nonetheless had been good enough to make the varsity soccer team. He was the only sophomore I had ever seen make the varsity soccer team. Mira Mesa was the largest high school in San Diego—my graduating class had over a thousand kids—and our soccer team was best in the county; we were undefeated. Despite being on the same team, we had never spoken.

"Who else?" I asked.

"There are more, but I'm not going to tell you. I gave you enough to get started."

Terry turned to leave, but I lightly touched his arm with just the tip of my index finger. He stopped short so violently that it was as though he were a mechanical dog and I had pushed his stop button.

"All right, Terry, I won't squeeze the life out of you today and make you give up all the names if you tell me in advance when the next egging will be. Deal?"

"Yeah," he said, rubbing his throat and looking at me sorely, in both senses of the word.

That Thursday in homeroom he walked by and said, "Tonight."

I was gracious enough to say thank you.

That night I sat in the tall fir trees of my front driveway holding a steel baseball bat—steel, not wood—the kind that can smash your bones to cat litter with one swing. Not wanting to miss the big night, I climbed into the trees at first dark, at eight o'clock. I waited for over four hours.

It wasn't until after midnight that a van drove up fast and slammed to a halt right in front of my driveway. *Eureka.* I had more adrenaline pumping through me than a Navy SEAL does before he gets to murder someone on foreign soil. Four kids, all wearing ski masks, jumped out of the car, ran onto my driveway, and started throwing eggs at my garage door.

I let it happen. *Live it up, you fuckers.*

At just the right moment, I leaped out of the fir trees with the metal bat, screaming, "Die, assholes!"

Three of the kids took off running extremely fast, so I couldn't catch them while holding the bat. I was sure that Bryan was one of them. One of the kids was slow, though, and I ran that one down with surprising ease. Filled with rage, I lifted the tip of the bat all the way up to the moon so I could bring it down on the kid's spine with enough force to sever it in two, shattering it like a glass coffee table. Or perhaps I'd bring the bat around in a fastball line drive and break the kid's knees, sending him to wheelchair-ville for life. But at the end of the day, I'm not Tony Soprano; I'm a good kid. So I dropped the bat and tackled the kid like a cheetah bringing down a zebra in the Serengeti. We collapsed together on the hard cement of the sidewalk.

"*Owwww!*" the kid screamed.

It was a girl's voice. I was surprised. That would explain why she ran so slow. I turned her over like a Thanksgiving turkey and ripped off her ski mask. It was a fat girl I recognized but again, had never spoken to. I had seen her, of course, in the incestuous petri dish, controlled science experiment known as high school. She was the striker on the girls' junior varsity soccer team. She was two grades below me too.

Bad move messing with a senior.

"What the fuck!" I screamed.

She quailed, openly terrified. I couldn't hurt a girl, of course, and wouldn't even hurt a guy if you really want to know the truth, but I was no less angry that these jerks were egging my house every week, and always on nights when I was working and not here to defend my family.

Someone on the inside at El Torito was obviously feeding them my schedule of shifts. I had an idea who it might be; I would deal with him later. He would meet the inside of a walk-in freezer in the restaurant kitchen in a week or so. Those lock from the outside. The temperature control was also on the outside and could be lowered below freezing.

Terrified, the girl shook like someone receiving electroshock therapy with that wooden popsicle stick clenched between their teeth. It was obvious she had been on these runs before and had grown accustomed to no one being at the castle when they arrived.

The other three, all guys on the soccer team, were already in the van, which now rolled up quietly in front of us. I lifted the girl to her feet by the front of her shirt, ruining the shirt's neck. I swung her around and, holding her by the back of her collar as my prisoner, walked her forward so that the others could see their woman, my hostage, in my capture.

"So help me God, if I ever see any of you here again, next time I will swing this bat and break your legs. Do you understand?" I asked them. "Do you fuckers ever want to play soccer again?"

The girl said nothing. Her face was as white as a polygamous Mormon's. I pushed her into the van, where she collapsed facedown like a wet noodle. She wasn't moving. I think she might have fainted. A ski-masked face leaned out the passenger window. I looked into the icy blue eyes—Bryan.

"If I ever see you here again, I will fuck you up," I said, pointing the tip of the bat at him. "And I really do hope you test me on that, because honestly I would love to."

The van drove off.

I know—I'm surprised I had it in me too. But the firstborn son of a single mother will act crazy if he feels she's threatened, especially when he's a teenager, even if those feelings of protection are completely misguided and she's been playing you for a fool all of your sixteen years. You may have forgotten how you felt in high school, but at that age you just have so many emotions roiling around inside you. Oh, who am I kidding, I still have those same emotions roiling inside me now.

Bryan wasn't smart enough to get into my AP Advanced Placement classes (I grudgingly concede he was a better soccer player than me; I sure as hell didn't make the varsity team as a sophomore), so I trailed behind him to his dummy class the next day at school. I was pretty good at tracking people undetected, stalking prey like the grim reaper. I would make a pretty good spy, I think. I melt into my surroundings, even into other nationalities, like Zelig.

I skipped class and waited until Bryan's was finished. I didn't know him as well as Terry, who had been in the same classes with me since the seventh grade. Bryan was silent, and we had never shared a word, except for me screaming at him on the soccer field to pass me the ball, which he duly ignored.

Filled with righteous anger, I once again leaned on my signature move. I waited for him to descend the bungalow's ramp, and then I circled around, grabbed him, and picked him up like a bag of groceries. He was small enough that I didn't have to grab him by his throat. I shook him out like a bathmat and slammed him against the wall of the bungalow three times.

"Are you the ringleader of this little operation?" I demanded.

He looked into my face with such arrogance that I was startled, for a moment taken aback, but I had the answer to my question. He was the ringleader, a guy whom I had never spoken to but was on the soccer team with.

"You tapeworm, you pint-sized little fuck." I shook him like a cocktail shaker. "I work on Friday and Saturday nights. I'm not even there when you joyriders come egg my house. My mother is there alone. I will end your life if you ever show up there again. Do you understand?"

True to our history, Bryan didn't say a word, but I looked into his arrogant eyes and I do think he was rattled, or at least surprised. I already knew that bullies are thin-skinned cowards beneath their initial attack and thus nothing to be afraid of. Nothing to lose even. Things can only get better for you after you stand up to a bully. Stand up to them, and they will shrink back faster than expected.

I dropped him like an elf, and he fell the height of the Empire State Building to the ground.

No one ever came to our house again.

I couldn't punch Janine in the nose, of course, or chuck her into the company atrium, though I would have been broadly cheered had I done so. She was a viper thrashing around in our sandbox. Janine was dirty. I should've complained to Maxine, my ally and Janine's boss. In the midst of this Maxine was handing me scripts to read and asking for my opinion on them, whether I thought the studio should acquire them or not. It would have been so easy to tell her about Janine's harassing me. Why didn't I? Because it was nonsense. Because I didn't want to bother Maxine with it. A desire to avoid conflict at work? Fear of retaliation from Janine once she found out I had gone to her boss? Janine was already retaliating against me; there was nothing to lose by speaking up about it.

At the same time a deeper problem was unfolding—a lack of meaning in my marketing job. The stupidity of five databases for one release date and the increasingly clerical nature of my job was a slow deadly drip-drip that finally led me to realize I was in the wrong place. Though glamor surrounded me on the lot, I couldn't escape the bad boss and tedium that populate corporate workplaces everywhere. I felt more and more distant from the creative life I wanted and had positioned myself close to at the studio but not into.

All my life I've been passionate about movies. But since early childhood I was even more passionate about writing. Storytelling and the English language are my real life's love affair. Sony would have been the perfect place to write a screenplay or novel and sell it to producers who were right there on the lot. But the idea didn't come to me until I went out into the real world and experienced real life beyond the cocooned, cozy borders of studio life. After gaining rough and hard experiences in the world, I finally had something to write about. I had original stories to tell. And I began to write them down.

11

The School of Enlightenment

Janine's obsessive, Javert-like campaign to undermine me didn't cause me to leave Sony right away. That period when I was trying to write coincided with an increasing desire for meaning in life. I had written short stories prolifically until I was a teenager, but now, struggling to write something for the first time since childhood gave rise to a windswept, restless feeling like autumn leaves swirling in an empty city street—an aching, yearning feeling in the hollow of my chest for something out there that I didn't quite know.

At the same time I started sometimes attending spiritual seminars put on by a small organization called the Learning Annex. The Learning Annex operates across the United States in major cities, and you may have seen their advertisement in the back of some free magazine, which you no doubt ignored because you were enjoying your life. I was one of the very few people in their twenties who took an interest in it. I was probably the *only person* in their twenties in the entire country who took an interest in it. I never saw another young person in all the events I attended there. All the other attendees were middle-aged or old. It was a terrible place to pick up girls.

Far from having the pull of Oprah Winfrey, the Learning Annex was closer to a scrappy start-up that aggressively pursued famous speakers—like Rhonda Byrne of *The Secret* (snake oil telling people they can get rich without working) to Oprah herself—but they couldn't attract these big names, so they got lesser-known self-help authors and pseudospiritual teachers eager for an audience to promote their work, with more than a few dilettantes and clowns among them. Indeed, there was a circuslike quality to the Learning Annex. And yet it was the only thing that felt real in my life at the time. It was just weird enough to have a little authenticity about it.

Some of the Annex's teachers felt like fraudsters. One woman whose books have sold relatively well had some good material during the first hour of her lecture but then she launched into a sidebar about how the human race first arrived on earth on spaceships. At first I thought she was joking and I belly-laughed out loud hard until I noticed that no one else in the room was laughing. As she kept talking, I realized she truly believed it. Until she started talking about aliens and having been a guest on the mothership where the aliens served her peppermint schnapps and tea, she had sounded entirely credible. It's a reminder of just how many crackpots there are in the world.

I know what you're thinking. Why was I in a place like that? The Learning Annex should have been a depressing place for a strapping twenty-seven-year-old buck like me. And sometimes it was. But the part of me that felt spiritually undernourished appreciated it. It was the only thing I had to look forward to at the time, because it was the only place that had the capacity to surprise me, where I might learn something new. I wasn't learning anything new at work, where Janine had never taught me anything new after day one, or even tried to, because she couldn't. Her desire was not to bring out the best in juniors but to feel power by rewarding sycophants and punishing individuals, whom she viewed as threats, like some Cinderella's stepmother. Because my situation at work was just wrong, or in spite of it, life felt unfulfilling and dulled, devoid of purpose and meaning, replaced instead by ennui and malaise, as though I were living underwater or looking out at life from behind a screen. Basically, I just wasn't present. The Learning Annex was my lighthouse on a lonely cliff, sanctuary at world's end, temporary way station between where I was and where I was going.

The Learning Annex was where I first encountered Deepak Chopra, by far the annex's biggest star. I was excited to come hear such a big name speak. I went to two or three of his lectures. At first I found his ideas stimulating, but at some point gleaned that they were all derivative. His talking points were all lifted from other people's work. He had no original content. And sometimes he stumbled badly when asked a straightforward question he hadn't preresearched the answer to. Instead of admitting he didn't know the answer like a normal person, he tried to contrive his way through, and sometimes his answers rang jarringly false. I'd catch the slightly bug-eyed, sweaty look of uncertainty on his face when he'd gone off the rails and was pretending to know something he didn't fully understand.

Wayne Dyer was much the same. I like Wayne more, though, because his heart is in the right place. He has less ego than Chopra; he's more humble. Wayne has no talent other than a vaguely haunted smile, but he is a genuinely nice guy and has been a chest-thumping fanboy of spiritual enlightenment since at least the 1970s. He and Chopra both blithely lift their material from the true source teachers and regurgitate it in their own works. They are really enthusiasts. Which puts us in similar company because that's what I am too, but as a wannabe disciple looking for a wise master, I was in the wrong place. As I would soon discover, the real enlightened ones, the true teachers, are not enthusiasts at all. They just *are*, without ever trying to become enlightened, indeed without having any interest in spiritual matters at all. Before they became enlightened, they had no interest in spirituality.

They were atheists.

That's what separates the true spiritual teachers from the many charlatans in the world.

Fraudsters and con men say that you can become enlightened if only you pay for their courses and buy their books. In reality, though, no one can become enlightened purely through study. The closest you can get is a little wiser, a little more tolerant toward others and yourself, more openminded. For the ordinary person, true enlightenment simply isn't possible.

Yes, you read that correctly.

Those few enlightened people—the ones who give birth to the source knowledge—are not self-taught. They're not born that way either, as it turns out. They're all hit with it, slapped upside the head with it in middle life and transformed into a different person. More accurately, they're the same person but now an enlightened one. These rarest of people, these snow leopards, are homegrown and came to be enlightened entirely by accident, never by wanting or seeking it. In fact, it happened against their will. So anyone seeking enlightenment should understand it simply isn't going to happen to you.

Right now Deepak Chopra is saying, "Tom, shut the fuck up. I have books to sell." Deepak would not want me saying this to his core audience.

Just when I was about to give up on the Learning Annex because I could see they hadn't found any true teacher, they found one. Most of their speakers were churned over and over—*ugh, Louise Hay again?*—a sure sign a business is struggling. But on what turned out to be the very last Learning Annex I ever attended, a brand-new person, a woman from the desert near Barstow, California, named Katie, came to Los Angeles to speak at the annex. By sheer luck, or perhaps because I had been seeking a master so intently that the universe divined me one, Katie turned out to be one of two enlightened people on the planet.

It was pure providence that she happened to live in California. And another miracle that her first Learning Annex coincided with my last.

Katie had been an unremarkable girl with no interest in spiritual things and little interest in school either. She could be described as ordinary, interested in what every young girl is—boys. She went to Arizona State, where she was an indifferent student earning mostly Cs and Ds. She got pregnant and dropped out of college. From then on she was basically a mother, and had a string of jobs. She divorced and married again, had more children.

At forty-two years old she was a housewife living in Barstow, severely depressed, and, as she put it, "in a near-constant state of rage." She didn't go into the source of her rage, perhaps because she didn't know or it didn't matter. But in the midst of a gradually deepening depression, one night she found herself sleeping on the floor beside her bed. She felt so unworthy that she no longer felt she deserved to sleep in a bed. This continued night after night. Her husband was at his wit's end trying to get her to sleep in the bed, but she wouldn't budge. Couldn't budge is more accurate. It wasn't a petulant tantrum. She just found herself there; it was the best she could manage.

She described becoming so depressed that it became a monumental task just to brush her teeth in the mornings. She felt so worthless and irredeemable that the simple action of brushing her teeth became insurmountable, like a staircase she no longer had the will to climb. The thought of her teeth rotting and falling out no longer concerned her. And still her depression only deepened. Crippling, powerful feelings of worthlessness engulfed her. Her primary urge became to disappear. She began to contemplate suicide as a way out. She no longer felt worthy enough even for the floor beside her bed, so she crawled up into the attic at night, where she could be out of sight of humanity. She slept on the dirty floor in the stale, musty dark. There seemed to be no bottom, no floor, to the abyss of her rage. It just kept expanding downward deeper and deeper. She hadn't asked for this—to be alive. She craved obliteration, annihilation.

One summer night shortly after her forty-third birthday when she was lying on the floor of the attic in the warm desert night, she felt something brush across her leg. A large cockroach was crawling on her leg. In her suicidal state she didn't even bother to brush it off. Normally as squeamish as anyone, she just let it roam freely over her body all night.

At some point during the darkest hour of night, just before dawn, something happened. A kind of contraction occurred inside her mind—an intense pulling back to a singularity, like a star being drowned by a black hole. Absolute darkness.

Frightened by the strange experience, she looked around the attic in panic. It was pitch-black. She couldn't see anything. It was predawn, the darkest hour of night, and yet the attic was far blacker than it should have been. It was deepest black. She had fallen so deep inside the well of her fear that she finally seemed to have touched bottom—the floor of depression. And what she saw there was raw terror. Too scared even to cry, she lay quivering on the floor in profound, hopeless despair. She thought she was going to die. Suddenly she was grabbed roughly from behind by a shadow, something she didn't see, and jerked backward over a black waterfall into a void that devoured her like Cronus devoured his own children.

She seemed to have been swallowed by herself.

A split had occurred inside her mind, a fracture, but one from insanity back to sanity, from unreality to reality. She had an awakening. A new dawn was born inside the tortured prison of her mind. No longer able to withstand the enormous negative pressure inflicted by the intensity of her false mind, a true break had caused her real self to irrevocably split clean away from the unhappy self (the ego). Such a seismic sundering inside her mind left her real self clearly delineated in the pre-ego state, or post-ego state, and for the first time she had so unalterably broken away from the false self (the ego), that she was immune to it and there was no chance it could ever take control of her mind again. This meant she could never be depressed again. When the break happens, it is final. The change is permanent. And then happiness is permanent—because the ego has been vanquished, permanently defeated. Perhaps this is the true meaning of heaven. The mind completely free of the false self, the ego.

The reason behind the mind split could be medical as much as spiritual, but no scientist has ever studied it because it is so infinitely rare that only two known people on the planet have ever experienced it. So no one knows. A complete and irreversible separation of one's real self from the false mind/ego such as Katie experienced can only happen on its own—it cannot be coerced or triggered, at least not yet. So no depressed person can ever be guaranteed it would happen to them, no matter how depressed they become. Odds are that it won't. For now it remains an act of grace. A mystery. And yet a future where this rupture and pathway to heaven (enlightenment) becomes common, independent of any teacher, study, or medical procedure, remains a tantalizing possibility.

After the split, Katie lay on the floor in the attic in silence in the dark. When she opened her eyes, the first thing she noticed was that all her pain and rage were completely gone. She felt fine. She passed into a deep, dreamless sleep.

In the morning when Katie's eyes flew open, the world was new.

Literally new, as in everything looked totally different.

She saw the world as it really is. She saw the matrix.

Katie told us that when she opened her eyes in the morning it was like seeing the world for the very first time. She saw the world like the first human ever to see it, like an alien from outer space seeing our world for the first time. She saw everything with fresh eyes, as though she had just been born, but with an adult's developed mind instead of a baby's. Everything she rested her eyes upon she saw without any story behind it, without any history, as a first-timer. Every single thing carried the fingerprints of the Creator. Every bookcase, armchair, and windowpane was redolent with the overwhelming power of creation. The creative power is playful, even mischievous, and has an astonishing, surprising sense of humor. At the bottom there's only laughter. Laughter is the deepest part of the well.

Consider a tree. Can you imagine what a tree would look like if you didn't know it was called a tree, if it had never been named so? What would it look like if you didn't know what it was, if you were looking at it as an alien from another planet where there are no trees? A tree looks like the *strangest damn thing* you ever saw! Try to see it as the first person ever to see one. From the beginner's mind. And the kicker is, *that's what it really is*—that strange bewildering twisting thing, utterly mysterious and, in a very real sense, unknowable. Only humans gave it a name out of the mind's compulsion to label and classify everything in sight. A name robs a thing of its essential mystery, its peculiar beauty.

Classification is just human invention; there's nothing real about it. Imagine things before classification. That's what they are. And even then, what is it? Mathematical tables, taxonomies, graphs, periodic charts, names, labels, systems—they all come from the human obsession to categorize what in truth is nameless. That thing we call a tree is not a tree at all. Look at it again without the name. What the hell is it? Once you name something you cease to notice it. It becomes covered by the name and its beauty diminishes. If you didn't name the things around you, they would retain their intriguing value. That fragile, somehow precious trinket you picked up on vacation is beautiful *precisely because you don't know what the hell it is*. Why do you think people are so fascinated by aliens and snow leopards? *Because no one's ever seen one, that's why.*

Katie said that seeing things as they are, before they were labeled, is breathtaking, exhilarating, and nothing short of miraculous. Everything she lays her eyes on is literally a miracle.

Is there any other way to live?

The joy that floods in from the nameless space is boundless, infinite. When you see the nameless without knowing what it is, you tap into that infiniteness. That same expansiveness fills you up inside and broadens and deepens your experience of life. That mystery has always been there and is still intact under the name, before it. If you unname something and look at it again from the beginner's mind, you will feel the unharnessed joy of the universe flow into you through its mysterious creation.

For a brief period following her awakening, Katie had no thoughts at all. She walked downstairs, straight out of her house, and into the desert. She didn't stop walking. She wandered and slept in the desert for ten days straight, just reveling in the multitude of miracles, the rapture of every object—wind, sand, sun, moon, desert, sky—the whimsical wonder of creation, all color, unique, and very much alive. She slept in the sand under the stars and forewent food for the duration. The California desert is warm and balmy in the summer at night, and she could live in it as easily as the geckos and desert birds.

The only other enlightened person on the planet is Eckhart Tolle, whom I didn't discover until much later, not via the Learning Annex but through a coworker at the Aspen Lodging Company. I read his book in the Yukon when I was riding my motorcycle back from Alaska, and was startled to discover that his origin story was identical to Katie's.

Tolle was a twenty-nine-year-old German graduate student at Cambridge in London, severely depressed. He was in a near-constant state of anxiety so crippling that it overwhelmed his daily life, and although he was a graduate student, he doesn't remember studying; it was just a blur. The same thing that happened to Katie happened to him. In the middle of the night he was lying awake with feelings of profound worthlessness and paralyzing dread, contemplating suicide in a depression deeper than the Mariana Trench, when in his darkest hour, as he described it, there was suddenly a contraction in his mind, and he was pulled backward into a "vortex." In a moment of pure terror he was swallowed by the vortex, and then he knew nothing, but noticed that all of his pain had packed up and left, like an abusive lover kicked to the curb. It was like coming home one day to find one's dirty apartment empty and clean, except this apartment was his mind.

To hear Tolle tell it in *The Power of Now*:

> Until my thirtieth year, I lived in a state of almost continuous anxiety interspersed with periods of suicidal depression. One night not long after my twenty-ninth birthday, I woke up in the early hours with a feeling of absolute dread. I had woken up with such a feeling many times before, but this time it was more intense than it had ever been. Everything felt so alien, so hostile, and so utterly meaningless that it created in me a deep loathing of the world. The most loathsome thing of all, however, was my own existence. What was the point in continuing to live with this burden of misery? I could feel that a deep longing for annihilation, for nonexistence, was now becoming much stronger than the instinctive desire to continue to live.
>
> "I cannot live with myself any longer." This was the thought that kept repeating itself in my mind. Then suddenly I became aware of what a peculiar thought

it was. "Am I one or two? If I cannot live with myself, there must be two of me: the 'I' and the 'self' I cannot live with." "Maybe," I thought, "only one of them is real."

I was so stunned by this strange realization that my mind stopped. I was fully conscious, but there were no more thoughts. Then I felt drawn into what seemed like a vortex of energy. It was a slow movement at first and then accelerated. I was gripped by an intense fear. I could feel myself being sucked into a void. It was as if the void was inside myself rather than outside. Suddenly there was no more fear, and I let myself fall into that void. I have no recollection of what happened after that.

In the morning I opened my eyes. I recognized the room, and yet I knew that I had never truly seen it before. Everything was fresh and pristine, as if it had just come into existence. That day I walked around the city in utter amazement at the miracle of life on earth, as if I had just been born into this world. For the next five months, I lived in a state of uninterrupted deep peace and bliss.[1]

Though Tolle was in London and Katie was in Barstow, California, and they had never heard of each other, they had both had the same experience.

Tolle goes on:

It wasn't until several years later that I realized that what everybody was looking for had already

---

[1] Eckhart Tolle, *The Power of Now: A Guide to Spiritual Enlightenment*.

to me. The intense pressure of suffering that night must have forced my consciousness to withdraw from its identification with the unhappy and deeply fearful self, which is ultimately a fiction of the mind. This withdrawal must have been so complete that this false, suffering self immediately collapsed, just as if a plug had been pulled out of an inflatable toy.

I don't know if I'm the only person who has noticed that Tolle's experience was the same as Katie's, but I have never seen anyone point out before that the only two enlightened people in the world had the exact same experience on opposite sides of the globe.

At the Learning Annex, Katie dropped a casual aside that those few who wanted to "go really deep" could attend the "school for the work in the desert." That batted around in my subconscious like a pinball.

I checked Katie's website and saw that she offered a ten-day School of Enlightenment—deep immersion into the mechanics of her own enlightenment and how to replicate it in ourselves. Too intriguing! It was exactly what I had been searching for the last two years. The course, as described, was exactly the sort of course I would want to attend if I had written the script in my head. Near her home in Barstow in the California desert, the ten-day course was designed to recreate her first ten days alone in the desert as an enlightened person. She had reverse engineered what had happened to her so that we could approach it from the nonenlightened side. She needed to house and feed everyone, though, so she moved the course over to a lodge in nearby Joshua Tree, still in the desert.

I had to go and see what was going on out there for ten days; I could just feel it was juicy. I had seen Katie and knew that she was authentic and not a charlatan, so whatever she had cooked up, I was interested in it. I had just missed the Joshua Tree school, so rather than wait another year, I signed up for the next school, which was in Los Angeles near the airport, just a couple of miles from where I lived.

The contents of the school were kept under wraps. The website made no promises other than that you would leave the school more enlightened than you came in—no breathless promises but reasonable expectations of success. Another sign it might be good was its outlandishly expensive price, which could be a good sign or a bad sign. Some charlatans offer cheap courses in the hope of attracting more customers. As with all things, I followed my nose and took the School of Enlightenment's outrageously expensive price tag as a sign that it was good, perhaps very good. For ten days the course alone cost $3,500. It was also mandatory to stay in the five-star luxury hotel Katie had chosen, which would add an additional $1,200 to the cost.

I guess enlightenment and a luxury lifestyle are not incompatible. Good to know. Not only do the rich have access to better food and better seats on an airplane, but they have an edge in access to enlightenment as well.

On the plus side, the hotel cost had been discounted due to the school holding the course in some of the hotel's ballrooms and bringing in around a hundred guests, and due to our being forced to share a room with another student. There was no option to choose your roommate; you could not even room with your spouse or opt out of a roommate if you could afford to pay for your own crib. Those coming with spouses would be pried apart at the door and paired with someone of the same sex. The course would be sexless and romance-free. Also, all meals would be vegetarian. Same as in vipassana. What do enlightened people have against meat anyway? Where did this myth come from that vegetarianism is healthier? I eat meat for every single meal of every day, so this would be a challenge for me. We were advised that the rules of the school were nonnegotiable and would be strictly enforced. Like vipassana in India, the course was billed as only for those serious about reaching enlightenment. The road would be arduous, and those not up to it should not come.

Including the mandatory hotel cost for nine nights, the grand total of the course came out to $4,700, a lot for a twenty-seven-year-old earning $50,000 a year at a movie studio. I was interested in the course but not willing to shell out $4,700 for it. I could backpack around the world for a year on the same amount. In fact, I did. On the website there was a form to apply for a scholarship to the school if you couldn't afford to go. They called it a "hardship application." It said you had to prove financial hardship to get the scholarship, which I could not do, since actually I could have paid their fee but simply didn't want to. The form said not to apply for hardship dispensation if you didn't meet the standard of need and that only one or two scholarship applications are approved per school. Two out of a hundred.

Not bad odds.

I've faced worse.

The form asked what my annual salary was. I do not lie, and I told the truth. But I wrote in the comments that I was only twenty-seven and while I was very interested in enlightenment, the course was obviously obscenely overpriced and I wasn't interested in enriching the founders and especially did not need to be enlightened in a five-star hotel. I could get enlightened just as easily in a roach motel or in a ditch on the side of the road. I suggested that I save the $1,200 hotel cost by sleeping at my apartment, which was just five minutes away, and driving in each morning instead.

The reply hit my inbox a week later. To my continuing astonishment I was ... approved! By Katie herself. But my request to stay at home had been rejected. They said being paired with a roommate "you don't like" was a "core requirement" of the course, which sounded ominous, but I eagerly agreed. The $3,500 would be waived for me. I only had to pay $1,200 for the five-star hotel accommodations to get the deep-dive course in enlightenment. Bargain!

The next obstacle was my insecure, untruthful boss. I didn't have any vacation days left, and Janine, rooted in rules and personal hatred of yours truly, was predictably emphatic I couldn't go.

"You don't have any vacation days left," she said.

Finally fed up with allowing her to treat me so badly and lie on my reviews for years, tired of standing by and letting her do a Lucy with the football on my Charlie Brown over and over again, I finally—belatedly but finally—stood up to her. Over her furious yelling that I couldn't go, I told her that I was, in fact, going.

"I'm going. I already signed up and paid. Fire me if you want to, but I'm going," I said. What was difficult for me to say before for once came easily. She went mute. The threat had worked.

I didn't know it then, but the School of Enlightenment would change the course of my life, and I never considered until now that it was only because Katie approved my scholarship application. If I had been declined—which I was expecting since I admitted I earned $50,000 a year, which I assume did not meet the hardship threshold—I would not have gone. I didn't want it that badly. I would have let it go. Probably there were people who earned less but paid the full amount. Another thing I knew was that a charlatan who is primarily interested in money would not have approved my application. The fact that Katie did when she didn't have to—indeed when I didn't deserve it—reinforced my impression that she really was enlightened.

After several unfulfilling years in Los Angeles, something was happening at last! I had sorely missed the feeling of forward momentum, of being in motion, of the wheel of life turning. I love the feeling of change. After two years in a moribund stasis, I had the delicious feeling of life moving ahead once again.

Spiritual Practice 1: Give Away

Similar to vipassana, the School of Enlightenment provided no advance specifics but only promised to be intense and to surgically cut through your bullshit like one of the Empire's planet-destroying lasers. They did not lie.

I arrived at the hotel's reception hall and checked in. I moved for the entrance, but found my way blocked by a Native American woman of around forty who stood four feet and ten inches high. She slid in front of me and glowered up at me.

"Give me your most valuable possession," she said.

"I beg your pardon?"

"You heard me." Her mouth was a slit the size of a paper cut. "Give it up—now!"

I hesitated.

"Don't hold out!"

"Fine," I said.

I reached down and took off my Justin cowboy boots and handed them to her. They had cost $300, and I had just bought them a month ago. She noticed the Justin label affixed. Being Native American, she knew her cowboy boots. Her eyebrows rose slightly and the corners of her mouth turned downward in a sign she was impressed. She gave me a curt nod and jabbed her head toward a doorway like a soccer player headbutting a ball into the goal.

My offering to the gods of enlightenment had passed muster. I could almost hear the ghost in *Indiana Jones* saying, *You have chosen ... wisely.* Like in *The NeverEnding Story*, I had passed the first two gates, where all people discover they are really cowards, and I could now visit the Southern Oracle, who in real life turns out to be Katie. Would she tell me that I had to go beyond the boundaries of Fantasia to find the answers to my questions? One year later the fortune-teller at Sony's Christmas party would tell me much the same thing.

I asked the Native American woman what she was going to do with the boots. She said they'd be given to a homeless man. I said that sounded fine to me. Fortunately I'd brought a pair of running shoes, naively thinking I would have time to exercise, and wore those for the rest of the course instead. The woman handed me a single red rose, and I passed through the doorway.

The room was empty except for a long red carpet flanked on both sides by rows of lighted candles. I followed the solitary path alone for a while until I heard voices. A small cluster of people materialized ahead. The men all held red roses, and the women held white. It was romantic and beautiful. I am sensitive to overt displays of beauty as you may have gleaned from these pages, and as I passed into the atrium, a choir of cascading voices drifted down from on high as though the von Trapp family was singing on a green hilltop just out of view. It was surprising and beautiful, more than I expected, and my eyes might have misted. Taking an enlightenment course in luxury isn't all bad, I thought.

As I took in my lush new surroundings—the binary roses, the singing, over one hundred people milling about—a woman in a crushed-velvet purple pantsuit with silver hair the color of the crescent moon emerged from a backdoor and strode out onto the dais. She had perfectly erect posture and moved with swiftness and purpose, as all good leaders do.

She took a seat in a plush red chair on the stage and poured herself a cup of tea from a small pot. She had a distinctively Western face in that it resembled nothing so much as a falcon or hawk, a bird of prey from the forests, the deserts, the mountains. She sat quietly for the next ten minutes without speaking, just looking around and taking us in. After everyone had wandered into the room, the singing stopped.

"Please sit down," the woman said.

We sat.

"Hi," she said slowly, looking around with eyes that were piercingly blue and as clear and penetrating as a hawk's. Her light blue eyes were startlingly vivid and so clear that they seemed to stand up on the whites behind them. The color was profoundly unmarred by any extra pigments or blemishes, so that they gave the impression of caves or doorways one could climb into. It was the falcon's gaze.

"I'm Katie. Welcome."

She began by describing our goals for the course, what we were here to accomplish. Achieving enlightenment required following a set of four steps recreated from her original experience. If followed to the letter, these four steps would allow us to experience the same peace and freedom she had been graced with.

No details of the school's curriculum were revealed. Katie said that we would be given instructions only right before we were to do something. No communication at all with the outside world would be permitted over the next ten days. No emails, no phone calls to loved ones, no checking on the kids.

Zilch.

We were going on lockdown, off the grid. We were to consider ourselves stranded on a floating berg in the middle of the Pacific Ocean with no way off it. No phone, no letter-carrying owl, no safe word, no panic button, no break-in-case-of-emergency escape hatch. Mobile phones were forbidden and taken from us—meaning no internet as well—and as a precaution the school had sabotaged all the pay phones in the hotel. They'd literally blocked up and taped over the coin slots, rendering them useless. We were not given key cards to the business center, pool, or gym. Anything pleasurable in the hotel was strictly off limits to us. We were all forced to wear nametags so that we couldn't disguise our identities inside the hotel. We would be watched by Katie's staff at all times. There was no free time. Similar to vipassana, we were forbidden to go outside or to leave the hotel; the hotel staff had been ordered to bar students from leaving through the front or back doors; security detail was posted at every exit. We were all under constant surveillance. Katie said that anyone not willing to follow the rules should leave now. Last chance. (No word on whether you got your favorite possession back if you left.)

No one moved. No one breathed. A couple of beats passed. Katie scanned the room. Everyone remained dead silent.

Finally her mouth split open in a wide grin, and with enormous warmth and depth in her voice she said, "*Well ...*" and held out her arms in an embrace large enough to hug the entire room.

The room tittered a little, and the tension collapsed into nervous giggles.

"During this course you will be pushed to your physical and emotional limits, to your breaking point and beyond," Katie said.

Some of the older participants shifted uncomfortably in their seats at these words. Some of the men scratched their patchy beards and their eyes went distant. These were not words that retirees, snowbirds, and older attendees want to hear on an expensive five-star retreat. They'd probably been expecting some HBO-like group play—laying hands on each other, maybe rubbing hot mud onto each other's backs to rekindle the spark like some couples retreat in Sedona, Arizona.

If so, they had come to the wrong place.

Katie said that if we stayed we would irreversibly be putting ourselves in her hands. "There will be no going back," she said. "Consider yourselves warned."

A few people seemed to be reconsidering Katie's offer to leave while they still could before her minions barred the doors for good. The course sounded extreme and juicy to me, but I saw a lot of concerned faces around the room. Katie's staff passed around an affidavit for everyone to sign—a legal waiver that said Katie was not responsible for anything that happened to us during the school, including rape, dismemberment, and death.

Seriously.

Frowns shot around the room like a staph infection as people read the document.

Death?

Dismemberment?

People's eyes glazed over and became unfocused. After fifteen or twenty seconds, though, they began to come back again. The people in the room collectively shook their heads like cows shaking the flies off—*all just a bad dream*. They sat there smiling, and merrily signed the waiver. They just didn't believe it.

They would believe it before the week was out.

"All right then!" Katie said as she collected the signed affidavits and tucked them away inside her pantsuit. She clapped her hands together and beamed a great smile at us.

She had one of the freest, most liberated smiles I have ever seen. Her piercing blue eyes were as bright as a thousand-watt lightbulb. I had the sense that every day was Christmas for her. Katie said that what we had done to start the course, giving away our favorite material possession, was one of three powerful spiritual practices. She invited us to feel the loss of our favorite object, to miss it, to grieve it as we may. She said learning to let go of possessions we're attached to is a spiritually potent act that benefits us far more than we know.

I listened and watched her closely. She was not an imposter or false prophet. I have a keen eye both for talent and fraud in people. My circumstantial (okay, lifelong) interest in spiritual matters has led me to believe that 99 percent of supposedly enlightened people are charlatans. Katie was authentic. I could feel it in my bones the way a Bedouin can feel a good rug or a good camel. I felt excited. This was going to be good.

We broke for vegetarian dinner. When we returned to the main hall at seven for the evening session, I was surprised to see that the herd had thinned itself by half. The room was significantly emptier. A full half of attendees had fled the scene, the hotel, and presumably Los Angeles following Katie's portentous edict. I guess Katie knew the ones who were too scared would become a problem later. She didn't want to deal with them, and now that I think about it, neither did I. They probably shouldn't have come in the first place. Who knows—they might have died during whatever nightmare Katie had concocted for us. Katie didn't seem to mind losing customers at all. She just closed her eyes, tilted her face back toward the ceiling, basked in something somewhere, breathed in deeply, and smiled in supreme satisfaction. I assumed the people who had vacated the premises faster than a banana republic's government fleeing a coup d'état would at least get some of their money back, but who knows?

We sat on the floor and waited in silence. Eventually Katie came down from whatever heaven she was in. She opened her eyes and stared out at us beatifically.

She was not displeased.

She said in a somewhat musical cadence, "So you're the ones who stayed."

She smiled, and the warmth of her smile radiated through the whole room like a uranium-enrichment centrifuge in Iran. Then she cried out, "Congratulations! You're in for the trip of a lifetime!"

I was the only one who threw my arm in the air and yelled, "Yeah!"

Yes, I was loving it already. I could tell this was going to be good. Now that Katie had weeded out the people who would not have made it anyway, she began to describe the course in more detail. As she spoke I scanned the room to see who my coconspirators, my fellow subversives and seekers in enlightenment were. Other than one young woman with blonde ringlets who was about my age, I was by far the youngest person at the school. That was not surprising—the course was too expensive for anyone under thirty-five to realistically afford, so young people would naturally be precluded based on cost alone. As a result, the participants were older, especially the men. There were a handful of women in their thirties, a few of them attractive, but a full 90 percent of attendees were over forty years old. As with the Learning Annex, it turns out that enlightenment, or enlightenment in five-star hotels at least, is largely the purview of the affluent and elderly. That's fine. Young people should be out making love and exploring the world in wide-eyed wonder rather than being in places like this. I think I might have been scraped by God upon exiting the birth canal or something, because I have always been interested in this sort of thing. At least three times during the school people came up to me unprompted and remarked with a wisp of melancholy how lucky I was to have discovered this while I was so young. Perhaps that's why Katie had accepted my application for a scholarship. It wasn't so bad to have a young person here just for diversity's sake. As a strapping male it was nice to be the beneficiary of affirmative action for the first time. Free largesse feels good—I'll take it.

Or perhaps she'd accepted me for a different reason.

The other young person, the girl with blonde ringlets, was visibly distraught, openly depressed, and to call her a trainwreck would be an insult to real trainwrecks. I have never seen a young person look so miserable, ever. She sat on the floor wailing and slouched over her two ramrod-straight legs in a sad sack Eeyore posture, her back rounded like Quasimodo's. She was a quivering pile of baggy clothes, blonde hair, and snot. Tears streamed openly down her face. She was a grim sight to behold. One hundred students sat all around her watching her shake, snuffle, and sob. By her sheer misery you'd have thought she was living in Calcutta or at the beginning of a lifetime sentence in Evin Prison in Tehran.

I grimaced and turned away.

Later I found out that she was not rich and had skimped to pay the full $4,700 tuition. I told her I filled out a form and got in for free.

"*Bah!*" she screamed at me.

Katie explained that her goal was to give us "the gap," that additional dimension of space in one's head that she had been graced with that grants full separation from one's thoughts. It is the ability to observe one's thoughts from afar, but never be taken in or controlled by them. She described to us again what that looked like: she'd woken up in the morning and seen the world as it really is—as a visitor from the Pleistocene epoch might if one day they magically woke up in our time—seeing everything as it is, an absolute miracle: strange, wondrous, bizarre, outlandish. That *is* our world without our conditioned stories about it.

For a few minutes after Katie awoke, she said she had no thoughts at all. Then the first thought flew into her mind. But she could now see that the thought was a foreign entity that hadn't originated inside her but rather had been flung into her mind from somewhere outside like a baseball.

Seeing this allowed her to say of the thought, "That's not true."

When the next thought came, she could see that one wasn't true either. Thoughts kept flying in, as they do, faster and faster, yet each time she saw that none of them were true.

As the thoughts continued to come into her mind, she was able to say of each one, "That's not true. That's not true. That one's not true …"

They were all false, illusory holograms entering her mind from external—insubstantial facsimiles with no relationship to truth. The thoughts that stay in your mind are only the thoughts you believe. Those are the ones you have to undo, simply by "unbelieving" them.

All enlightenment is really a process of undoing and unlearning what you thought you knew. The upshot is that all negative thoughts are false, so don't believe them. Simply reject them.

By the same token, if you have a negative thought, you can simply *accept* it without agreeing with it. The important thing is not to resist it. It's the resistance that causes your stress, not the underlying thought, which can be neutralized by either dismissing or accepting it. The stress you feel is from internal resistance or *opposition* to the thought, which is always completely false and unreal. Accept the thought or problem, even invite it in, embrace it, without agreeing with it, and the stress will vanish. Accepting or dismissing, not resisting, will bring you present.

Seized by a sudden strong desire to teach others what she had been blessed with, Katie distilled enlightenment into a process of four simple steps she called "The Work"—so called because it's spiritual work—to help others break out of the false prison of their thinking. These four steps seem to echo Siddhartha's Four Noble Truths.

The crux of it is that any stressful thought isn't true.

If you understand this, you don't need the Work.

The only thing you really have to do is conquer your own negativity. Your negativity is only a trick by your mind to keep you out of the present moment.

Worrying about the past and future is the other trick by your mind to keep you out of the present moment. They are shallow tricks a child would play on another child. The ego is an insecure child, when you understand it, and the real you is an innocent child, whom the insecure child plays these tricks on. The ego's whole purpose is to keep you out of the present moment. Our journey in life is to stay in the present moment.

Katie's process, if you follow it without questioning it, does lead you to where she lives on a permanent basis—in the permanent now.

You begin by acknowledging the thought that's bothering you and ask, "How does this thought make me feel?" The point is to become aware of the direct link between the negative thought and how it makes you feel. It's important to make the distinction that it's actually the thought that makes you feel bad, not the event the thought is about. The very fact the thought makes you feel bad is the ancient linkage between you and the universe or God telling you that it isn't true.

In the first step, of the upsetting thought ask yourself, "Is it true?"

During the course people often became unsure at this moment, but since they were so wedded to their thoughts, most of them decided, "Yes, it's true."

They believed it was true.

In the second step, Katie asked again, "Are you *absolutely sure* it's true? Can you be absolutely sure?"

Here, every time, in the end everyone was forced to answer, "No."

There's no way to be absolutely sure if a negative thought is true or not. There's no way to be 100 percent sure. And that's for a very good reason—because it's not true. This is the beginning of loosening the tyrannical yoke of your false mind.

In the third step, ask yourself, "Who would I be without this thought?" or "Who was I before this thought?" If you think about it, before you had the thought you were fine. Before the thought entered your mind, you were probably skipping down the sidewalk happy as a clam, not thinking about anything. It was only the *thought* that disturbed you, not anything real.

Finally, the powerful fourth step is to *turn the thought around*, which means reverse the negative thought to its polar opposite. Anytime you are upset by a thought, it means you're attaching to a lie, believing a lie, a thought that isn't true, so you want to cut the attachment. Stop thinking, if possible. Stop the mind. If not, the quickest way back to truth is simply *to reverse the thought* that is making you feel bad. Whatever's bothering you, literally say aloud its polar opposite. See how you feel. You will instantly feel lighter and better. *Feeling lighter means it's true.* Your body is jumper-cabled directly into the universe at large, remember? No exceptions.

When students were surprised to learn that they did in fact feel demonstrably lighter—less burdened—after the turnaround, even if they didn't understand or completely believe the turnaround, Katie would smile and say, "And isn't that what you wanted all along? To feel better? To feel good again? To be at peace?"

When someone asked how could they know whether their turnaround was true or not, Katie replied, "Don't think about it. It's not intellectual. Intellectual is still thinking, and you let the thought in again through a backdoor. As long as the turnaround makes you feel better, that's it. You don't need to immediately understand why it makes you feel better or whether the turnaround is true. You will understand all that in time. For now it's enough simply to do the Work and feel better." She had a wonderfully plainspoken way of explaining things.

Katie understood that the truth lies in opposites. The answers to all of life's riddles lie in their opposites; and it is the ultimate secret to vanquishing the ego. When something feels jarring or emotionally upsetting, that means its opposite is true. It can take a long time to understand this, and a leap of faith at first, but once it clicks it makes perfect sense.

The Work sounds exceedingly simple, right? Yet for everyone at the school, fully believing the conclusions reached in the third and fourth steps proved extremely difficult. At the end of the day, people just don't want to accept that their thoughts aren't true, that they're being deceived by their minds. They seem to love their negative thoughts and the drama they create. Katie said that people are addicted to the drama in their heads the way they are to sugar. People are desperate to hold on to their thoughts as if they were Willy Wonka golden tickets, as though giving them up would cause their whole world to collapse, vanish, cease to exist—a terrifying prospect the ego would do anything to avoid, which is why most people are still under its spell.

Katie would rejoice at such a prospect though and say, "Good! And who would you be without your thoughts? Who would you be if your whole world vanished? Who would you be without your dysfunctional world? Wouldn't it be glorious to find out?"

Katie was so committed to the truth that stepping on people's sensitivities, hobbyhorses, or sacred cows was of little consequence to her, as though the truth could not bear even the whitest lie. She spoke remarkably bluntly to people "to cut through the mind's misdirection." Katie spoke only the truth, if you could handle it. Many times she seemed wise beyond the normal confines of time and space. By some numinous power, she seemed to know each person's individual character traits and flaws before she had even spoken to them, and her words carried insights particular to that person. She was kind to some people and tough on others (I, apparently, was a tough-love candidate).

One day Katie casually told us a startling tale. While sitting on a suicide hotline once, a caller told her he had a gun pointed to his head and that if she didn't give him one reason why he should want to live, he would pull the trigger and blow his brains out right there on the call. There was a clicking sound on the other end like a gun safety being turned off, Katie said.

She was silent.

After a few moments the man said, "Well? Now or never."

Katie said, "You know, I thought about it, but I just couldn't think of one."

The audience gasped.

"What?" The man said. *"You can't?"*

"Nope."

"You can't think of one reason why I should want to live?"

"Not really," Katie said. "I tried, but I couldn't think of one."

There was a long silence on the other end. Finally Katie heard faint snuffling sounds and the clanging of metal that might have been a gun being dropped. The man spoke.

"Thank you for your honesty," he said. "That's all I wanted—for just one person to be honest with me just once. For just one person to stop lying and tell me the truth."

He went on to say that if she had told him anything else—given him reasons why he should live or why he shouldn't kill himself—that he would have pulled the trigger and blown his brains out right there.

"Have a nice day," Katie said.

"Thanks, you too ... Wait. *Who are you?*"

It's a good thing Katie wasn't one of us average people, I thought. That man owed his life to the fact there was an enlightened person on the other end of that call. I'm not sure whether Katie's answer would've worked in every situation, but I believe that by some supernatural power she knew what was needed there. Or maybe it was just the truth.

Questioning your thoughts was central to the Work. Step 2 is crucial: *Are you absolutely sure the thought is true?*

Well, no. If you even have to ask the question, then it's not true. If it was true, you'd know it in your bones. You wouldn't have to ask.

Step 3 also cuts to the quick of enlightenment: *Who would you be without your thought?* You'd be a fucking cruise missile—taking action fearlessly, without hesitation or regret.

Katie poured herself into the school with enormous energy. She worked a staggering number of hours during the ten days. She barely slept. Katie said that ever since she woke up to living in the permanent now, she'd had enormous stamina and energy, and she didn't feel tired anymore. It showed. Though she only slept a few hours a night, she seemed always fresh and alert, never tired, not even once.

Many participants' pain revolved around family members they were quarreling with and in some cases, not speaking to at all. Most painful was family members they had fallen out with completely, such as children they were no longer allowed to see. These issues were enormously upsetting to people, and the pain from them inevitably bubbled up, reducing them to crying blobs. I watched these people bathe in emotional pain on stage for all to see. They had signed up for the course for a reason, and in many cases this was it: estrangement from a loved one. I have lost a family member and can confirm it is uniquely, even exquisitely painful. Katie wisely counseled just to let the bad actor go, because what else can you do?

"It's out of your control," she said. "Just let them go, until they come back to you on their own. Forgive them. Love them in your heart. Love them from afar."

As always, Katie was right. I never saw her wrong, not once.

"Your family should love you," Katie said to a participant on stage. "What's the turnaround?"

The woman on stage was quiet. Katie waited.

"Your family *shouldn't* love you?" the woman asked, her voice trembling.

"Or …?" Katie said.

"Your family should *hurt* you."

"How do you feel?" Katie asked. "Do you feel lighter?"

"Why, yes," the woman said. "That's a depressing thought, but somehow, yes, I do feel lighter. I don't know why."

"Because it's true," Katie said. "Who knows how to hurt you better than your family? They know everything about you, all your weak points. They're tied to you emotionally. They want to pass their pain on to you—unconsciously perhaps, but still, they do. It's up to you to decide how much time you want to spend with people who hurt you."

Another time a woman was wailing on stage, grieving that her daughter wouldn't let her see her grandchild. Katie calmed the woman the way Crocodile Dundee calmed a water buffalo. She said, "Why can't you be with the person you love? You can be with them anytime you want, in your mind."

The woman looked doubtful.

"Think about it," Katie said. "Even when you're with the person in real life in the same room, the experience is mostly happening in your mind anyway. The joy, the happiness, the emotion, are all experienced in the mind whether the person is physically in the room or not. And how often did you see your daughter and grandchild anyway? Twice a year?"

"Once a year," the woman answered. "They live in another state."

"They live in another state," Katie said, smiling. "They do indeed."

The audience laughed.

"Think about it, dear," Katie said. "You see them, what, eight hours out of nine thousand hours in a year? The rest of the time you're only visiting them in your mind already. So what's really changed? You can visit them in your mind anytime you want—just be with them. Be with their best selves, the way you like to remember them."

The woman's face was streaked with tears, but she was no longer crying.

Many people were afflicted by a divorce or a partner who had dumped them. When someone complained about being dumped, Katie always replied, "Nope, you've been spared." She was adamant about that. "You've been spared, dear. Trust me. You've been spared. Next!"

Katie told us, "Life will give you everything you need, bring every problem you haven't yet solved right to your doorstep."

The audience chuckled knowingly.

"All your weak points, what you haven't faced yet, life will serve it up to you again and again. The same issue will keep arising until you solve it. You solve it by doing the Work on it. Once you undo it—and all spiritual work is really *unlearning* the false things you've learned across a lifetime—you'll find that life no longer serves up that particular problem to you anymore. It moves on to the next one, to the remaining issues you haven't yet dealt with." She smiled and tossed up her hands. "It's like a video game," she said. "Congratulations, you get to move on to the next level."

Laughter in the hall.

"So I suggest you solve what's bothering you as quickly as possible so you can move on to the next one. Your problem is always really an internal one in how you're perceiving, or rather misperceiving something, never an external person or situation."

Katie sat up straight. "There are people who have become so enlightened that they actually seek out problems, seek out what's left inside of them to dissolve because they want to live the rest of their lives as freely as possible. They've internalized the Work to such a degree that they can undo virtually any stressful thought, so they no longer fear problems. Finding what's left to undo becomes like sport or play for them.

"The ego will stick with whatever has been working for it so far, which is whatever you're willing to believe, whatever your mind keeps chewing on, usually the same one or two stressful thoughts that keep recycling in your mind over and over endlessly. And if you finally forget about one of those, a new thought quickly arises to take its place, doesn't it, so once again you're chewing on the same one or two thoughts. And dear, that's just not an interesting way to live."

Laughter.

"So if you simply refuse to accommodate those one or two thoughts, if you decide to banish them from your mind forever and refuse to take on new ones, your ego will just burn up, immolate.

"Negative thoughts and their resulting feelings are like little bits of bad weather. Don't make a big deal about the weather. Ignore it.

"Enlightenment is about undoing, letting go. When you let go, when you forgive, you're free from whatever you thought mattered. There is no problem when you're not thinking."

A hand raised. "What was the happiest time in your life?" a student asked.

Katie paused, considering the question. "Right now," she said.

"If you could go anywhere, where would you go?"

Katie thought about it. "Here," she said suddenly, looking up brightly. "I'd be here, with you now."

The crazy thing is, she meant it.

"If you could meet anyone in human history, who would it be?"

She pondered the question. "You," she said finally, her eyes shining. Some of the students frowned. Katie laughed. "You don't believe me," she said. "I mean it. I would rather be here with you, now. Because here is where I am and you're who I'm with. Why would I want to be anywhere other than where I am? That's not possible. *Now* is the only time; *here* the only place. I'm here, until I'm not. When I go somewhere else, then I'm there. But to want to be anywhere other than where you are doesn't make any sense. Besides ..." She suddenly beamed and stretched her arms out to all of us. "Look how beautiful you all are. *Of course* this is where I want to be. Why would I want to be with anyone else?"

"The past is gone. It doesn't exist. It existed only in the moment it was the present, and then it was gone. Poof." Katie snapped her fingers. "The future doesn't exist other than as a thought in your mind, as a concept. The future looks like this—it's now ..." She waited one second, two seconds. "Now it's now," she said, snapping her fingers each time she said *now*. "Now, now, now ... Do you see? The future only ever arrives as the present moment. There is no future. There's only now. Your future is the byproduct of what you're doing now. The future grows out of the now. What you're doing now is what you will be in the future. Your future is determined by your present. So whatever you want to be in the future, do it right now. Now is the only time you can do anything anyway."

Someone stood up and marched for the exit.

"Well, maybe not *right now*," Katie said, and everyone laughed.

"And that is the real purpose of life," Katie continued, the flock watching her rapt. "To become so present that you don't need the Work anymore. The four steps become so internalized in you from repeated use that they start to live inside you, and they respond to thoughts instantaneously, automatically. You find yourself in perfect harmony and alignment with life—not wrestling or fighting it anymore—and that's when life's deeper purpose starts to unfold and flow through you, and your actions become inspired because you're no longer resisting; you become a clear conduit for life to work its magic through you. And that's when you can start to influence life and mold to some degree what happens to you."

After lunch on the first full day, Katie asked, "How many of you have been raped?"

I was startled to see a full third of the women in the room raise their hands. I think that number is consistent with national statistics: about one-third. One man raised his hand too. I looked away, ashamed for him. Katie asked the women who had raised their hands to stand in a straight line. Then she ordered all the men to line up facing them, one man in front of each woman. Katie said she was going to turn off the lights and that for the next three minutes the men could put their hands on the women wherever they liked and could do whatever they wanted to them.

I thought I heard a zipper being pulled down prematurely.

The women looked horrified.

Katie instructed them not to move a muscle in resistance. The men stood still as refrigerators, poker-faced, as if any facial response would betray the lust, intrigue, or just plain embarrassment they were feeling. I stood opposite a youngish woman in her early thirties. I shrugged, embarrassed. She blushed but didn't avert her eyes from mine.

"Ready!" shouted Katie.

Standing grimly in a line as though facing a firing squad, the women braced themselves to be assaulted all over again. One poor middle-aged woman was clenching her eyes so tightly shut, girding herself for the sequel to whatever horror had happened to her long ago, that my heart went out to her. Amazingly none of the women made a break for the exit. They looked on despairingly, though, as Katie's staff deadbolted the doors to cancel any hopes of escape. A whiff of atrocity lurked over the room as though the ceiling's fire sprinklers were filled with poison gas. I could scarcely believe this was the school's inaugural event.

Katie took a deep breath, about to shout "Go!" when a woman down the row let out a high, plangent scream, a piercing cry of black terror. It sounded horrible, like a handicapped person being tortured. Katie gave her no quarter. She sternly reminded us that we had all signed affidavits to follow her orders, whatever they may be, after making the choice to stay.

A dial was turned and the lights extinguished. I didn't move. I could hear the women breathing in rapid spurts in the moist, cloistered darkness as they prepared to be assaulted. Like an animal in the forest rounding the watering hole at midnight, my ears pricked up for sounds of abuse down the line—the sound of more zippers being pulled down, bodices being ripped, garters being yanked down and snapped, hands slapping flesh and leaving large red handprints on women's lily white bare behinds, the goosebumps standing up on their suddenly exposed flesh where the blood and air were rushing to it—wondering whether anyone was really having a go at it.

I didn't hear anything other than clipped, hurried breathing. The clock ticked on. We had each been ordered to stand directly in front of our partner, mere inches from her face to make touching her easier, and I felt my partner's hot breath wash over my face like a small warm wave lapping over a beach. Her breath smelled like strawberries. The room was close; it felt like a womb or a bed. I had the feeling of water rushing between reeds, the closest thing to an ancient pre-mating ritual in a dark cave I can imagine. My partner's body heat crossed the slender gap between us like microwaves. She was shapely with soft curves and a pretty face. She was attractive, and after a minute I had a wild, involuntary urge to reach out and clasp her bosom against my chest in the bedroom closet-like darkness. But of course I didn't.

Suddenly the lights flickered on. I looked down the line. To my astonishment, about half the men were hugging the woman across from them. Just embracing them! I couldn't believe it. I had missed my chance to hug the attractive woman opposite me. Dammit! Most of the women stood rigid as stone, their arms hanging limply by their sides. Only one woman was half-heartedly hugging the man across from her back, her face miserable. Half the men stood back, as I did, doing nothing. There was a collective exhalation of relief from the women when the lights came back on. They had survived the school's first test; they had not been raped again.

"Bathroom break!" Katie called out cheerfully, and her minions unbolted the doors.

When we returned, Katie asked the women, "Are you okay?"

The women nodded. If none of the men really understood the purpose of the exercise, it seemed from the silent communication between Katie and the women that they did.

On the fourth morning we came downstairs to find the breakfast buffet cart gone. Vanished. The room was empty. I laughed. This was one of the school's surprises. No breakfast this morning. Some of the participants were milling about the empty room like confused cows, as though if they just kept milling around, breakfast would magically reappear. Losing breakfast was so profoundly unacceptable to them that they refused to believe the evidence of their own senses.

Stomachs rumbling, we straggled into the main hall to begin the day. As we sat down, Katie announced that we were going on indefinite fast. We would have no food at all for the foreseeable future. The fast could last until the end of the course—another seven days.

"Not to worry, though," Katie said, smiling, "there will be plenty of water stations on hand."

My roommate, Bruce, an obese psychologist from Iowa, snorted in disbelief. The students were spending $5,000—most of them more than that due to airfare to Los Angeles which wasn't included in the price—for a recondite course in enlightenment in a luxury hotel that they now discovered provided no food after the first three days.

Hilarious.

I thought about how much profit Katie must be raking in not providing food to a hundred-plus people for seven out of ten days. Her overhead had just disappeared. Actually, since all her workers were volunteers, there were now no costs to her side at all by my calculation. As I said before, the price of enlightenment is steep.

At lunchtime the buffet table had been put back, but it was empty aside from two bins filled with green "vegetable water." Yummy.

Katie's minions told us that the water was "infused with boiled-down vegetable parts" and therefore was more nourishing than ordinary water. Bruce didn't look impressed. He gave a great heaving moan like an orca giving birth. Nearly all the students, other than a few granola hippie types, looked glum. And wouldn't you be if you were an affluent couple of lawyers in their forties who had just shelled out $10,000 to be enlightened in luxury only to discover they had no access to the filet mignon being served in the hotel restaurant down the hall and had to get by on fasting and vegetable water instead? I'm sure a few people wondered where their money was going. I took a sip of the vegetable water. It tasted as awful as you would expect. Like green peas. I set my glass down. I'll just have regular water, I thought.

Three days later, on the morning of the seventh day, I was starving. Bruce looked positively woozy and disoriented from hunger. He was swaying gently from side to side like a palm tree in a soft Hawaiian breeze. If you didn't know Bruce was just really, really hungry, you'd be forgiven for thinking he was staggering drunk. After three days of fasting he was as obese as ever, even more so. Cruel twist of fate—fat man stops eating, only gets fatter.

On the eighth day, when Bruce entered the dining room and saw the buffet cart empty yet again—our fourth consecutive day without any food—it seemed to trigger some ancient trauma that pushed him past his breaking point. I watched Bruce stare into the empty cart for a long time without moving. His eyes were watery and distant, as though his mind was in another galaxy billions of light-years away.

His expression betrayed a curious mix of desperation and self-pity. After three days of fasting he had really been expecting there to be food on the fourth morning. And doesn't that make sense? Three days of fasting sounds right, followed by food on the fourth day? I had watched

Bruce sit on the edge of his bed in our room that morning and do what he had taught a thousand of his patients to do: visualize it.

Visualize it. Get it.

He had visualized a mountain of scrambled eggs and a Roman Emperor's share of bacon.

But reality doesn't give a shit about what they teach shrinks in shrink school. Reality is much closer to the Old Testament—no justice, no mercy, no remorse, and most importantly, no food. Bruce scratched his patchy beard as though he were in sub-Sahara Africa and flies were in it. His eyes watered to the brink of tears, and another huge, heaving sigh exited his vast frame as though he were a sperm whale watching a sunset. The next thing I knew, Bruce had waddled over to the buffet float and gripped its lip with both hands. He leaned over the empty cart and hung his head in the tins in despair. Staring into the empty tins, he seemed to be trying to will food into them Mary Poppins–style. For just a moment, perhaps, a great smell of breakfast wafted into his nostrils as towers of eggs, miles of sausage links, and buckets of Belgian waffles materialized before him like Valhalla. If so, the mirage was only that—a mirage. Bruce swayed gently from side to side, his eyes pressed tightly shut. He was either dreaming of food or about to pass out. The swaying palm tree began to sway a bit unrealistically—the parabola of his movement became too wide for his feet, which were cemented to the floor as though packed into cinder blocks. Suddenly Bruce's knees buckled, and he collapsed on the spot.

"*Bruce!*" I cried out and ran to him.

I slid to the floor over my roommate. I patted his cheek. Was he dead? I hoped I would not have to perform mouth-to-mouth CPR on him, but I was prepared to do it. Bruce lay on the floor, his eyes open but as vacant as his stomach. I half expected him to say, "Take me now, God. I'm ready." I stared into his sad, pouchy face. It wasn't just hunger. There was definitely an emotional component to his anxiety at not getting food. Breakfast was like morphine to him. His opioid, his poppy. Bruce was reaching his tipping point. He wanted to eat more than he wanted enlightenment.

Me, I was still holding out for enlightenment.

I enlisted another man's help and together we peeled Bruce off the floor and propped him against the empty buffet cart like a scarecrow or a warning to would-be assassins. Physically depleted from the effort of moving him and hungry ourselves, we straggled over to the main hall.

Katie was smiling serenely on stage. She clearly had no problem starving herself. In fact, she seemed to enjoy it.

Spiritual Practice 2: Face Your Fear

From her perch on stage Katie declared that today would be our first real test.

"Are you afraid of being murdered? Raped?"

Again the preoccupation with rape—I wondered whether Katie herself had had an experience when she was young. Every time Katie asked this question, the same woman who had cried out during the first exercise issued a banshee-like shriek from the back of the room. Her scream was long and tortured like the scream from a lobster being lowered into a vat of boiling water in a Red Lobster kitchen. Katie sat placidly while the woman screamed unabated for a full two minutes. Then Katie apparently had had enough because she told the woman to be quiet.

"Are you afraid of being murdered?" Katie repeated. "Afraid of being abandoned, destitute, alone and penniless?"

Yes, we nodded dutifully. Yes, we were. I wondered what horror was in store for us.

Katie instructed us to go up to our rooms and leave behind our wallets, money, identification, keys—everything. A bus was idling out front. We were to board it in ten minutes with nothing but the clothes on our backs. We would be driven to the worst area in Los Angeles—Crenshaw in the South Central part of the city—and be abandoned there overnight. We would be forced to survive on our own for twenty-four hours straight without help, without a quarter to drop into a pay phone or a safe word to cry out if we'd had enough and wanted to exit this twisted game. We would have to survive a night on the meanest streets in the most dangerous neighborhood in America with no protection and no possible escape. Katie said that the bus would return the following day "to collect whoever was still alive." She reminded us that we had signed affidavits indemnifying the School of Enlightenment of any responsibility for anything that happened to us.

The audience blanched. Someone was dry heaving. This was too much. People leaped to their feet in panic, in a frenzy as though they had just been bitten on the ass by angry rats. Katie smiled broadly from ear to ear as chaos and terror ravaged the room like a monsoon. She drank it all in rapturously. Seeing people freak out and losing their minds only seemed to juice her.

"You lost your mind? Great! Celebrate!" Katie cried out, nodding. "Good! What's wrong with losing your mind when your mind is the whole problem in the first place? Sounds like a good beginning," she said.

She sighed with pleasure. "Ah, so many unfinished areas left to dig into."

It's become fashionable to declutter your home. Katie's passion is decluttering the mind. As I watched middle-aged people run around the room in loopy, ranting terror like wildebeests hemmed in by a pride of lions, I smiled. I was probably the only other person in the room who was excited. At last, something truly provocative! Katie held up her hand with a look of admonition as she waited for the panicked students to settle down.

"There's more," she said. "Listen up."

Besides having no money, phones, wallets, or identification, we would not be allowed to speak to anyone. We were permitted to say only three things:

1. Feed me.
2. Thank you.
3. No.

You might have guessed—and if you did, congratulations—that no was added only belatedly to fend off the rape that would inevitably occur by a denizen of South Central Los Angeles.

We were absolutely forbidden to say anything other than these three phrases. We were not allowed to go to the police. We could not ask for help. "Help!" was not one of the approved three phrases.

Our task, Katie explained, was to walk up to strangers and say, "Feed me." She pointed out that because we had been starved for the last four days, our request should be convincing. In our weakened, malnourished state it would be clear to people that we really were hungry.

"You won't have to pretend!" she exulted.

Our hunger would give us that "extra push" to not be shy about approaching strangers in Crenshaw utterly defenseless other than for our destitution, which should be abject enough to backfoot even the most violent killer, and asking them to feed us.

Ten minutes later we all boarded the bus in silence. It was like the Trail of Tears. Dread permeated the procession like a death fugue. The women especially looked terrified, their faces drained of color, white as marble. They stared into space, numb. They had already shut themselves down, resigned that they probably wouldn't survive the night. The bus rolled out of the luxury hotel with the sickening feeling that it was transporting us to a concentration camp. After an hour wending through the streets of downtown Los Angeles, the bus slid like a submarine into the impoverished neighborhoods of Inglewood and Crenshaw.

First everyone on the street was Latino. Then everyone was black. Abandoned La-Z-Boys, sofas with no cushions, rusted box springs, and mounds of broken furniture formed topographical mountain ranges inside fenced-in yards in front of ramshackle broken-down houses. A group of about twenty shirtless young black men in jeans and do-rags hoisted forty-ounce bottles of liquor to the sky and shook their fists at the bus, this strange leviathan that had no place in their neighborhood. A forty-year-old red-haired woman who had been vivacious earlier in the week sat beside me. She stared straight ahead, gripping the handlebar above her white-knuckled like a parachute ripcord, her face contorted in open, free-flowing terror.

But there was no ripcord out of this situation.

"It's just a penis," she said aloud to no one, in a detached, clinical voice. "He'll put it in … It'll go on for a few minutes … Then it'll stop. It won't kill me. It's just a penis …"

Her eyes glazed over. She had mentally checked out, and her medulla oblongata, the lizard brain at the base of her brainpan, had returned from one hundred thousand years ago to take control of the console again and map out a plan for her to survive. *We knew your pansy-ass developed brain didn't have the stones when it counted. Now back the fuck up. We're here to clean up your mess yet again.*

"It'll happen … then it'll be over," she mumbled, still checked out behind her eyes.

Suddenly she swiveled toward me, sallow and moonfaced, and frowned. I frowned back and turned away to look out the window. The apocalypse loomed just outside these Plexiglas windows. I wanted to say to the woman, "I'll protect you," but honestly was not sure I could.

I scanned the unforgiving urban jungle. This was by far the most dangerous jungle in the world. This place made Syria look like Club Med. Enormous men who could play in the NFL were shirtless or wearing wifebeaters, drinking forties, and smoking spliffs of marijuana the length of my full arm. It looked like a healthy environment. The locals watched the bus peel by, a fish out of water, until their curiosity gradually and inevitably gave way to venom. Roving throngs of young black men swarmed into the street, lured by the gravitational pull of the bus, like a black hole zeroing in on a dwarf star. The men shouted and shook their fists at the bus as we passed. It looked tribal. We had their full attention now.

A couple of shirtless teenagers jumped onto bicycles and started pedaling furiously behind the bus.

"Are they armed?" an elderly white woman asked.

"Probably," I answered. "I would be if I lived here. The gat is tucked inside their shorts."

On hearing this, the woman in the seat in front of me swooned. Her eyes rolled back inside her skull, a small moan issued from her mouth, and she fainted right there in her seat, dead to the world. I thought being unconscious might well be the best way to get through the next twenty-four hours.

Everyone was terrified but rather bravely seemed to accept that we had no choice but to somehow make it through the night in the most dangerous neighborhood in America. I felt a flinty determination begin to set in among the students, an obsidian grit, and maybe some good old-fashioned American toughness. *The British are coming. Time to kick their asses. Go time. Let's do this.*

The students were steeling themselves for a night of horrors that was coming up real fast now. The violation of our bodies, a beating for sure, and possibly death awaited us in this neighborhood. Yet these soft-bodied, middle-aged people were actually going to go through with it. They were tougher than they looked. Tougher than me.

One sane woman suddenly jerked around in her seat and asked, quite logically, "Guys, why are we doing this? Are we nuts? Why do we trust Katie? Just because we paid her a lot of money? Have we been brainwashed into joining a cult?"

"Probably," the red-haired woman next to me answered detachedly. "We have been brainwashed into a cult; we haven't been brainwashed ... Either could be true. So, yeah, we probably joined a cult."

Thank you, grasshopper. I didn't know whether it was an enlightened response or not, but at least the woman wasn't freaking out, which under the circumstances would have been more than justified.

The bus trundled on, and throngs of black youth coalesced around us like covalent bonds. Some of them started banging their fists on the bus' exterior. *Bang! Bang! Bang!* The hollow metal sheeting reverberated disproportionately loudly inside the bus, like a kettledrum, further frightening us. As the mob closed in, hemming us in like a net rising from below to swallow a school of fish, my mind drifted back to when I was twenty-one years old, shortly after I graduated from UCLA.

I lived in a tiny apartment in Santa Monica on Third Street and Rose, just above Main Street, a fashionable area. Rose Avenue was the effective demarcation line between affluent Santa Monica and impoverished Venice. It was like a sovereign country's border—on one side was the first world, on the other side was Somalia. I had just returned from traveling around Europe for five months and was working in a small diner. Another waiter at the diner was a young French migrant who lived three streets down from me on the Venice side of Rose.

One night he invited me over. It was close enough that I decided to walk.

It was pitch-black outside. The night coming off the ocean was as dense and black as octopus ink. There were no streetlamps on the boardwalk on Santa Monica Beach, so you could hear the surf roaring in the distance but couldn't see it. At the time, Venice Beach and Santa Monica Beach were overrun by vagrants and drug addicts and I would have hesitated to go down to the beach at night. The beach was a lampless gaping hole and I feared that if I entered it, I would never return.

Crossing Rose Avenue into Venice was like crossing the Rubicon into hell. I had a clear sense of walking into danger but not enough to stop me. I peered into the moonless murk. I felt alert, my senses heightened. Shortly after crossing Rose, I looked down and saw white tape spackled on the sidewalk in the outline of a human being, about six feet tall. I had seen that somewhere before, on crime TV. But here it was in real life. Someone had been murdered in this very spot in the last twenty-four hours, and the police had framed the body in white tape before carrying away the corpse, leaving behind only this eerie silhouette, a sort of grave in the urban jungle, that most dangerous of the world's jungles.

Yellow crime scene tape hung down in shredded ribbons from a stop sign and a fence where it had once protected the urban grave. But the ribbons had been slashed and viciously ripped apart as if by some virulent vampire dog, some bloodthirsty animal. I stared at the human outline commemorated on concrete. It was my first time to encounter death up close. I realized a man, probably a black man, had been murdered in this spot as recently as a few hours ago. I looked around but the darkness was impenetrable. I couldn't see a thing. It was dead silent.

I moved on to the next street, and that's when it happened. A gang of fifteen black kids between the ages of six and fifteen emerged like wraiths from the darkness. With astonishing speed they zoomed at me in a pack like an amoeba. It happened so fast that I did not run. I stood perfectly still and just absorbed them, intensely alert. The boys closed around me in a tight circle and pressed their bodies up against mine. I realized it was dangerous because I couldn't see their hands. If they wanted to, they could have started stabbing me with knives and killed me right there quite easily. One of the little boys, perhaps eight years old, tipped his face back to look up at mine. I clenched my stomach to absorb a knife thrust. But his face suddenly split into a pearly-white smile. His teeth were so white that they glowed in the dark.

He reached down. I flinched. Then he whipped out a baggie filled with white powder—cocaine. I had never seen cocaine before; it looked like laundry detergent. I held up my hands in the universal "No, thank you" gesture. The boys giggled as a collective unit, and like a blob with fifteen pairs of feet underneath, they crabbed off into the darkness. I was left alone on the street. Beyond a single streetlamp, the darkness once again was inscrutable, thick and menacing, binding, old. Threats of untold number lurked beyond that solitary lamp in the mine-like darkness. *Wow,* I thought. *Los Angeles has a lot of bad areas.* After that experience I stayed out of Venice at night. I saw that Venice was frankly more dangerous than Afghanistan.

That memory came back to me as the bus snaked through Crenshaw, and then Inglewood. I kept thinking the bus was about to stop and we'd be ordered to get out. But it kept driving. Another hour passed. I could see that everyone was wondering the same thing: *Why hasn't the bus stopped yet?* Was it possible we were heading to an even worse part of Los Angeles?

Suddenly the bus took a hard right turn and abruptly changed directions. Before long we pulled out of the bad area completely. I smelled brine and saw that we were driving north up the Pacific Coast Highway. The primal fear everyone palpably felt suddenly gave way to confusion. No one thought we were out of the woods just yet, and

I still wondered whether this was just a detour to a worse area. But as the bus kept rolling in the direction of Santa Monica, it dawned on me that perhaps we were not going to be abandoned in the projects that night. Had they driven us through that neighborhood just to scare us?

We finally pulled onto the wood-ribbed deck of the Santa Monica pier, and the bus cantered to a leisurely stop. Exhalations of relief flooded out of the students when the driver yanked the gearshift into park. It appeared we were not going to be raped and murdered, at least not today. The dialed-up-to-the-maximum tension eased just a little. A little air came out of the tires.

"Get out," Katie said.

It's great to be ordered around and humiliated when you're paying $5,000 a head for it.

It was one in the afternoon. Katie didn't tell us that we wouldn't have to spend the night out here, but she did tell us to return to the pier at seven that evening. The students exchanged glances. Katie said to remember the first exercise on the first day—giving away our most valuable possession. That was powerful spiritual practice, she said, one that benefits us far more than we know. Today we would learn the second powerful spiritual practice, second of three. She knew we were hungry, she said, and on our fourth consecutive day without food.

"Now go out and get someone to feed you," she said.

We would be shadowed by her minions to ensure we didn't say anything other than the three allowed phrases. She urged us to take full advantage of the exercise, to be bold and not to run away and hide in the sand somewhere—we would only be shortchanging our own chance of enlightenment if we did that.

"And isn't that why you came in the first place?" she reminded us.

I wandered down to the beach in the direction of the Chess Park, an old sanctuary of mine from when I lived on Third Street that first year out of college. I won the Maryland State Chess Championship when I was eight years old in the fourteen-years-old-and-under division, but I'd been astonished to lose regularly to the genius savants who live in the chess park. The park was my second home, though as an ultracompetitive person, it always stings me bitterly to lose a game of chess. There's nothing like being an eight-year-old state chess champion and then meeting an esoteric group of people who can kick your ass every time. It's humbling.

One guy who obviously had severe mental problems played with all ten of his fingers caked in blood from his literally eating the ends of his fingers off. He was young, in his early twenties, with black hair and stubble, and quite handsome in a James Dean way. We called him Grandmaster Bloodyfingers. He was a legitimate genius and had the corresponding insanity to back it up. He was the only person who could beat a fat man named Duckworth. Duckworth had an impressively high rating of 2400 on the professional chess circuit, ranking him among the best players in the United States, and yet Grandmaster Bloodyfingers beat him every time.

I marshaled the courage to play Bloodyfingers once. He only played for money, as most of the good players did, so we played for five dollars. Everyone in the park played with a time clock to force players to move quickly to prevent games from slowing down. Bloodyfingers gave me ten minutes of total game time, while he gave himself only thirty seconds to play his entire game. The clock counts down only on your turn. After you make a move, you punch the clock and then it ticks down for the other player. You lose the game either when you run out of time or are checkmated. All I had to do to win five dollars was stretch out the game long enough for him to use cumulative thirty seconds and run out of time. I had a leisurely ten minutes, twenty times his amount of time, so I could afford to think longer between moves. I thought I should be able to win this. Halfway through the game, he spent fifteen seconds, half of his total game time, on a single move.

After he moved, he was down to less than ten seconds left to last him the rest of the game. No pieces had come off the board yet, and we were roughly even.

He won.

He checkmated me with one second left on his clock. Humiliating to be sure, but I was playing a bona fide genius of the sort I have never encountered since. I had never seen a chess player who saw through the game instead of having to go through complex mental calculations the way the rest of us did. Bloodyfingers never spoke, but he occasionally cackled wide-eyed like a goose surprised by a water sprinkler erupting under its bottom.

"Duckworth is one of the best players in the country, and you beat him every time," I said as I handed him five dollars. "You're as good as Bobby Fischer. Why don't you play professionally?"

He smiled, revealing a cavernous maw of empty black gums with only five teeth left, one of them dangling by a single thread and about to fall out.

Oh, that's why, I thought.

I avoided the chess park today. I was not going to ask those people to feed me. There is no one cheaper than a homeless chess genius.

I scanned the people on the beach. A young Mexican father, about thirty years old, with his perhaps ten-year-old son, stood nearby. I walked up to him. I felt a little nervous.

"Feed me," I said, choking on the words but looking him straight in the eye.

The Mexican stared back at me. He scanned me from head to toe in my rather well-appointed clothing. His eyebrows quivered, and for just a moment his whole face shook as though it were being kneaded into bread. Suddenly his head flew backward and he erupted in laughter.

He thought I was joking.

"You are *loco*! That is hilarious, dude!" he laughed.

But I didn't smile. My face was as implacable as a Serbian war criminal's. He stopped laughing. To my astonishment, he reached into his pocket and handed me a five-dollar bill.

My God, I had just made five dollars simply by asking a stranger on the beach for it!

My jaw dropped to the floor. "Thank you," I said, amazed. I had already used two of the allotted three phrases. I didn't anticipate needing to say no, nevertheless no is always a useful card to carry in one's back pocket.

How kind, I thought, suddenly filled with a deep appreciation for the man and his generosity. I knew he probably didn't have much wiggle room in his budget, and yet he had helped me anyway. I will always remember my Mexican friends.

A stand-alone Hot Dog on a Stick materialized on the boardwalk ahead of me. I marched up and bought a hot dog on a stick and a lemonade for four dollars. That left me with one dollar left to play with, which I stuffed back into my pocket. I inhaled the hot dog in one bite and flushed it down with the lemonade. It was beyond delicious, but the entire thing was gone in less than a second. My stomach rejoiced. Hunger turns eating into a sensuous experience. It had been so long since I'd had food that I could literally feel the nutrients from the hot dog shoot out on platelets across my bloodstream, distributed to the four corners of my body. A deep sense of well-being radiated through me. The best part about a Paleolithic lifestyle is definitely still the eating.

Emboldened by my success, I didn't hesitate. I zeroed in on an affluent-looking white woman in her forties with a string of pearls around her neck. Rich lady: low-hanging fruit. She was walking on the boardwalk in the direction of the pier with her husband. If the Mexican man had given me money, this ought to be a slam dunk. I headed straight for her and bisected her path.

"Feed me."

The woman stared at me. For just a moment her face went slack like the painting *The Scream,* in blank precomprehension. Then her face contorted grotesquely into a horror show that was far scarier than *The Scream.*

"*Go awaaay!*" she screamed at the top of her lungs, her face twisted like a gargoyle's.

She swung around and, roping along her husband who looked mortified by her behavior, scuttled down the boardwalk like a beetle.

I was disappointed. My own whities, so worthless. Judging by the pearls and handbag and designer clothes she was wearing, she could easily have afforded to give me a dollar. The Mexican had given me five dollars he probably could scarcely afford. I recalled my Sunday school lessons from childhood: *"Blessed are the poor in spirit, for theirs is the kingdom of heaven."* Blessed are the humble and the kind, it means, and heaven is theirs. I knew the Mexican man would be taken care of in the next life. The middle-aged woman, who I had the distinct feeling had married into money rather than make it herself, would return in the next life as, perhaps, a bug of one kind or another.

I walked to Santa Monica's Third Street Promenade. It was a place I knew well. In my life before the school I came here every week for a Bryan Kest *ashtanga* power-yoga class and yuppie-hipster shot of wheatgrass at Jamba Juice afterward. Wheatgrass tasted awful but the marketing had worked, and somehow I felt cool swallowing it, like it was snake blood in Thailand or something. I felt like a hipster, the very person I don't want to be.

Sometimes I woke early on Saturday mornings for an 8:30 a.m. yoga class and had breakfast afterward on the promenade, thereby negating the exercise I had just done, followed by time in the bookstore. Now I was entering the promenade as a wraith, as someone from the hungry, homeless netherworld. I walked up to a young girl my age.

"Feed me."

She looked at me like I was insane. But then she looked in my eyes and saw I wasn't crazy. She giggled a little, and then promptly turned around and fled. I realized asking an attractive girl my age probably wouldn't work. In the brief moment when we had first made eye contact and I had started speaking, her eyes lit up happily until the words "Feed me" escaped my lips. She probably thought I was going to ask her out. Which in retrospect I should have done since she was cute. *Dammit!*

But asking her out wasn't one of the approved three phrases.

The next woman I approached was in her early thirties. "Feed me." I was getting used to saying it now without thinking, and my delivery had improved. She shot me a quizzical look and thought about it for a moment.

"Okay, come with me," she said. She cocked her head toward a pretzel shop.

I think she thought I was retarded.

Which, as a strategy, actually worked quite well.

We stood in line, and she paid $1.50 for a pretzel, which I wolfed down right in front of her, the crumbs falling all over my shirt. It was part of my new mentally-challenged act. Although truth be told, the crumbs would have fallen on my shirt anyway. Again the food was gone in less than a second.

"Thank you," I said.

She didn't buy me a drink. I was thirsty.

I noticed that in the time since I'd eaten the hot dog on a stick and now the pretzel, my hunger had, out of nowhere, suddenly intensified violently and had morphed into an alien with an angry head that was thrashing around inside my stomach. The first twenty-four hours of the fast had been rough, but I had not felt too hungry since then, nothing too uncomfortable. The third day of a fast has a golden reputation for being sublime: like after a colonoscopy, you feel amazingly light, clean, as though your whole body had had a good spring-cleaning. But eating again in very small quantities today had ruined the fast I'd gradually built up and ignited a surprisingly ferocious hunger in my belly, something vile. It was a wretched, poverty-level hunger that I had never known in all my life. It was an awful new feeling.

I moved around the Third Street Promenade like a ghost, or some kind of ravenous wolf. Only an hour remained until it would be time to return to the bus. I wanted to replicate my beginner's luck one more time and see if I could get another stranger to give me money simply by asking for it, to prove that the first time had not been a fluke. I scouted possible targets and finally settled on a youngish woman around thirty-five. "Feed me." Without hesitation she reached in her purse and handed me a five-dollar bill.

Disco!

With the dollar in my pocket I now had six dollars, enough to buy a Double-Double burger with fries and a Coke at In-N-Out Burger. Success! I stood in line and bought it to go. I was proud of myself. This was really earning my dinner. I had this wondrous burger, this ambrosia, food of the gods, in my hand. In my hand! It was exactly what I wanted and needed. I decided to celebrate by taking it down to the beach and eat while watching the sunset.

As I crossed Second Street heading toward the Pacific Coast Highway, out of the corner of my eye I spied a homeless man lying dejectedly on the sidewalk, his back propped up against a brick wall as though it were the masthead of his bed. I moved to walk around him, but … too late; I had seen him. Maybe I had been indoctrinated by the school. Maybe it was just my basic nature. But a small voice in the back of my head said, *Give the Double-Double burger to that man on the street. You are in the School of Enlightenment for Chrissakes! Try to act like it!*

The frontal lobe of my brain shot back, *No, I worked hard for this. I'm starving too. I'm going to eat it. I earned it. I begged harder than he did. I begged better. Screw him. And screw you too!*

But I already knew what I would do. My decision had been made, and I wasn't going to reverse it. I walked up to the homeless man and asked if he wanted my In-N-Out burger. He looked up at me, bleary-eyed.

"Yeah," he said.

I handed it to him and walked away. I turned around at the corner and waited until he bit into the burger. I wanted to make sure that if I gave it to him he actually ate it. He didn't touch the fries, I noticed resentfully.

The *moment* after the burger had left my fingertips I profoundly regretted my decision. I thought I was practicing spiritual enlightenment. I thought I was getting my money's worth from the course. But as if my stomach was a separate organism with a brain all its own, the split second after the burger left my hand, my already rumbling stomach exploded into a truly vicious hunger—an African famine type of hunger that wipes out millions from the human race every year. For the first time in my life I knew how these people felt. I was quite cranky and fiercely berated myself. *Dammit, what are you doing?* I punched myself in the face. I almost went back to the homeless man and snatched the remaining half of the burger out of his hand.

"I made a mistake. I want that back," I was going to say. As the man looked up at me eating the burger, I was going to say, "Sorry, but I'm hungrier than you. Next time you beg, really put your back into it. Beg like you mean it."

It was now seven, and I had to return to the pier. Drawn by the phantom lure of the food as though it were a tractor beam, I poured salt in my wound by gratuitously walking past the homeless man once again. As I walked past, he pushed the last piece of hamburger into his mouth. His vacant eyes stared straight ahead, uncomprehending. He was probably barely conscious. An ugly pang of hunger stabbed the inner wall of my stomach like an alien trying to break out. *At least the bum ate the burger,* I thought bitterly.

In college I'd experimented with buying food for the many homeless people in Westwood. I'd bought Diddy Riese cookies and coffee for them, only to have my offer rebuffed. I had been startled to discover that homeless people very often will turn down food. I will accept free food even when I'm full. I can't imagine turning down food under any circumstances.

I crossed the Pacific Coast Highway and made my way back to the Santa Monica Pier. The iconic Ferris wheel gleamed in the night sky high above the Pacific Ocean. The wheel was so bright that aliens from outer space could use it as a homing beacon to plan some future attack on our planet.

Katie stood alone on the pier—elfin, luminous, ascendant—gleaming in an emerald summer dress that whipped around her ankles in the warm summer wind that drove out of the Pacific and engulfed the pier. She raised her outstretched arms toward us in an embrace that was large enough to take in the entire world. A radiant expression of deepest joy shone on her face. You could tell that this exercise at the school was her favorite.

"Huddle in, team!" she called.

Hungry and dragging our feet like rented donkeys, we collected around her like refugees who had just arrived in the cargo hold of a slave ship from Cambodia. Katie slowly clapped her hands together. Clap … clap … clap … clap … clap, clap, clap, clap!

"Bravo!" she cried out, clapping faster now. "Bravo! Well done!"

She leaned in. Her eyes were glittering as she searched our faces. Her blue eyes were all alight, ignited in blue flame. From head to toe she was lit up phosphorescent, incandescent, framed from behind by the electric Ferris wheel.

"Do you know what the purpose of that test was?" she asked, her voice louder than usual.

No one tried to answer. Even the brownnosers were silent this time. Everyone was too downtrodden. "We'll talk about it later," Katie said, happy as could be. "How many of you approached strangers, asked them to feed you?"

About 75 percent of people raised their hands. The others, more than I'd have thought, had slithered away and hidden under a rock somewhere to run out the clock.

"And did they feed you?"

Most people had had some success, as I did. Only three people, one glowering woman and two Indian IT people, said no one had given them a goddamn thing.

Katie huddled with us, quarterback to our ramshackle football team. "I know you haven't eaten for days," she said. She flashed us a conspiratorial look, as if we were all in this together. "Come with me."

She smiled impishly and gestured toward the side of the pier as though Christmas stockings hung off the end of it. I perked up at her words. I was dreaming of a rib eye and a baked potato with sour cream. Perhaps the mistake I had made giving the hamburger away would soon be redressed. I would be rewarded for my good works.

"Behold," Katie cried out with a flourish, sweeping her arm down toward the parking lot beneath the pier.

I strained to see what she was pointing at. A large area had been cordoned off and the buffet table from the hotel had been transported here and erected down on the asphalt below.

We stumbled down the cliff like migrants looking for oranges. Some people were literally rolling head over heels down the side of the hill, their clothes caked in dirt. Acute hunger had degraded their motor functions. Would Katie finally give us some meat? The whole school had been only vegetarian up until now. She must know how hungry we were.

I padded up to the buffet like a kid in pajamas on Christmas morning, excited to see what sumptuous wonders lay inside. I peered inside the tins. Disappointment hit me like a dick punch. There was only the dreary vegetable water from the last four days and some tofu eggplant garbage, none of which I can stand. If I eat tofu or eggplant, I puke. Who can stand it?

I was so disappointed I actually cried aloud, "Dammit!" no longer caring who heard me.

The food could not have been worse. I looked around desperately, but the parking lot was empty. I was flooded with crazy ideas that suddenly seemed plausible, like punching a stranger and stealing their wallet for food, or running back up to Third Street Promenade and renew my begging with fresh vigor. I had already thought of a few new strategies I might try. *If I begged for a burger before, I can do it again.*

Katie made a nifty little bow in front of her surprise dinner, sweeping one arm across her waist and throwing the other in the air like a theater actor. She sure seemed pleased with herself for providing what was essentially pig slop.

"Dig in!" she cried out ecstatically, as if she'd just driven us in to Bob's Big Boy.

I tried some vegetable water. It tasted horrible. It tasted like ass. Because I was so hungry, I nibbled on a little eggplant. I nearly vomited. My stomach rejected it outright. I doubled over and dry heaved in the parking lot. I happened to be standing right in front of Katie while I dry heaved. She blithely ignored me as I loudly retched.

She stared over my doubled-over body and, holding up a wad of eggplant that looked like an alien fetus, shouted to everyone, "Mmm, delicious. Have some!"

My body craved In-N-Out hamburger, goddammit, the very thing I had just *given away*. I craved rich foods—pork, sour cream, cheese. These magical foods held no dominion over Katie, though, a converted vegetarian since a year after her enlightenment. *What the hell does vegetarianism have to do with enlightenment anyway?* Jesus ate meat and the Bible endorses it 100 percent. I found myself looking up at the gulls in the sky. *If only I could shoot one down.*

I was surly during the entire bus ride back to the hotel. Who the hell stays in a five-star hotel and is starved for four days? "Fuck this." I slammed my fist into the Plexiglas window. No one cared, least of all the window. My hand hurt. I growled like a wild thing, like a wolf-man who had somehow boarded our bus. Aggravated hunger was driving me crazy.

I had followed the rules up until now; I had been a good boy. Just like at work, where I was being falsely smeared by a jealous boss, I had behaved and been good all my life, and it had gotten me nowhere. Everything they teach you as a kid is wrong. Being good gets you nowhere.

That night after we got back, feeling desperate but armed with a plan and thus newly determined, no longer the altar boy I once had been, beaten down by haters and control freaks, buffeted by enemies on all sides, I decided that if no one would help me in life, I would have to help myself. While the main exit to the hotel was barred by Katie's goons, there *was* a coffee shop in the hotel lobby. I waited until Bruce had waddled into the bathroom, and then grabbed a fistful of dollars from my wallet. I waited until everyone had gone to sleep, and then just before the coffee shop closed at eleven, cleaving to shadow I slid downstairs and whispered my deepest desire in the ear of the prettiest college student you have ever seen manning a cake display.

I bought a hunk of carrot cake and a mug of coffee, breaking protocol at the school for the first time. The hunk of carrot cake was the size of a soccer ball, and I inhaled it like it was the last gasp of oxygen on a failing mission to Mars. It was the best goddamn thing I have ever tasted in all my life. It tasted better than filet mignon and lobster with a pound of foie gras on top by a measure of a thousand. I drowned down the cake with the steaming hot mug of acrid black coffee, guzzling it like it was Gatorade. Coffee, too, had never tasted so good.

It's amazing how Katie's vegetarian slush had not ameliorated my hunger one bit but, on the contrary, had only amplified it. Eating carrot cake, not even meat, was strangely more filling than I could have ever imagined. About five minutes later my hunger magically disappeared, and I was satiated nearly to full satisfaction. I was shocked that was all it had taken. The curiously potent mix of a slab of carrot cake the size of a pay phone and a cup of pungent black coffee had cured all of my ills in one swoop. I decided I would have to add carrot cake to my list of magical foods alongside eggs, bacon, pancakes, and coffee. I said a little thank-you to God that I had survived that nasty, virulent hunger.

The next morning I came down to breakfast to discover the buffet table had been reinstated with full benefits as it had been the first three days … with the usual unsatisfying vegetarian swill. Still, this food was okay for me. There was rice and a bin of steaming fried vegetables with a hot, thick vegetable sludge that I could pour over it to make a sort of vegetable curry that was enough to satisfy my hunger. I could thank the rice for that. Thank God hippies and beatniks don't have a problem with rice.

Katie was serene as she greeted us that morning. I wondered whether the gradually building tension of the first eight days had peaked in the starvation exercise and we would now be descending into a kind of milk-and-honey homecoming.

Katie began by asking us again whether we understood the purpose of yesterday's harrowing exercise. Only one or two people tried to answer, and I realized that no one in the room knew the purpose of begging for food in Santa Monica.

Katie said that for most people, nearly every decision they make in life is based on fear—fear of being alone, fear of being broke, friendless, abandoned, destitute.

"What would happen if you didn't make choices based on fear?" Katie asked. "What would happen if instead you made decisions that are most in tune with who you are, most aligned with your true nature, instead of choosing what you *don't want* out of fear of being forsaken or left penniless in the street?"

The question hung in the air.

"So," Katie said, "I thought I would destroy your world."

The woman sitting next to me shifted in her seat.

Katie said, "What would happen if your worst-case scenario came true? Your worst fear? And make no mistake, we all have the same worst fear—that we wind up alone and homeless in the street, hungry, with no shelter, no bed, no food. Now take it even further. From moneyless and homeless on the street, what's next? Death, of course. You die alone on the street."

Silence fell over the room. But it wasn't a completely uncomfortable silence. I could feel that it was almost a relief someone had finally said it. It's taboo, but for the first time our shared primordial fear had been voiced and laid bare at our feet. Katie had dared to speak it, and she appeared to be right. That fear drives our choices and our economies. Economically it may be a good thing.

"But," Katie asked, "is making choices based on fear a good thing *for you*? Of course not. Who would you be if you didn't make your decisions based on fear? Who could you be? Who would you become?"

The question lingered.

"Who would you be?" was a question she often put to us at the school. "Who would you be without your thoughts?"

A fucking cruise missile. No fear, no hesitation, and no regrets.

Katie leaned in and her voice, which always had a musical cadence, suddenly cut sharp like a knife. "The truth is, even in your worst nightmare, you would not die," she said. "You will *not* die. Do you see? You proved it yesterday. With no money, no voice to negotiate with, only five words to speak, no friends or family to call, no help from any of your lifelines, no help of any kind, all you had to do was ask a stranger on the street to feed you … and they did. They did, didn't they?" A shiver ran down my spine and I realized she was saying something powerful. "Strangers fed you, and all you did was ask them to. They would clothe and shelter you too, if you asked them. After I awakened, I knew it before I ever tried it myself."

She stood on the dais. "God will not let you die, no matter how moneyless, destitute, or alone you are." She looked at us with a fierceness that pierced me like a sword. "Practically speaking, you have nothing to fear in this life, nothing at all. Even if you were totally alone with nothing on the street, you would still be okay."

The only way Katie could ever prove this to us, because no one would believe her if she just said it to them, was to literally put us through it. She had thrown us out into the streets hungry, with nothing. It occurred to me that she was right. In the course of five hours I had made almost twelve dollars. If I begged for eight hours, I was sure I could average twenty dollars a day, enough for breakfast, lunch, and dinner on the Third Street Promenade.

"Of course," Katie continued, "just in practical terms, you cannot die. Not only will you not die, but you cannot."

A primal scream of the deepest anguish filled the air, like a twelve-year-old boy being castrated for his induction into the Vienna Boys' Choir. "How is that possible?" the woman, Katie's foil, howled from the back of the room. "My brother is dead! Both my parents are dead! Everyone I ever loved—*dead!*"

"If you were dead, how would you know it?" Katie shot back. The voice in the back of the room screamed in what can only be described as fathomless pain. Katie raised her voice. *"How would you know you were dead?"* The wail fell silent; it slithered back inside its shell. "You wouldn't know," Katie continued. "You can't *be dead*. If you were dead, you would never know it. You can only be alive. Do you see? It's only possible to be alive. You cannot '*be dead*.' It's impossible."

It's good to be enlightened, I thought as the room tried to absorb the radical yet true notion that we couldn't die.

Spiritual Practice 3: Moment of Truth

On the tenth day, the last full day, Katie said it was time for the final exercise—the third spiritual practice. We were instructed to go up to our rooms with our roommates, the strangers we'd been bunking with since we arrived, sit down on the edge of the bed with them, look them straight in the eye, and tell them the five things we hated most about them.

Yes, that's right.

Katie exhorted us to be brutally honest. Being fiercely honest is a crucial part of being an authentic person, she said, of not being disconnected from yourself or "acting" various roles through life—not pretending to be a different person to get acceptance from your spouse, your boss, your friends, your parents, your yoga instructor, and so on. When people are disconnected from themselves, they come across as fake to others. We all know people like this, especially living in cities, often shallow blondes, behaving so superficially that they seem to have lost all touch with their real selves, so much so that you wonder who the real person once was. They are constantly playing a role to be perfect, to be positive, to be sunny. Katie said healthy people always behave the same, as themselves, regardless of who they're with.

As I was here to get my money's worth, I went into the exercise with characteristic gusto. I decided to be completely honest and not leave anything out on the playing field. Bruce, over three hundred pounds and obese, was an extremely kind and decent man, belying his wearing the same T-shirt all week that said Bite Me in huge block letters across the front. He had a curious nature, as most people at the school did, and I could see he was devoted to his job as a psychologist. He had come to the school because he was genuinely interested to see whether Katie could offer something that traditional medicine could not. He could also expense the cost of the school as research, he confided to me out the side of his mouth. Up in our room, he asked whether I wanted to go first. I said sure. The rules were that after each honest remark, the other person had to take it in deeply and reply, "Thank you," no matter what had been said. The person was not allowed to make any rebuttal or say anything else.

I began, "Bruce, you're obese. You should really take better care of yourself."

Maybe I was naive, but I thought this was the whole point of the exercise, to really go for it; I wasn't going to leave anything out on the floor. Bruce's eyes watered. After a long time, he swallowed, and whispered through clenched teeth, "Thank you, Tom."

I continued, "You snore all night long. It's really annoying."

Katie had told us just to let it rip, and I didn't see any reason not to. Bruce's eyes watered again. I wondered what he was experiencing behind them. After what seemed like an eternity, he wheezed, "Thank you."

"Bruce, you're monopolizing the bathroom with your stuff—gels, shaving cream, fragrances, hair spray, beard trimmer. I only have a toothbrush and a comb. You have thirty more items. What do you need all that stuff for?"

Bruce's chin drooped to his chest. "Thank you," he managed.

"You're also taking up most of the space in the room; your clothes are everywhere. Shouldn't you be a little more organized as a professional therapist? What would your patients think if they saw your slovenly habits?"

A long delay.

"Thank you … Tom."

"You should get more exercise."

He didn't answer.

Bruce's eyes were distant, far away in that galaxy light-years away again. Or perhaps he had gone to his shrink's happy place, usually an island in the Bahamas. My items were done, and I girded myself for whatever horrors Bruce might lob my way. He started in.

"I think you're a very nice young man."

"Thank you."

"I would say you've been a delight to share a room with."

"Thank you."

"I've enjoyed being roommates so much. I hope we can keep in touch."

"Thank you."

"I have no complaints about our time together whatsoever."

"Thank you, Bruce."

"I'm sorry for any inconvenience I might have caused you."

I stared at him.

Suddenly I couldn't make eye contact with him anymore. I felt too ashamed. I looked at the floor and wished it would fly up and smack me in the face. The room went deathly quiet. I listened to the sound of the clock's second hand tick remorselessly by. Finally I looked into Bruce's face. His gaze was still distant and opaque.

I clapped my hands together loudly.

"Well, Bruce, thanks. Let's exchange email addresses then, shall we?"

The school's final event was the graduation ceremony. But graduation was not assured. Katie said that we had all been secretly observed, graded, and written up all week by her minions. Most of the staff wore nametags that said "Staff" or "Group Leader." Two hard-looking women with butch haircuts wore "Director" tags.

Earlier in the week, a first-time staff person, an overweight young woman, had criticized me for skipping the first two steps of the Work during facilitation practice. I'd replied that I didn't need to repeat steps I already implicitly understood, but she ordered me to repeat each step by the book anyway.

"Fine," I said, and did as she asked.

The next day one of the staff members who was friendly to me came up and told me that the overweight woman had spent no fewer than thirty minutes ranting about me in their evening staff meeting the night before in front of all of the staff including Katie.

"What!" I said.

"She said you were a 'nightmare' to facilitate. She actually called you 'the student from hell' and said you wouldn't do the Work as prescribed."

"I wouldn't say that," I said. "I don't need to do the first two steps, so I skipped ahead to the last two. She told me not to do it, and I said fine and did as she asked. What's the problem?"

"Well, it seems she's made you a target now. Her goal is to see that you don't graduate from the school."

Great, I thought. Janine had followed me to the school and reincarnated as this obese woman. How the hell do I get away from these people?

"What's worse," my friend said, "is that if you fail the school, your scholarship will be revoked, and you'll be forced to pay the additional $3,500 that was previously waived for you."

"*What?*" I said. "What's wrong with these people?"

That afternoon the young woman who'd complained about me trotted up and gloated that I'd been "flagged" as a troublemaker, a dissident, an undesirable who didn't do the Work in the approved way.

"You don't follow the rules," she sneered.

"No, I don't," I said, without really paying attention to what I was saying.

"A director will shadow you at all times for the remainder of the course."

"What?" I said. "That's absurd. You asked me to do all four steps, and I said okay. So what's the problem?"

She looked at me with a kind of leering pleasure, as though I was the sugar that had made her fat. "If I have anything to do with it, you won't graduate the school," she said. "I'll have you thrown out of here."

"Listen," I said. "I'm here on scholarship. They say if I don't graduate, I'll have to pay for this shakedown."

"Not my problem," she said gleefully, and stalked off.

Unbelievable. This was the School of Enlightenment, but the staff seemed less interested in enlightening people than in power-tripping, no different from any kibbutz or utopia commune anywhere. I didn't care whether their kangaroo court graduated me or not, but I did care if they revoked my scholarship and I had to pay the full tuition.

The next day I was doing the Work in the afternoon session when I glanced down. An old woman with a face like a prune was lying on the floor under my chair and staring up into my crotch. Her wrinkled nose was mere inches from my scrotum. It was one of the directors. I recoiled in horror.

"What the fuck!" I screamed, cupping my balls with both hands. *"What the hell are you doing down there?"*

"Making sure you're doing the Work properly," she seethed. "You're on probation."

I'm on probation at the School of Enlightenment. It was too absurd to take seriously, and yet I had to if I didn't want to be out two months' salary soon.

I decided to take matters into my own hands. After failing to stand up to Janine for years, I'd finally had enough of this kind of person. The best defense is a strong offense. The director clearly didn't give a shit about being enlightened—she was about as nurturing as broken glass in your throat—but she was smarter than the obese young woman who was trashing me in their nightly meetings. Because the director wasn't stupid, I thought there was a chance she might be fair and listen to reason.

"Can I talk to you?" I asked her. "If you would kindly remove your face from my crotch?"

She lay still for a moment, thinking. Finally she shrugged. "Okay," she said.

I roped her into a corner. The woman had a mullet that looked like a beaver had sat on top of her head and died there. I explained that the overweight woman was out for my blood.

The director shrugged.

I said, "If she has a problem, why doesn't she do the Work on it? Isn't that what the fucking Work is for?" The director yawned. I shook my head and tried again. "Worst of all, when she facilitates the Work with students, she asks the four questions mechanically. She looked at her watch when the student was answering. She was bored. She doesn't give a shit about people and their problems."

For whatever reason, this hit home. The director looked at me sharply. "She facilitates mechanically?" she asked.

"You're goddamn right she does," I said louder now, puffing out my chest like a red-breasted robin.

"Hmm." The director frowned. "Let's talk about this later." She nodded to me with military curtness and strode off, crossing the entire room in three strides.

The next day someone tapped me on the shoulder. It was the director. She actually smiled at me. "I spoke to Katie," she said. "I put in a good word for you." She winked at me.

"Thank you!" I gushed. Hot gratitude welled up in me. I almost hugged her.

"And," the woman continued, "I heard what you did—giving those new cowboy boots to the homeless. I started to think you got a raw deal yesterday."

"I most certainly did," I piped up. Technicolor was returning to my world again.

The suspense held up right until the graduation ceremony. Katie stood on stage and announced each person's name through a bullhorn, shouting, "Passed!" and then the person came up to receive their diploma. When she got to my name near the end, she paused ... and paused ... Then she frowned. "We have a problem here," she said through the bullhorn. *Fuck! I knew it!* It was the first time during the ceremony she had said anything other than "Passed!" *She's really not going to pass me. I'm going to be the first person ever to fail the School of Enlightenment.*

"Just kidding!" Katie finally said. "Passed!"

Ha, ha ... very funny. I didn't know she had such a sense of humor.

I was often shy in groups and hadn't asked Katie any questions during the school. I had one burning question, though, and in the final session, not knowing whether I would ever have the chance to speak with her again, I went for it and raised my hand.

"Yes?"

Katie's expression whenever she looked at me was neutral and uninterested. She never betrayed even the slightest hint that she recognized me or was interested in me. Whatever charms I possess with the female sex were utterly lost on Katie. That's the surest way I knew she really was enlightened.

Suddenly flustered, my longtime frustration bubbled out of the deep. An unexpected torrent of emotion gushed up, and I blurted, "Katie, everyone at the school always has a problem with someone else—mother, father, brother, sister—and it seems quite easy to do the Work on another person. My problem has never been with another person; it's always been with myself. I can't stand my own mistakes. I can't stand it when I screw up. I can never forgive my own mistakes. Doing the Work on myself isn't working, because I still don't believe I made the right decision. Can you help me?"

It all just came tumbling out in a raw unvarnished moment. It was a testament to how much I trusted Katie, as I rarely, probably never, open up to anyone. I knew she had no agenda, so knew I was in a safe place. She was the only truly wise person I have ever met, and suddenly I felt quite grateful that she existed on the earth. I had finally worked up the courage to ask her the burning question I had wanted to ask all along and was surely one of the reasons I had come to the Learning Annex in the first place.

Katie replied, "Just keep doing the Work. Do it for breakfast, do it for lunch, do it for dinner. Is it true? The answer will come."

"No, no," I pleaded. "I can already figure out the answers to the Work. More repetition will not help. My problem is deeper. Please give me something else."

I felt frustrated, desperate for a more direct way, anything that would stop the reflexive self-punishing, self-criticizing hammer I had been beating myself up with, I just realized, ever since my parents' divorce when I was five years old.

Katie saw my anguish. Finally she sighed. "Okay," she said reluctantly, in what appeared to be a rare moment of being forced to go someplace she would rather not go. "Come here." I approached and knelt at her feet, broken like a baby. "Look at me," she said. I raised my eyes and looked into her bright blue eyes. Truly, they were the bluest eyes I had ever seen. Then she said something I could not have imagined.

"Do you always believe your memory?"

"What?" I asked. "My memory?"

"Yes," she said, "your memories—do you believe them?"

"Well, yes," I stammered, "of course I believe my memories."

"Well, don't," Katie said. Her eyes lifted to the stars, and her lips parted in a smile. "Your memories ... are not true. You don't remember what happened; you only think you do. If you could go back right now to the exact same time and place, you would discover that what you thought happened didn't. What you think happened is not what happened."

She looked straight at me. "Don't believe your memories." She slapped me hard on the cheek twice like the Godfather slapping his manservant.

She paused for a moment and seemed to reflect.

"Who knows what you'll do with this someday?" she said, gesturing out toward the school. "Now go, get out of here." And she shoved me like the falcon master pushing the bird off into the sky.

On the final day of the school I had a brief exchange with the young English girl with blonde ringlets who had looked so miserable earlier. Her name was Gemma. I knew her story well from the public sessions—she had come to the school because her husband had cheated on her with a woman named Fiesta. Gemma was young and innocent and had been especially devastated by her husband's affair. She was a smart girl apparently, had gone to Oxford, and she'd gotten married at age twenty to a Latino man who had bussed her table both literally and figuratively in a restaurant.

I asked her why she had married so young, and she said, "It was kind of cool to be married during university."

That didn't make any sense to me, but I said okay. It shows you that not everyone at Oxford is a genius. Gemma and I had never spoken until now. She had looked absolutely miserable all week sitting on the floor slouched over her ramrod-straight legs in baggy Charlie Chaplin pants, her neck drooped and back rounded, tear-soaked strands of long blonde hair plastered to her face like papier-mâché. She was like Eeyore and Puddleglum fused together in some sick science experiment to create a mutant whose superpower is being depressed.

In such a state of abject despair I had never really noticed her. But with young men scarce, as Jane Austen might have astutely observed, Gemma and I had, unspeaking, come together and danced one song at the school-ending dance party. I gave her a few swings and a dip and she smiled at me, and I guess that's when she first noticed me.

The evening the school ended, we went out with a group of eight students back to Santa Monica Beach, the scene of the hunger games two days before, to watch the sun set and take in just a little more spiritual glory. We would have to supervise our own enlightenment now as there was no one on the planet higher than Katie in that regard. I learned from Katie that the amount of time we have on earth is so finite and so precious that I feel obligated to enjoy all of it, every second I can. I don't want to waste a minute being narrow-minded, unhappy, bored, or dissatisfied.

Living in the moment recreates the deeply present feeling we felt at camp, playing sports, in love, in childhood, running around the neighborhood with your brother on Halloween looking for porch lights switched on and collecting candy—the happiest moments of our lives. The reason those moments were so happy is because we were so immersed in them. There were no seams between us and life then. There was no daylight between us and life. We weren't thinking, we were just engaged, experiencing. That feeling can be refound anytime simply by pulling tightly into this moment, whatever it is. You have to embrace and fully accept the present moment in whatever form it takes to surge ahead with it and change your life. You cannot be separate from or resisting it. Life feels light and like play when you are actively living in the present moment, especially when it's married to a purpose or a goal. Life is richest and grandest when you're climbing the mountain toward the summit.

After sunset Gemma, two other young people, and I broke off to a Mexican place for dinner at, you guessed it, the Third Street Promenade. I had been a ghost here two days ago. It felt strange to be back again, this time feeling much more alive and present than the disillusioned yuppie I had been.

One of the girls was a cool, good-looking, hippie-ish girl from Colorado named Rachel. She would have been perfect at Haight-Ashbury in the summer of 1967, and I felt a little bad she had clearly been born in the wrong era. She was more of an authentic hippie than anyone I had ever met. Rachel believed in all that stuff too—flower child stuff, yoga, three-way sexual adventures. She was my age and had been a first-time staff member at the school. (Staff members had to complete one school as a student before they could join as staff.)

Sipping margaritas and eating real food (meat!), we chatted and got to know each other. Gemma said she was supposed to stay with her aunt down in Anaheim, a good hour's drive away. She was trying to put off going back to England because she didn't want to see her cheating husband again. In fact, she declared bravely, during the school she had decided to divorce him and stay in America.

"Wow ..." said Rachel, smiling.

I don't think anyone at that table particularly believed her. Rachel, in the best tradition of hippies, was enormously candid, open, and generous, and she offered to let Gemma stay with her at a friend's house in Santa Monica. Gemma gratefully accepted.

Rachel had an easygoing nature. She was natively honest in a way few people are anymore, and I liked her instantly. She was hot too, and if she had been a little less hippie perhaps, I would have loved to have dated her, but I sensed that her tastes ran a little granola for me. The guy she was into was openly bisexual, she said, her chest swelling with pride.

"We had a three-way, twice, once with a man and once with a woman, my best friend, Sara," Rachel declared proudly. "I'm also bi," she added, in case I missed that part.

She was so animated when talking on this subject that it was clear she considered three-way sexual orgies an accomplishment in and of themselves. I would consider them an accomplishment too if I could just get one going. I did have two hot women right in front of me, and Rachel was so into it that I doubt she would have said no if I proposed one. The other one was desperate to stay in America and presumably would do anything to make it a reality. Yet it still seemed somehow out of reach. At root I come from conservative Swiss stock. Three-ways with homosexuals are not really in the cards for me.

On Facebook almost all of Rachel's posts are about something called OM, which I thought might be the *om* signifying worldly perfection that Siddhartha discovered while listening to the disparate sounds burbling from a river, or the *om* meditation Franny obsessed over in *Franny and Zooey*—until I finally clicked on the link and discovered it actually stands for Orgasmic Meditation. Rachel's bio reads that she is a certified teacher and a trainer/coach of Orgasmic Meditation. She attends large events called TurnON with Facebook invite lists of over a thousand people. The event's "About" section says, "The TurnON games are designed to create the visceral sensation of orgasm in your body. A partner strokes a woman's clitoris for fifteen minutes with no goal other than to feel, connect, and be present."

Good morning! I can imagine the creepy guys that show up at those events. Like men who start salsa dancing so they can dance with young women. Rachel invited me to drop by her OM class "to stroke some pussy." I politely declined.

Though Rachel was orgy obsessed, tree hugging, and sexually progressive to the furthest extent one can be, she didn't smoke or do drugs, and she possessed that ineffable sense of having been raised well and loved by two doting parents. Her good upbringing was unmistakable beneath the group sex veneer. It wasn't a complete surprise then when we learned that Rachel hailed from one of America's wealthiest enclaves, Aspen, Colorado, where she had recently bought one of her parents' starter homes.

As we talked deeper into the night, Rachel, at some point, in a spontaneous, warm gesture, invited us to winter with her in Aspen. My eyes brightened at the offer. It felt like an opening, a breath of fresh air, an escape from the prison my life had become without my ever intending it to become so. Rachel offered to rent me a room in her house for $300 a month, surely the cheapest rent in the most expensive town in America. When I heard the offer, I knew I wanted it. As one of the least decisive people in history, for once I was crystal clear that I wanted this. It felt like freedom. It felt like the new beginning my stagnant life was crying out for. I longed to break free and to feel alive again.

I felt like I was drowning, though in reality I wasn't—my heightened sensitivity had deceived me into feeling like more was wrong than it was. Of course, some of it was wrong. It caused me to see Rachel's offer as a gorgeous lifeline. There was a whole world out there, a world beyond the same commute to work five days out of every seven for the last five years straight and the same unenthusiastic trudging out to bars on weekends with so-called friends with gossamer-thin alliances—a world beyond this superficial life. Why would I waste another day hunkered down behind a desk doing brain-bleedingly boring clerical work when a whole world beckoned outside these narrow walls? There's a whole world out there beyond spreadsheets and dating apps. Or had I forgotten?

To me it was a no-brainer.

Benighted and lost, I reached for the light instead.

Stories of wonder and faraway places like Morocco and Tibet had long captured my imagination. Since early childhood I had always been drawn to the world's farthest corners, its most distant places—I have no idea why and still don't. I simply have the most fervent desire to explore the most remote and least known places on the planet. Almost before I could talk, I stenciled out maps of the world, colored them in with crayon, and taped them to the back of my mother's bedroom door. After etching in the United States, I moved straight on to drawing Antarctica and the North Pole, and then the Orient. I was just following my bliss. I wanted adventure—to see strange lands, imbibe exotic fragrances, climb steep windswept mountain faces, dive down hidden alleyways, pry open locked doors, carry a light inside dark rooms, cross oceans, and wash up on the unknown shores of the furthest sea.

Isn't that better than wasting your life behind a desk?

You're goddamn right it is!

As for me, I am tormented with an everlasting itch for things remote.
I love to sail forbidden seas, and land on barbarous coasts.

—Herman Melville, 1851

The Journey Begins

I quit my job on a Tuesday. That night at eight o'clock I drove out of Los Angeles on Interstate 15, heading north to Las Vegas en route to Aspen. That night on the dark highway, pulling away for good, was perhaps the happiest night of my life. I had moved out of my apartment and given away my possessions. Everything I owned now existed in a single duffel bag in the trunk of my car. I didn't even miss the cowboy boots. I felt fleet-footed, light—physically light, light of things, light of heart, exactly the way I wanted to feel. I learned the delicious suspension of gravity and the airy feeling of lightness that comes from having no possessions or almost no possessions.

I still remember the joy of sliding out onto the open highway in the desert at night. It was a weekday and there were no other cars on the I-15N save for a few long-distance eighteen-wheelers. The yellow dash of the highway dividing line streamed by in the slipstream of my car's high beams. The white light of the high beams and the softly gleaming blue dashboard lights were all that separated me from the infinite dark.

After what felt like an eternity driving into the pitch-black desert night, some distant galaxy—a gauzy ribbon of inchoate light—twinkled faintly on the farthest edge of vision way out beyond where the horizon should be. It pulsed and vanished, quivered and vanished. Like a distant star, if I looked straight at it, it disappeared. I had to look slightly off to one side to glimpse it in my peripheral vision. It was a constellation of planets light-years away on the retreating edge of space moving through the cosmos without human concern. We're microscopic compared to it; that greatness would no more consider us than we would a microbe. Nothing we do matters. Therefore we might as well do everything—do everything we want to do.

The inchoate, gauzy ribbon of light was no more than a distant blur in the primordial darkness. After driving toward it for what felt like forever, the lights morphed slightly—smeared and blurred together like watercolors—until all at once they sharpened into a stark clarity. Now it was a string of Christmas tree lights flung overboard off a cruise liner in the dead of night, dashed out to sea and floating on the black water.

After a very long time, the lights seemed to quiver and swell, bulge and fall back again, until all at once they blossomed into an arc of lights slung out before me like glittering jewels in the dark, a lost city of gold on the endless plain. That dark plain was so vast, so empty, that I felt it stretching on forever without end—infinite.

The golden cities of Nevada sprang up from the depths of blackest night like Monte Cristo's treasure shimmering beneath dark waves in the chilly night sea. Those shimmering cities in the dark, the ghostly oases of Primm and Jean, had a vivid, haunting beauty as of a grave in water, an elegiac beauty that I have never quite surpassed in terms of sheer aesthetic beauty.

Sometimes you can feel it. Your soul, the hollow in your chest, is scraped by God. The abrasion on your soul, like a bruise on your shin, is a raw, windswept, aching feeling—the feeling of a wound being grazed. Some bliss or ecstasy enters through the cavity in your chest and for a moment you can scarcely breathe, so overwhelmed by the beauty of creation you are, of the windswept desert at night, the window rolled down and the hot desert air beating your face. So stung by its beauty that for a moment you feel the full brunt of it drilling down on you like a mountain of bricks or a tidal wave collapsing on top of you until you almost can't stand it.

It's arresting, the scope of the American West—it's vast and thrilling, magical country to me. That drive would inform my life for many years to come. The real reason for my joy that night was that I was back in the unknown, where the world is forever changing, forever fresh and new.

A few years later, I was looking up through smeared red and green watercolors on rain-streaked windows of black skyscrapers as I waded through a sea of red umbrellas in the Shibuya scramble cross, the busiest pedestrian intersection in the world. I was living in the heart of Tokyo, Japan.

I had just turned thirty years old. A new decade spanned ahead.

Long hanging signs and giant television display screens on the exterior of business buildings in Shibuya and Shinjuku broadcast a steady stream of bizarre images and symbols so foreign that they looked like the progeny of Klingon and hieroglyphics, and I was gripped by a sudden urge to unravel their meaning. Many people who stay in Japan too long begin with a desire to unthread the mysterious ornate kanji runes.

I looked out over a sea of black hair and red umbrellas in the rain-soaked cityscape. A cornucopia of intensely vivid colors burst out at me, and I had the feeling I might be here for a while. I gazed out over the bay. Junks drifted across the rippling black water. On the other side of the Rainbow Bridge, billions of neon lights illuminated skyscrapers thrusting up into the night sky like tombstones.

Asia would prove an easier mistress to enter than to leave, with its exotic rhythms and strange attractions, the mysteries of the Far East. It was perhaps not unlike what Alexander found when he marched into Babylon, Persia, the capital of the ancient world in 331 BC, and discovered a magical place, a sort of Disneyland for adults in much the same way Tokyo is today, a mysterious, haunting place he ultimately would never return home from.

I'm the sort of person who when I see waves lapping on the shore, my gaze immediately turns up to the horizon, and my spirit and every cell in my body yearns to move toward that horizon, to reach for it, explore it. I feel always and forever the itch for adventure, the curse of the curious, the rapture of new experiences. I could easily spend two years circumnavigating a ship around the globe. Our ancestors had the opportunity to sail through the Strait of Magellan and around the Cape of Good Hope. They got to discover the New World and be paid handsomely for it by queens of empire. They had the chance to ride horses across plush virgin country to deliver the mail, and push east in search of a new Silk Road and a passage to India.

Lewis and Clark had the thrill of being the first settlers to follow the Snake River across the New World to the Pacific Ocean. Can you imagine the excitement they must have felt on that unknowable journey? It must have been like Kirk and Spock touching down on some strange new planet to explore. Lewis and Clark had no idea what was out there, where they were going, how long it would take, or even whether there was an ocean on the other side or not. The New World could have been like Asia, with the coast ten thousand miles away, and they would have just kept going either until they reached it or until they died. Some might believe they were scared, but I'm quite sure they were not. I believe they were just excited. Today when the world has largely been discovered, how can one do that? Today's jobs are mostly for desk jockeys. We only get to spend a few finite years on earth. Don't we want something better than sitting behind a desk?

Explorers have to find a different way today, usually their own way to do it. Queen Isabella is no longer handing out large commissions to sail into wild uncharted oceans in search of new sea roads, rare commodities, and lands to conquer. You no longer get paid to draw maps of a place for the first time. Can you imagine drawing the first map of an undiscovered country? How rich and satisfying an experience would that be? It's nice to live in the age of air travel and business class, but living in the fifteenth century would have been fun too. When adventure was a job and not a vacation, I would have excelled. The thirst for adventure, the curiosity, it never stops, it never ends: the desire for an intellectually and physically stimulating life, the wish that it could go on forever, and then reset and start all over again.

Usually the mores of books such as these is that in the end the prodigal traveler, the lost young man, finds himself and returns home and settles down. Is that not the custom? I have read so many books like that. Indeed, Odysseus in the *Odyssey*, the first story all the others seem based upon, did finally return home to Ithaca and Penelope after twenty lost years. And what of my lost years? Where is my triumphant return home, my hard-won peace? What do I seek? What if the answer is not immediately clear? Does that mean terror and panic? Then again, do we really want the journey to end?

As with the ship that sails firmly away from land and moves confidently toward the sunrise in the east, that horizon you burn to explore and will yourself to reach, without any known plan of return, that ship goes to where we do not know. It goes in search of the unknown, to find new worlds.

A deep pleasure is excited inside me, a shiver of aliveness shudders down in my core, and my heart soars in union with the crisp morning dawn—that dawn that is forever fresh and new—and I am at one with the world. In my heart the white sails are forever pulling away from shore, forever being raised up to the sky to catch those trade winds. My soul stirs with adventure, my heart swells with the waves. It lies out there somewhere, somewhere in the unknown world.

Acknowledgments

To my girlfriend, who got me to write this book and without whom it would not have been written. And to Ray Bradbury for your friendship, inspiration, and visits to UCLA, where you wrote *Fahrenheit 451* in the library basement, and for showing us how to live in uninterrupted wonder. Love you, Ray! Your spirit carries on, and indeed you did live forever.

www.ingramcontent.com/pod-product-compliance
Lightning Source LLC
Chambersburg PA
CBHW050120170426
43197CB00011B/1648